CHINESE GLEAMS OF SUFI LIGHT

CHINESE GLEAMS OF SUFI LIGHT

Wang Tai-yü's *Great Learning of the Pure and Real* and Liu Chih's *Displaying the Concealment of the Real Realm*

With a New Translation of Jāmī's *Lawāʾiḥ* from the Persian
by
William C. Chittick

Sachiko Murata

With a Foreword by Tu Weiming

State University of New York Press

Published by
State University of New York Press, Albany

Printed in the United States of America

For information, address the State University of New York Press,
State University Plaza, Albany, NY 12246

Production by Marilyn P. Semerad
Marketing by Anne M. Valentine

Library of Congress Cataloging-in-Publication Data

Murata, Sachiko, (date)
Chinese gleams of sufi light : Wang Tai-yü's Great learning of the pure and real and Liu Chih's Displaying the concealment of the real realm ; with a new translation of Jāmī's Lawāʾiḥ from the Persian by William C. Chittick / by Sachiko Murata ; with a foreword by Tu Weiming
p. cm.
Includes bibliographical references and index.
ISBN 0–7914–4637–9 (alk. paper) — ISBN 0–7914–4638–7 (pbk. : alk. paper)
1. Sufism—doctrine. 2. Islam—China. 3. Wang Tai-yü. Ch'ing-chen ta-hsüeh. 4. Liu, Chih, ca. 1662–1730. Chen ching chao wei. I. Chittick, William C. II. Jāmī, 1414–1492. Lawāʾiḥ. English. III.Wang Tai-yü. Ch'ing-chen ta-hsüeh. English. IV. Liu, Chih, ca. 1662–1730. Chen-ching chao-wei. English. V. Title.

BP189.3 .M87 2000
297.4'0951—dc21

00–020625
CIP

10 9 8 7 6 5 4 3 2 1

Contents

Foreword

When the Prophet Muhammad instructed, "Seek knowledge, even unto China," the rhetorical significance of China was perhaps its remoteness, an unlikely place for Muslims to travel for economic, political, or social reasons. Therefore Islam's arrival in China in the Tang dynasty (618–907), probably within the first generation of Muhammad's disciples, is quite remarkable. The Muslims in Tang China were mainly traders who, protected by extraterritorial rights and confined to specifically designated port cities, preserved their Arabic names, native tongues (primarily Persian), and original dress. Although they led a separate religious and social life of their own, they built mosques in more than a dozen cities, notably Guangzhou, Quanzhou, Hangzhou, and Chang'an. With the expansion of maritime trade in Song China (960–1279), the number of Muslims increased and their presence in the mainstream of Chinese society was reflected in art, architecture, and literature. Those who settled permanently in the Middle Kingdom married Chinese women or adopted Chinese children, especially in times of famine.[1]

The Mongol conquest of China (1278–1368) provided an unusual opportunity for Central Asian peoples to serve as advisors and officials in the Chinese court. As a result, several Muslims became ministers. One of the most prominent was Sayyid Ajall, whose legacy as the governor of Yunnan province is ingrained in the collective memory of the local culture and an integral part of its ethico-religious identity.[2] By the time of the Ming dynasty (1368–1644), according to Donald Leslie and others, Muslims in China had been thoroughly transformed into "Chinese Muslims" and the Hui Hui (as Sinicized or, at least, Chinese-speaking Muslims, called themselves and were designated in public discourse) were a conspicuous presence on the Chinese religious landscape.[3]

Nevertheless, an intellectual effervescence among a coterie of theologically sophisticated Muslim scholars did not begin until the seventeenth century, specifically in the transition between late Ming and early Qing (1644–1912). For the first time in the history of Islam in China, the ulama significantly enriched the intellectual life of the Chinese Muslim community by producing highly sophisticated theological works. Why the late seventeenth and early eighteenth-century Muslim teachers felt the need to articulate a pattern of fruitful interaction between their faith community and the larger society which had been profoundly shaped by Confucian values is a fascinating area of inquiry for intellectual historians, comparative religionists, and theologically-oriented philosophers.[4] It has also recently attracted the attention of Islamic scholars, especially those in Cultural China.

Before answering this challenging question one must first inquire what the creative minds among the ulama actually produced as the result of their philosophical reflections and how they responded to this perceived need. Such an inquiry entails a concerted effort to recognize, understand, and appreciate the best of the cultural production that is still available to us. Archival work, textual analysis, bibliographic research, philological study, and translation are necessary steps toward a preliminary interpretation. Sachiko Murata, through painstaking archaeological digging and patient attentiveness, is instrumental in opening up this field to the international scholarly community. I am privileged and grateful to have been associated with her project from the very beginning. It has been an intellectually enticing and spiritually uplifting experience.

I first encountered Islamic philosophy in the early 1960s, through a comparative religion course with Wilfred Cantwell Smith focusing on the perceptions of religious communities outside the Christian West. Smith's sympathetic reading of the Koran as a committed Christian thinker was a source of inspiration to me and enhanced my ability to appreciate the three Abrahamic spiritual traditions from a Confucian perspective. Later, I also benefited greatly from Huston Smith's sensitive and humane approach to the world's religions. His admiration for Frithjof Schuon's insight into the perennial philosophy also helped me cherish the quintessential values of Sufism. Annemarie Schimmel's masterly depiction of the mystical dimensions of Islam heightened my fascination with the experiential side as well as the intellectual understanding of the Prophet's message. My meeting with Professor Toshihiko Izutsu at the East-West Philosophers' Conference in Honolulu in 1969 and at several subsequent international gatherings offered me a rare opportunity to think philosophically about Sufism from a Sinic perspective. I am proud to have played a part in reissuing his seminal work, *Sufism and Taoism,* in North America by the University of California Press. However, it was my collaboration with Seyyed Hossein Nasr and Osman Bakar in a series of Islamic–Confucian dialogues in Cambridge, Massachusetts, and in Kuala Lumpur, Malaysia, in 1995 that enabled me to truly immerse myself in the study of Islamic philosophy in classical Chinese.

I learned from Sachiko Murata and William Chittick that Wang Tai-yü and Liu Chih's philosophical reflections on Islam represent the earliest instance in which Muslim thinkers wrote their treatises in a major intellectual language other than Arabic or Persian. Even the Muslim appropriation of Greek philosophy to construct a new theological synthesis was in Arabic. In choosing to express themselves in classical Chinese, the Chinese ulama were compelled to use a non-Islamic idiom as a medium of communication. This obliged them to respond to the Confucian intellectual world. The case of Matteo Ricci and his Jesuit colleagues readily comes to mind for comparison.

It is often assumed that Ricci deliberately adopted an accommodating strategy to make his Catholic message acceptable to Confucian literati. By emphasizing the compatibility of the Christian idea of God with the classical Confucian notion of Heaven, he intended to convey that believing in God was a return to the source of the sagely teaching that had been lost in Neo-Confucian moral metaphysics. His teaching that the real meaning of the Lord on High, far from an alien conception, is rooted in the core of Confucian orthodoxy and orthopraxy had a sympathetic resonance in the minds of his converts. Recent scholarship suggests that, as an envoy from the Vatican, Ricci had a more grandiose design than simple accommodation. Whether or not he really meant to colonize the Chinese mind, his evocation of classical Confucian religiosity was a deliberate attempt to deconstruct the Neo-Confucian faith of forming one body with Heaven, Earth, and the myriad things. Indeed, only by denying the truth of the Neo-Confucian core idea of the unity and continuity of all beings was Ricci able to demonstrate the necessity of radical transcendence as the defining characteristic of the Lord on High as the Creator.[5]

By contrast, the Chinese Muslim theologians were so seasoned in the Neo-Confucian mode of thinking that they philosophized from the core of its concerns: understanding things, refining knowledge, authenticating intentions, purifying hearts and minds, cultivating bodies, harmonizing family relationships, governing states, and bringing peace to the whole world. Intent on educating members of their own faith, they elucidated the basic tenets of Islamic thought for the purpose of self-reflection and mutual learning, rather than advocacy, let alone conversion. The Neo-Confucian value system implicit in their philosophical exposition was an integral part of what they considered self-evidently true. The Neo-Confucian code of ethics constituted a significant part of their belief, commitment, and action as well. They did not try to accommodate their theology to the Neo-Confucian mold, nor did they appropriate the Neo-Confucian frame of reference to make their theological ideas more palatable to the larger society. They were so steeped in the ambiance of the Neo-Confucian world that they took it for granted that "this culture of ours" provided the solid ground for them to flourish as Muslims.

It would be misleading, however, to give the impression that the Chinese ulama somehow effortlessly integrated Neo-Confucianism and Islam into a new synthesis. Actually, it was against overwhelming odds that the first generation of Chinese Muslim thinkers attained such interpretive brilliance. The story of Wang Tai-yü is truly exceptional. Widely acclaimed as the first major Chinese Muslim thinker, Wang wrote at least three seminal texts: *Cheng-chiao chen-ch'uan* ("The real interpretation of the orthodox teaching"), *Ch'ing-chen ta-hsüeh* ("The great learning of the pure and real"), and *Hsi-chen cheng-ta* ("True answers on the unique real"). Wang was conversant with the Four Teachings (Islam, Confucianism, Taoism, and Buddhism), and involved in a variety of inter-religious dialogues from the Islamic perspective. His versatility in engaging non-Muslim scholars in an extended conversation earned him the reputation of Chen-hui Lao-jen—literally, "the old man of Islam."

Yet, Wang was not raised in a Chinese literary family, nor was he ever formally tutored in Confucian classics. Born in a Muslim family of Central Asian ancestry, Wang received a religious education typical of youth of similar background. Since there was virtually no Chinese literature on Islamic teachings, Chinese who could not read Arabic or Persian would not have the direct access to the sacred Islamic text and its commentaries. Wang's study of Islam was understandably in Arabic and Persian. There is no way to gauge how he charted a course of action in the symbolic universe where most of the people he encountered spoke Chinese. Nor is there solid evidence of his meeting with the Jesuits, even though the temple that he later associated with for expounding the message of "pure and real" was adjacent to the religious base of his contemporary Ricci in Nanking.

According to his autobiographic note, Wang Tai-yü began learning classical Chinese in his late teens. While the need to acquire enough linguistic proficiency to discuss meaningfully the Islamic truth with members of his own faith community and scholars in the larger society is obvious, it seems evident that there was also intrinsic value in his sustained effort to become educated in Confucian classics. The perceived or suspected instrumental rationality seen in Ricci's case was absent. There was no comparable institutional pressure for Wang to make his work accountable to a higher authority in the religious hierarchy. As an aspiring member of the ulama class leading the life of the faithful, his orthodoxy and orthopraxy were never judged by his missionary work, no matter how broadly that is defined. Surely, his family, his teachers, the Muslim community in Nanking, Islam in China, the spread of Catholicism in the Confucian intelligentsia, the popularity of Pure Land Buddhism and religious Taoism, the vibrancy of the folk traditions, and a host of non-religious factors all weighed in Wang's educational choice.

But, there is no reason to doubt that his commitment to Confucian learning was also an integral part of his own self-cultivation—a holistic way of learning to be a good Muslim in a predominantly Confucian society. Wang was empowered by his profound "personal knowledge" and intimate "tacit understanding" of Neo-Confucian moral metaphysics to articulate his Islamic theology in a Chinese idiom. His creativity in constructing a Chinese Islamic world view is an original contribution to Neo-Confucian thinking. In a strict sense, he did not use Confucian terminology to articulate his ultimate concern. Rather, by embodying his transcending vision in the local knowledge, he offered a nuanced and subtle description of how the truth of Islam can be concretely realized in Confucian China. What he proposed was not an alternative path but a mutually beneficial joint venture. His acceptance of Confucian humanism as his own culture enriched his ordinary daily experience as a Muslim intellectual in a cosmopolitan Chinese city. His broad and deep understanding of Islamic philosophy added a new dimension to and a fresh perspective on his conversations with like-minded Confucian literati, Buddhist monks, and Taoist scholars.

In our pluralistic religious world, Wang Tai-yü can be easily categorized as a Confucian Muslim. From the perspective of the dialogue among civilizations, the meetings in Cambridge and Kuala Lumpur affirmed the authentic possibility of mutual reference, fruitful interaction, and genuine collaboration between Islamic and Confucian civilizations. As we embark on the twenty-first century, we begin to imagine the shapes of this kind of creative synthesis in North America and Southeast Asia. Wang single-handedly and powerfully demonstrated that it could be done. Moreover, in a systematic and conscientious way, he put into practice a concrete procedure to seamlessly interweave the core curriculum for Islamic studies with a richly textured exposition of Confucian learning. Without a full understanding of his own Islamic faith and the Confucian wisdom he had gained through the daily ritual of painstaking reading, cogitation, deliberation, and writing, such an inspiring exercise in analogical imagination was virtually impossible. *Great Learning of the Pure and Real* is the fruition of Wang's labor of love.

It is remarkable that the dialogue that Wang initiated in the middle of the seventeenth century continued to gather momentum in subsequent generations and produced a series of significant contribution by what Kuwata Rokuro, An Mu-t'ao, and others identified as "Muslim Confucian" (Hui-Ju) writers.[6] This trajectory reached its apex in the early eighteenth century, when one of the most sophisticated theological minds in the Chinese Islamic world, Liu Chih (c. 1662–1730), signaled the renaissance of Sinicized Islam. Among the themes Liu elucidated, the unity of Heaven and humanity is particularly intriguing. The motif in the *Doctrine of the Mean* featured prominently in Liu's ontological and epistemological exposition of apprehending the Supreme Lord. The anthropocosmic vision of the human participation in cosmic creativity in the *Doctrine* underlies Liu's project of a new fusion of the Islamic and Confucian horizons:

> Only those who are the most sincere (authentic, true and real) can fully realize their own nature;
> Able to fully realize their own nature, they can fully realize the nature of humanity;
> Able to fully realize the nature of humanity, they can fully realize the nature of things;
> Able to fully realize the nature of things, they can take part in the transforming and nourishing process of Heaven and Earth;
> Able to take part in the transforming and nourishing process of Heaven and Earth, they can form a trinity with Heaven and Earth.[7]

Liu's interpretation of Heaven/human, nature/destiny, substance/function is thoroughly Confucian. Yet, by grounding the discourse in Sufi teachings, he presented a coherent vision of the Islamic way of learning to be fully human. He successfully, if not effortlessly, incorporated Confucian notions of self-cultivation, sagehood, and ultimate transformation into an Islamic world view. At the same time, his Sufi vision, informed by the ideas of the unity of all realities, the continuity of being, and cosmic equilibrium, enabled him to appreciate the Confucian faith in the partnership between Heaven and humanity as co-creators.

Sachiko Murata's pioneering attempt to allow the shafts of Sufi light to shine through the opacity of Chinese Islamic theology illuminates a well-kept secret in the comparative study of religion. It has important implications for several other fields of inquiry, notably Chinese religion, East Asian thought, and comparative civilizational studies. It also helps us to place the Confucian-Christian dialogue in a broader context, categorize Chinese religions more ecumenically than the Three Teachings, and recognize the contours of Islamic studies in traditional China. Her view of the unfolding landscape is so enchanting that the promise of original research and productive scholarship seems limitless. I am grateful to her for inviting me to share a truly exceptional moment in the dialogue among civilizations.

TU WEIMING

Acknowledgments

I wish to express my gratitude to all the organizations and individuals that have made this research possible and assisted me along the way. I am grateful to Stony Brook for the junior faculty research leave that I received in the autumn of 1994 and the sabbatical leave in the spring of 1997, both of which allowed me to spend time at Harvard and the Yenching Institute. I am also grateful for the assistance given by the Harvard Yenching Library and Harvard's Center for the Study of World Religions. Most of all, I thank the National Endowment for the Humanities, whose generous support made possible the main body of my research. Several libraries in Japan, including the Library of Congress, Tōyō Bunka Kenkyūjo of Tokyo University, Tōyō Bunko, and the Tenri University Library, were generous in providing microfilms of Chinese works. My special thanks go to Mr. Yamamura of Tōyō Bunko and Miss Kobayashi of Tenri. I am also grateful to the Center for Civilizational Dialogue at the University of Malaya, which providing me with some assistance for my trip to China. Professor Tentaro Inoh of Chuo University kindly sent me various secondary sources on Islam that he had obtained more than fifty years ago when he was teaching in Beijing. Professor Chiyo Shima of Chiba University and my friend Hiroko Yamada helped me obtain documents from the Japan Library of Congress. Professor Sun Quanzhuo of Shanghai Foreign Language University and Professor Yu Weihan, former president of Harping Medical College, acted as my guides in China and gave me all sorts of assistance. Professor Yu Zhengui, director of the Academy of Social Sciences at Ningxia, and Professor Ma Ping of the same Academy were helpful to me in China. Several people assisted me in various stages of preparing this study, including Professors Shi-ming Hu and Sung-Bae Park of Stony Brook, Zou Qin of Harvard, and Mitsuko Collver of special collections at Stony Brook Library, who established a section for Islam in China. I am grateful to Professor Seyyed Hossein Nasr, who invited me to participate in an ongoing dialogue with Tu Weiming on Islamic and Confucian relations, and who has continued to encourage me to pursue my work on Chinese Islam. My good friends Dr. Alma Giese and Professor Wolfhart Heinrichs of Harvard not only encouraged and aided me in my research but also gave me a cozy place to stay in Boston whenever I needed it. Finally, I am extremely grateful to Professor Tu Weiming for his unstinting support despite the tremendous demands on his time. He patiently read with me the texts from cover to cover and gave me invaluable suggestions and advice, without which I could not have finalized the translations. Reading these texts with him while sipping the finest Chinese green tea offered me a glimpse into the domain of the Heavenly Immortals.

The calligraphic design on the front cover is taken from the frontispiece of *Jen-chi hsing-yü* by Ma Ming-lung, published in 1919. A copy of this work was kindly provided by the Tenri University library. The text reads as follows (Chinese indicated by italics, Arabic by roman letters):

> He said, *the sage said*, upon him be peace. "*At the time when the human recognizes himself clearly, he truly recognizes the Real Lord of protecting and nourishing.*" "He who knows himself has known his Lord."

Introduction

When *The Tao of Islam* was published in 1992, I knew little about Chinese Islam and had no thought of learning more about it. However, I had decided to continue my study of Neo-Confucian thinking, and, with the intention of reading Chinese texts under the guidance of Tu Weiming, I applied for a fellowship to spend time at the Center for the Study of World Religions at Harvard. I received the fellowship for the academic year 1994–95, and devoted my time there to studying Chinese cosmology. In March 1995, however, I attended a conference called "Islam and Confucianism: A Civilizational Dialogue" at the University of Malaya in Kuala Lumpur. Professor Lee Cheuk Yin of the National University of Singapore, a specialist in Chinese intellectual history, presented a paper there on Wang Tai-yü, the first Muslim thinker to write in Chinese. I was fascinated by his talk, and on my return to Harvard I immediately went to the library of the Yenching Institute to see if I could find any of Wang's books. The Yenching turned out to have one of the oldest known copies of Wang's major work in its rare book collection, and it also had a small shelf of works by Wang, Liu Chih, and other Chinese Muslim authors. Seeing the availability of these resources, I put aside my previous project and devoted myself to the study of the Chinese texts. I have not been able to put them down since. The present work is the first fruit of that change of direction.

In *The Tao of Islam*, I tried to examine Islamic thought with Far Eastern eyes. It became clear to me in carrying out research for the book that the manner in which Islamic intellectuality is portrayed by modern scholarship has at least as much to do with the preconceptions of Western scholars as with the actual texts. If scholars see the Islamic tradition as mired in either/or thinking and as antithetical to the Far Eastern concepts of balance and harmony, this is because they have been trained to think in terms of sharp dichotomies, not because the texts necessarily present the world in these terms. As soon as one searches Islamic texts for the idea of an overarching Tao that functions according to the complementarity of yin and yang, it turns up in a wide variety of texts, beginning with the Koran and the Hadith, and especially in the various forms of literature that employ imagery and symbolism, Sufi writings in particular. Even the famously rationalistic texts of the philosophers find plenty of room for such quasi-Far Eastern concepts, though it is far more difficult to find them in Kalam (dogmatic theology) and almost impossible in jurisprudence.

I based the Chinese side of *The Tao of Islam* on my own understanding of Chinese thought. It barely occurred to me that Muslim thinkers might already have covered some of the same ground. It was precisely the discovery that they had in fact dealt with similar issues that excited me the moment I heard Professor Lee speak about Wang Tai-yü. Here was a seventeenth-century Muslim discussing Islamic concepts in the Chinese language in a manner that immediately struck me as similar to what I had been trying to do, though his version was far more sophisticated than mine. My intention in spending a year at Harvard had been to continue the line of research that I had begun in *The Tao of Islam*. But the existence of texts by Wang and other Chinese Muslim thinkers made me think that I should rather investigate how Muslims themselves interacted with Chinese metaphysics, cosmology, and psychology.

In order to continue my research on Chinese Islam in a more concentrated manner, I applied to the National Endowment for the Humanities for a fellowship to study the works of Wang Tai-yü. I received support for the academic year 1997–98, and was also accepted as an associate at the Harvard Yenching Institute. In the preceding spring, I had used a sabbatical leave to undertake the first stage of my project. That was to look carefully at the handful of Persian texts that had been translated into Chinese in the seventeenth and eighteenth centuries, with the aim of grasping how Islamic ideas were transferred into the Chinese intellectual milieu. The second stage was to make a translation and careful study of Wang's major work, *The Real Commentary on the True Teaching*. As part of the preparatory research, I spent three months in Japan and China looking for manuscripts and old editions of the Chinese texts. During the fellowship year, I was not able to make a great deal of headway in translating Wang's long work, but I did make a careful study of one of the translated Persian texts, Liu Chih's *Displaying the Concealment of the Real Realm*, and one of Wang's shorter works, *The Great Learning of the Pure and Real*, and these are the texts presented here. I met with far more difficulties in understanding these texts than I would have expected, and several of my colleagues and friends from whom I sought help will surely attest that we are dealing with works that are challenging even to those who have a thorough knowledge of later Chinese intellectual history. Many passages would have been indecipherable without my own understanding of Islamic concepts paired with my colleagues' grasp of the niceties of Neo-Confucian and Buddhist thought.

Before even beginning to introduce Wang Tai-yü and Liu Chih, the greatest of the Chinese ulama, it may be useful to say something about the significance of their writings for our understanding of Islam in China. Any survey of the modern scholarship will reveal that very little is known about Chinese Islam, even though it is generally acknowledged that there have been Muslim communities in China for a thousand years. A good deal of research has been carried out on Islam in twentieth-century China, but little has been written on the Muslims' perception of themselves before the twentieth century. It is true that in the late nineteenth and early twentieth centuries, many scholars devoted efforts to surveying the Islamic writings in the Chinese language. Isaac Mason, among others, did pioneering work on bibliography, and he partially translated Liu Chih's life of the prophet Muhammad into English. All this secondary literature has been surveyed, summarized, and improved upon by the valuable books of Donald Leslie, *Islam in Traditional China* and *Islamic Literature in Chinese*. But despite all this research, little attention has been paid to the actual contents of the Chinese writings and how they relate to Islamic teachings. One of the few exceptions is provided by the excellent articles of Françoise Aubin.

Like Islam in other parts of the world, Chinese Islam has its local peculiarities, though these should not be exaggerated. As Joseph F. Fletcher has pointed out, early scholars of Chinese Islam often suggested that Islam in China had departed from the orthodoxy and orthopraxy of the central Islamic lands, but there is little evidence to support this claim. For, as Fletcher maintains, "The history of Muslims in China is not a history isolated from other Muslims."[1] Nonetheless, we meet formulations of Islamic teachings in the Chinese language that would certainly appear strange if they could be translated directly back into Persian or Arabic. The reason for this is that the most important determinant of the local peculiarities of Islamic teachings in Chinese is the Chinese language itself along with the great intellectual heritage for which it was the vehicle.

The specifically Chinese formulations of Islamic teachings do not begin appearing until the seventeenth century because, so far as is known, up until that time Chinese Muslims studied and wrote about Islamic topics in their own languages, mainly Persian. In 1642, Wang Tai-yü published his *Real Commentary on the True Teaching*, which is the first Chinese-language exposition of Islamic learning. By the end of that century, at least three books had been translated from Persian, and Liu Chih, the second towering figure of Chinese Islam, had begun his career.[2]

The Chinese ulama were not motivated primarily by the intention of making Islam known to non-Muslims. Rather, they were writing for their own co-religionists, who did not have sufficient acquaintance with the Islamic languages to master Islamic thinking, especially not when faced with the vast resources of the Chinese intellectual tradition. As J. F. Ford has written about Wang Tai-yü's major work, "[H]is book was not a work of proselytism, but was primarily aimed at educating in their own religion the Muslim community which already existed."[3] He points out that this was a period of accelerating assimilation of Muslims into the Chinese community.

> [I]n the new phase of their history when the bulk of them spoke only the Chinese which was now their mother tongue, and the original stock was diluted by accessions from the Han, their grasp of Islam was in danger of slipping unless they overhauled their methods. The faithful had to be provided with explanations in a language which they could understand, and Wang Tai-yü was the first to do it. His book also showed the Muslims the possibility of thinking and writing about their religion in the Chinese idiom.[4]

The Islamic community had reached a point where the ulama perceived the danger that Muslims would no longer be able to understand the principles of their own faith and the rationale for their own practices. All the early texts deal mainly with how to understand Islamic teachings, not how to put them into practice. Their primary concern is not to explain the Shariah or jurisprudence, nor the contents of the Koran and Hadith in any direct way. Rather, the writings elaborate on the nature of the Islamic perception of God, the universe, and the soul, that is, the domain that is traditionally called "the principles of the religion" (*uṣūl al-dīn*).

In short, the early Chinese texts were written to explain to Muslims why their tradition looks at the world the way it does. The language of these texts is mainly that of the dominant intellectual school of the day—Neo-Confucianism. These are not apologetic works written for non-Muslims, but expository works written for Muslims who themselves had become intellectually assimilated into Chinese civilization. As Leslie points out in his useful discussion of the whole issue of assimilation, "Minorities managed to survive, but individuals who wished to be accepted into Chinese society must by the nature of things become Confucian."[5] It seems to be precisely these "Confucian" Muslims who were being addressed in the Chinese texts, which were certainly not written for the "common man." If they were, then the common Muslim was familiar with the sophisticated discourse of Neo-Confucian scholarship and had a working knowledge of Buddhism and Taoism. Since this seems unlikely, we can safely conclude that they were written for Muslims who had been to some degree integrated into the educated elite of Chinese society.

It is of course true that there were other factors encouraging the ulama to write in Chinese. One in particular is worth mentioning, and that is the "rites controversy" that was caused by the objection of Franciscan and Dominican friars to the Jesuits' willingness to allow the continuation of "ancestor worship" among Christian converts. According to several Japanese scholars who have studied this period, this heated controversy encouraged Muslims to make their own positions available in Chinese so that they would not be criticized like the Christians (though there is no sign of the relevant issues in the texts translated here).[6]

Whatever the specific reasons that motivated the ulama to write in Chinese, there can be little doubt that they were following what Erik Zürcher calls a "cultural imperative" that had already been adopted by Buddhism, Judaism, and Christianity. In a brief comparison of the ways in which these four religions adapted themselves to the Chinese situation, Zürcher points out that there are consistent patterns of adaptation, all connected with the issues that were to flare up in the rites controversy—"theological terminology, adoption of Confucian values, Confucianism as an 'incomplete' secular doctrine, and . . . the constant tendency to quest for a common origin, going back to the teachings of the ancient saintly rulers. . . . The authority, the sheer mass and attractive power of Confucianism was such that any religious system from outside was caught in its field."[7]

If the Islamic texts in Chinese need to be understood and evaluated in terms of Chinese history, they also need to be investigated in terms of Islamic civilization. It is certainly not without interest for the history of Islamic thought that these works have no precedents in any other Islamic countries. Only in modern times have Muslims been faced with a similar intellectual challenge. The Chinese writings represent the first instance in which Muslims wrote major treatises in the language of one of the great, pre-existing intellectual traditions. Only the Indian, Buddhist, Greek, and Judeo-Christian traditions could compare with China in terms of the richness of philosophical, theological, cosmological, and psychological teachings. But Muslims never had to express themselves in the languages of any of those traditions. Wherever they went, they took their own languages with them—first Arabic, then Persian. Although Persia did have a pre-existing intellectual heritage, by the time Muslims began writing in Persian, the language had been totally transformed by

Arabic. The other languages that were used to express Islamic learning, like Turkish and Urdu, were also in effect new creations of Islamic civilization itself.

What the Chinese ulama did, then, was to write about Islam in a completely non-Islamic idiom. The only similar situation that had been experienced by Islamic civilization was the Muslim adoption of Greek thought during the first three or four centuries of Islam. The grand difference, however, is that the early Muslims wrote about Greek thought in Arabic, not in Greek, so they used Islamic terminology to make their points and they did not have to worry about responses by the Greek philosophers. In contrast, the Chinese ulama wrote in Chinese, so they had to use Neo-Confucian terminology. Their books were immediately printed and distributed, so they could not ignore the possible reactions of other Chinese intellectuals. Anyone who reads these texts with a knowledge of the Chinese ambiance of the seventeenth and eighteenth centuries can see that they are part of the ongoing discussion and debate among Chinese intellectuals concerning the nature of the quest for human perfection.

Given that these texts anticipate what Muslims would have to do in the modern world, studying them may suggest in unexpected ways the resources available to the Islamic tradition for dealing with alternative interpretations of the universe. Modern Muslims, for example, have written a good deal about Islam's theoretical and theological relations with other religions, Christianity in particular. Far too many of these writings, however, are marked by a surprising lack of understanding not only of the other religions, but also of Islam's own theoretical resources for dealing with religious diversity.

To cite one example of what I have in mind, it is commonly thought that Far Eastern metaphysics and cosmology are impersonal and therefore alien to the Islamic world view. But this was certainly not the way in which the Chinese ulama saw Confucianism. If we can learn only one thing from their writings, it is that the stereotypes about Islamic and Chinese thinking need to be discarded. Islam is indeed the third of the three Abrahamic monotheisms. There have been modes of Islamic thinking that tend toward a rather harsh exclusivism. But this does not mean that there have not been other modes of Islamic thinking that easily adapt to a much broader and more inclusivist view of things.

From another side, some of modern scholarship still maintains that Confucianism is not really a "religion," but rather a philosophy. This evaluation, of course, depends upon our definitions of the terms *religion* and *philosophy*, and it is heavily indebted to a Christian sensibility toward what may be properly called "religion." For their part, many of the Chinese Muslims saw Confucianism as an affirmation of the same transcendent principles that animate the Koran. They had no difficulty understanding the Confucian teachings as pertaining to the same order of reality as the Islamic teachings—which is not to say, however, that they had no criticisms to offer.

One of the things that is striking about these Chinese texts on Islam is the nonalignment of a good proportion of the contents with any specific teaching. My Confucian and Buddhist colleagues have been deeply struck by the manner in which the texts obliterate the modern stereotypes about Islam. When I spoke to Professor Lee about Wang at the conference in Kuala Lumpur, he explained that he had discovered one of Wang's books a short time before in a Chinese bookstore in Singapore. After telling me how the book had totally changed his preconceptions about Islam's role in China, he expressed an opinion that has been echoed by several others who have looked at these texts, if not in so many words: "If this is Islam," he said, "Islam is a wonderful religion."

To the question, "Is this Islam?," my own response is that it is as much Islam as any other seventeenth-century version of the faith, and a lot more so than anything that famously bears the name in the modern world. The fact that so many interpretations of Islam have now been narrowed down to fit into ideological frameworks is simply a reflection of modern Muslims' ignorance of the Islamic tradition and their sense of impotence in the face of the impersonal forces of modernity. It says nothing about the rich resources of the tradition itself.

I am not about to enter into a defense of these texts, however. They speak for themselves, and readers can take them or leave them. Rather, I would like to suggest some of the commonalities that the Muslim authors saw with the other Chinese traditions. This is, after all, the first instance in which Muslims wrote in the context of a foreign intellectual tradition, and as such, it does parallel the experience of modern Islam. But there is also a vast difference between seventeenth-century China and the modern intellectual environment. In China at that time, there was no basic conflict between the principles that underlie the Far Eastern religions and Islamic principles. In contrast, the principles that have molded modern thought are largely hostile to religion. I do not think that it is going too far to say that the contemporary intellectual environment is essentially hostile to religious teachings and only accidentally tolerant toward them. In contrast, the Chinese intellectual environment in which the Muslim scholars were living and writing was essentially congenial with religious teachings, and only critical of specific teachings, the specificities depending on who was writing—Neo-Confucian, Buddhist, Taoist, Muslim, etc. What I have in mind can quickly be grasped if we think about some of shared features of the traditions that were plain to the Chinese ulama. Five of these seem especially obvious.

The first principle of Islamic thinking is *tawḥīd*, the assertion of (God's) unity. The Arabic word means literally "making one" or "making into one" or, as it is sometimes translated into Chinese, "practicing one" (*hsi-i*). The most concise theological expression of *tawḥīd* is said to be the first half of the Shahadah, that is, the statement, "(There is) no god but God." As the first and most basic principle of faith, *tawḥīd* is the fountainhead of all theological thinking. By theological thinking I do not mean simply Kalam (dogmatic theology), but also philosophy, theoretical Sufism, and many other expressions of Islamic understanding—notably poetry, which is the chief vehicle for expressing theological ideas in accessible language.

Tawḥīd demands that all of existence be governed by a single, supreme Reality—which the Chinese ulama had no objection to calling by the Neo-Confucian term *Principle* (*li*). Everything comes from this One, Real Principle, and everything returns to it. The fact that much of Islamic discourse personifies this Principle and discusses it wholly in anthropomorphic terms does not detract from the fact that there is a complementary perspective found in the same Islamic discourse that declares the Principle's utter transcendence and ineffability, making personal and anthropomorphic language totally inappropriate. The twin ideas of transcendence and immanence, or asserting God's incomparability (*tanzīh*) and his similarity (*tashbīh*), are the yang and the yin of Islamic theological thinking.[8]

There is certainly no disagreement among the three Chinese traditions concerning the underlying unity of all reality, whatever the terminology that may be employed. Hence, the Islamic stress on unity appears as another version of a well known idea. Nor does the anthropomorphic pole of Islamic understanding pose any problem when the terminology is drawn from the three Chinese traditions. There is no concept of "God" per se in Chinese, so the highest principle cannot be named in the same personal terms that are usually used in Islamic languages. Nonetheless, many of the typical designations for God used by the Chinese ulama—such as "Real Lord"—are rooted in the ancient Chinese writings and Confucian imperial imagery, and such expressions are perfectly congenial with some of the Koranic divine names. On a more philosophical and metaphysical level, the abstract terms that Neo-Confucianism employs have plenty of parallels in Islamic texts, so it is easy to make the transition from one set of impersonal terminology to another.

In the works of the Chinese ulama, *tawḥīd* is a constant theme, even though they rarely employ the Arabic word. A prime example is Wang Tai-yü's *Great Learning of the Pure and Real*, which is translated here. The book is structured in terms of three meanings of the word "one," and it explains how all the distinctions that must be drawn in discussing God, the universe, and the human being are subsumed under the reality of unity. Although Wang deals with issues that are central to Islamic texts, he draws all his language and imagery from the Chinese tradition and employs numerous terms employed not only by Confucians, but also by Taoists and Buddhists.

A second point that illustrates the commonalities of the four traditions is the issue of what we nowadays call "nature"—heaven, earth, and the ten thousand things. Chinese thinking agrees on the revelatory and sacred role of the natural world, because it is the locus within which the Tao or the Buddha nature displays its own reality. Everyone knows that the concept of Tao has to do with the harmony of heaven and earth and the perfect balance among all the forces that drive the supernatural and natural worlds, but it is often forgotten that the Koran is full of discussion of God's signs in the natural world. The idea of the balance of heaven and earth is central to its message, as is recognized by much of the Islamic intellectual tradition. The Chinese ulama had no difficulty seeing the idea of cosmic equilibrium as a shared feature of the traditions.

It perhaps needs to be stressed that this is a dimension of Islamic teaching that tends to be forgotten in modern times, when Islamic countries have been rushing to adopt modern technology and institutions with all their implications for the destruction of the natural order. This helps explain why so much stress is laid in modern Islamic discourse on social and political teachings. As long as the cosmological teachings of Islam are ignored, it becomes easy to pretend that Islamic social teachings are the crux of the tradition and to ignore the intimate relationship that was always seen between society on the one side and, on the other, "heaven, earth, and everything between the two" (to use the Koranic expression).

A third major area of agreement between Islam and the Chinese traditions lies in the domain of "sagehood." All agree that the human models of the past are utterly essential for the quest to live in harmony with heaven and earth. In Islamic terms, this is the second principle of faith: prophecy. For the Chinese, the teachings of the ancient sages and worthies, the Buddhas, and the boddhisattvas, are indispensable. In all these traditions, the reasons for the indispensability of the guidance of the sages and prophets is that human beings cannot possibly achieve the goal of life without help from those who have already achieved it.

This brings us to a fourth point of commonality, which is that the goal of human life is clearly laid down and agreed upon by all four traditions. It is to achieve human perfection. As Tu Weiming has often said in characterizing Neo-Confucianism, the fundamental impulse of the tradition is "learning how to be human." This is also a key issue in Taoism and Buddhism, no matter how much the discussion of human nature may differ. In the Chinese Islamic texts, it is completely clear that the ulama saw "learning how to be human" as the fundamental purpose of all Islamic teachings. When the Prophet said, "Seek knowledge, even unto China," he meant knowledge of how to be human, of how to live up to the models established by the perfected human beings of the past. In contrast, if we try to sum up the general thrust of modern education and even modern civilization, it would be more accurate to say that it is "forgetting how to be human" in any sense of the word "human" that would have been meaningful in the pre-modern context. The very idea that there can be a human perfection of which the sages and prophets of the past were the models and toward which all human endeavor should strive has long since been discarded as outmoded and naive.

This brings us to a fifth, closely related point—the domain of social and political teachings. In the Far East, Confucians lay special stress on this domain. The Chinese ulama, in fact, found themselves almost completely in agreement with the Confucian teachings on social relationships, which they rarely criticize, in contrast to various Buddhist and Taoist concepts. The principle here is that if society is to achieve peace, harmony, and equilibrium, it must be built on individuals who conform to the Tao. Confucianism laid down this principle with stark clarity, and the Buddhists and Taoists do not deny it. If individuals fail to rectify their own individual relationships with the Tao, then the family, the nation, and the world will never be put back into order. The contrast with the modern situation, in which the domain of individual initiative and striving toward the ultimate is constantly being eroded by the vast, impersonal institutions of government and industry, and where all solutions are sought in further strengthening these same institutions, could hardly be starker.

In short, the Chinese ulama—and indeed, most ulama of pre-modern times—could only agree wholeheartedly with the following passage from the Confucian *Great Learning*:

> The ancients who wished to clarify their clear virtue under heaven would first govern their countries. Those who wished to govern their countries would first regulate their families. Those who wished to regulate their families would first cultivate their personal lives. Those who wished to cultivate their personal lives would first make their hearts true. Those who wished to make their hearts true would first make their intentions sincere. Those who wished to make their intentions sincere would first extend their knowledge. . . . From the Son of Heaven down to the common people, all must regard cultivation of the personal life as the root or foundation. There is never a case when the root is in disorder and yet the branches are in order.[9]

The present book is divided into seven parts. Part one describes the first appearance of Chinese-language works written by Muslims in the seventeenth and eighteenth centuries, introduces the two major Chinese Muslim scholars, Wang Tai-yü and Liu Chih, and describes some of the efforts carried out by Muslim scholars to translate Islamic books into Chinese. Part two introduces the writings of Wang Tai-yü in detail. Part three describes Wang's *Great Learning of the Pure and Real* (*Ch'ing-chen ta-hsüeh*) and situates it in the context of Chinese and Islamic teachings. Part four is a translation of Wang's *Great Learning*. Part five explains the importance of the Persian work *Gleams* (*Lawāʾiḥ*) by ʿAbd al-Raḥmān Jāmī and describes Liu Chih's translation of *Gleams* into Chinese with the title *Displaying the Concealment of the Real Realm* (*Chen-ching chao-wei*). Part six offers a new English translation of Jāmī's *Gleams* from the Persian. Part seven presents a translation of Liu Chih's *Displaying the Concealment of the Real Realm*. The two translations are arranged on facing pages so that readers can judge for themselves how Liu Chih modified the text to fit the Neo-Confucian context of Chinese thought. The translation of *Gleams* from Persian was made by my husband, William C. Chittick, whose editorial advice has been followed throughout the book, though I remain fully responsible for the final text.

1

Chinese-Language Islam

Estimates of the number of Muslims living in China today vary widely, but fifteen to twenty million seems to be the minimum. Ten Muslim nationalities are officially recognized by the government, nine of which speak their own languages and live in specific areas of China. The tenth, the so-called Hui, speak only Chinese (albeit with many words and expressions peculiar to themselves) and are scattered all over the country.[1]

Islam's history in China extends back to the seventh century, that is, the first century of Islam. The Chinese Muslims provide mythic accounts of how Islam came to China during the lifetime of the Prophet himself, who died in 632. It is known that China signed its first treaty with a Muslim mission in 651, the year of the final conquest of Persia, so the mythic accounts cannot be too far off. A second mission arrived in 655, and another forty are recorded as arriving by the end of the eighth century.[2] Opinions differ as to when immigrant Muslims may have formed some sort of community, and there is no strong evidence for a Chinese-speaking Muslim community until around the ninth century.[3]

No one knows to what extent the Islamic presence in China derived from immigrants or from Chinese converts. However this may be, many of the immigrants gradually became indistinguishable from the native Chinese, and a large population of Muslims who considered themselves Chinese became established. Until the seventeenth century, however, it seems that Islamic learning was transmitted in Persian and Arabic (and perhaps Turkic dialects as well), since we have no Chinese texts on Islam written by Chinese Muslims before this time.

Historians agree that Chinese Islam in general is heavily influenced by Persianate Islam. The Japanese historian Tazaka Kōdō, for example, analyzed several book lists provided by Japanese and European researchers in his monumental study of the history of Chinese Islam and came to the conclusion that the books used were mainly by Persian authors and mostly in Persian, though Arabic works also played a significant role. After all, Persian was the primary language of Islamic instruction from Persia east, and Arabic is the language of the Koran and of the majority of the Islamic classics.

China was one of the more isolated outposts of Islam, and it was also the site of an enormously rich indigenous civilization. Thus it is not surprising that Muslims eventually had to write in Chinese in order to pass on the Islamic tradition to fellow Muslims. What is surprising is that this movement did not begin until the seventeenth century. The historical factors that precipitated the decision to write in Chinese remain to be investigated. Here I will only suggest certain preliminary conclusions that can be gleaned from the writings themselves.

The Essentials of Islam

By the seventeenth century, Islamic literature in Arabic and Persian was enormously rich. The Islamic sciences had developed in several directions, and diverse writings were available within China itself. When the Chinese ulama decided to write in Chinese, their basic difficulties were how best to cull the essential teachings of Islam from the original sources and then express them in an appropriate idiom. To understand the nature of the problem that they faced, it is necessary to know something about the general situation of Islamic learning at this point in history.

To conceptualize their own religion, Muslims have traditionally divided Islam into complementary fields of knowledge. They considered all these to have roots in the Koran and the Sunnah (the words and acts of the Prophet), while they saw the religion itself as a flourishing tree, with clearly defined branches, each oriented toward the production of fruit. The fruit of Islam's tree is the perfection of human individuals, however this might be formulated in various schools of thought. Thus Islamic scholarship has always had its own criteria for distinguishing the essential from the accidental, the roots from the branches, and the flowers from the fruit.

In one of the basic ways of thinking about the tradition, Islam is viewed as a "religion" (*dīn*) with three fundamental dimensions. These are *islām* or submission to God's will, *īmān* or faith in God and his teachings, and *iḥsān* or virtue, sincerity, and beauty of character. One might also call these right action, right understanding, and right intention.[4] As the tree of Islamic learning developed, each of these dimensions grew into a major branch of learning with many boughs and twigs.

The branch of learning that addressed right activity came to be known as "jurisprudence," or the science of the Shariah (the revealed law). After Koranic Arabic, this has been the most commonly studied science among

Muslims. The Shariah delineates in clear detail what the Koran and the Sunnah teach about rites and various communal and societal actions. The so-called "Five Pillars of Islam" are the most basic rites, incumbent on all Muslims. But the Shariah, like Jewish law and Confucian social teachings, also deals with many issues that do not appear "religious"—and certainly not "spiritual"—to most people in the modern West. These include foods, business transactions, marriage, and inheritance. The Orientalist adage, "Islam is not a religion but a way of life," refers in part to this wide reach of the Shariah.

The second basic branch of Islamic learning addresses right understanding. The Koran commands faith in God, his angels, the scriptures, the prophets, and the Last Day, and it was clear to Muslims that people cannot have faith in things of which they have no knowledge. From earliest times, scholars devoted themselves to explicating these objects of faith. By the third/ninth century, this second branch of the tradition had subdivided into three major offshoots, each of which was well on its way to full flower. "Kalam" or dogmatic theology took a defensive and polemical view of Koranic teachings, depending on rational argument to convince doubters and disbelievers. "Philosophy" was heavily indebted to the Greek heritage and, like Kalam, took a rational approach to understanding, but it avoided Koranic language and often voiced opinions on Ultimate Reality and the prophets that blatantly contradicted the views of the Kalam authorities. "Theoretical Sufism" differed from the first two by stressing suprarational perception over reason. For the Sufi authorities, the key to understanding was not the acquisition of knowledge through study and investigation, but—much in the Taoist fashion—the emptying of the heart so that God might inspire it directly. The most common designation for the knowledge gained by this route is "unveiling" (*kashf*). Although these branches of learning tended to be distinct in their formative period, many scholars studied all of them and a number of famous authors wrote books in more than one branch or harmonized them in various ways.

The third basic branch of Islamic learning has to do with right intention, sincerity, purity of character, love for God and the neighbor, ethics, morality, interiority, and the spiritual path. This is the whole enterprise of strengthening one's personal connection with the divine, purifying the heart and mind, and attempting to live day-by-day in the awareness of God's presence. The most thorough explications of these issues are found in theoretical Sufism which, as noted, pertains to the domain of right understanding.

In all these branches of Islam, it was—and remains—difficult to speak of anything that might properly be called "orthodoxy," given that there has been no institution that might decree the correctness or incorrectness of various expressions. This is not to say that no one made claims to authority, simply that there was no church or hierarchy that could adjudicate the claims. As a result, Islamic norms became established through various sorts of consensus, but debates have always continued. Certainly Muslims agree on the basic principles, which are God's unity, the prophethood of Muhammad, and the divine origin of the Koran. But all these are terms that need definition, and diversity of opinion arises as soon as definitions are formulated. Some observers have suggested that "orthopraxy" was the criterion for Islamicity—that is, acknowledgment of the incumbency of the Shariah and observance of it. This is perhaps closer to the actual historical situation, but it also is problematic. It is true, however, that acceptance of the incumbency of the "Five Pillars" has been considered by most Muslim scholars as the least criterion for Islamic affiliation.

In the second branch of learning, which is the domain of right understanding, there are three foundational issues, often called the "three principles" of Islam—the assertion that God is one (*tawḥīd*), prophecy, and the Return to God. Each of the three branches of the tradition that dealt with right understanding discussed these issues in its own ways. Philosophy, for example, had several major schools, and the basic discussions were all rooted in the three principles. In the seventeenth century, most of the positions of the three major approaches to this field of learning were still being discussed. For example, Mullā Ṣadrā of Shiraz (d. 1640) presents in his *Asfār* an encyclopedic engagement with all the philosophical and theological positions of earlier schools of thought. Theoretical Sufism was especially rich in the diversity of its approaches to divine Unity, though by the seventeenth century the dominant themes were set by the school of Ibn al-ʿArabī (d. 1240).[5]

Sufism had several characteristics that made it adaptable to diverse cultural contexts. These help explain why Sufi teachers were commonly the means whereby Islam has expanded its borders, as can be witnessed in India, Indonesia, Central Asia, Africa, and, as scholars have often remarked, China. These characteristics can be boiled down to the fact that Sufism stresses the essential over the accidental. Always the Sufi teachers focus on "spirituality," which is to say that they stress the kernel over the shell, the meaning over the letter, the spirit over the body, and the subtle over the dense. If, for example, Rūmī's 25,000-verse didactic poem, the *Mathnawī*, has been called for centuries "the Koran in the Persian language," this is not to suggest that it has any formal similarity with the Koran. Rather, the *Mathnawī* succeeds in bringing out what Rūmī himself calls "the roots of the roots of the roots of the religion." It is this special ability to look beyond the form and into the divine intention that marks Sufi writings throughout Islamic history.

Traditional criticisms of the Sufis have come from two groups of scholars who have a vested interest in defending the formal dimensions of the religion. These are the jurists, who specialize in the Shariah, and the Kalam authorities, who defend the primacy of certain exteriorizing interpretations of the Koran. The Sufis have typically replied by agreeing upon the necessity of the formal observances as well as belief in the Koranic dogmas, but by criticizing the critics for not recognizing that all these things, no matter how necessary for Islamic faith and practice, are the body of Islam. Real Islam demands making contact with the heart and spirit of Islam.

The Chinese Language

It is worth remembering that the Chinese ulama were faced with a problem that was not present in any of the other languages used to express Islamic teachings. It would be next to impossible to write scholarly Chinese in the Arabic script, and only slightly less difficult to write Arabic in the Chinese script. When a language does employ the Arabic script, any Arabic word can be made part of it, so languages like Persian, Turkish, Urdu, Sindhi, Gujrati, and Malaysian have numerous Arabic loan-words, and indeed, a language deserves to be called an "Islamic" language largely because of the massive carryover of Arabic terminology. Even the European languages allow for a relatively simple transliteration of Arabic words. But the Chinese script simply does not permit transliteration except in an enormously awkward and even grotesque manner.[6] Thus the name Muhammad, which obviously had to be spelled out in Chinese at least on occasion, ended up being written in a half-dozen different ways, each of them a cumbersome attempt to present the word phonetically.

In short, it should not be surprising that the Chinese Muslim authors avoided using Arabic words. But this made their task unique in the Islamic world. Everywhere else, authors could simply employ the Arabic terms in their own languages, without having to worry too much about getting the exact meaning across. The Chinese ulama had to use preexisting Chinese words to render Islamic ideas, and every one of these words had precedents and connotations in one or more of the three Chinese traditions—Confucianism, Taoism, and Buddhism. The paucity of references in the Chinese works to the great personalities of Islamic history, unparalleled in Islamic literature, is tied directly to the difficulty of representing their names in Chinese characters.

There are numerous important terms known in the Islamic languages for which the Chinese authors had to find equivalents. What should be done, for example, with the word *Allah*? In Persian, the word is part of everyday speech, though people are just as likely to use the Persian equivalent (*khudā*). But there is no equivalent in Chinese. According to

Tazaka, to render the concept of God Muslims used "heaven" in the Tang period (618–907) and both "heaven" and "Buddha" in the Sung dynasty (960–1279). At the end of the Ming dynasty (1368–1644), when they had begun writing books in Chinese, they used words like "Real Lord" (*chen-chu*), "Real One" (*chen-i*), "Real Ruler" (*chen-tsai*), and "Lord" (*chu*).

"Real Lord" is especially interesting because Christians employed the expression "Heavenly Lord" (*t'ien-chu*). The very name of the Christian divinity would have caused difficulties for metaphysically minded Chinese, given that heaven and earth are inseparably linked, while the supreme principle must lie beyond the two. As it happens, the Koran frequently refers to God as "creator of heaven and earth," and the common Chinese expression "heaven, earth, and the ten thousand things" has its Koranic equivalent in "heaven, earth, and what is between the two," which occurs in some twenty verses.

The question of Islamic terminology in Chinese has yet to be investigated with any rigor, so a few examples will have to suffice. Muhammad was referred to as the "Sage" (*sheng*) or the "Utmost Sage" (*chih-sheng*)—"sage" being a term that was reserved for Confucius and the great teachers who had preceded him. Muhammad was also called the "Chief Servant" (*shou-p'u*) and the "Ambassador" (*ch'in-ch'a*), terms that reflect a standard version of the second half of the Shahadah (the testimony of faith), recited in the daily prayer— "I bear witness that Muhammad is His servant and His messenger." The Koran is the "classic" (*ching*), the "heavenly classic" (*t'ien-ching*), and the "real classic of the true mandate" (*shih-ming chen-ching*). The Islamic tradition itself is often called "the pure and real teaching" (*ch'ing-chen chiao*). Adam is the "human ancestor" (*jen-tsu*). The prophets (*anbiyā'*) and "friends" of God (or the "saints," *awliyā'*) are the "sages and worthies" (*sheng-hsien*). The angels are the "heavenly immortals" (*t'ien-hsien*), a term associated with Taoism. The jinn, who in Islamic terms are spiritual beings ranked below the angels and made of fire rather than light, are "spirits and demons" (*shen-kuei*). Satan is the "chief spirit" (*shou-shen*) or the "chief devil" (*shou-mo*). The vicegerent of God (Arabic *khalīfa*; English caliph), a term whose spiritual rather than political meaning is important in Chinese, is the "representative" (*tai-li*). Paradise is called "heaven country" (*t'ien-kuo*) or "ultimate happiness" (*chi-lo*). Hell is called "earth prohibited" (*ti-chin*) or "earth prison" (*ti-yü*). The daily prayer (Arabic *ṣalāt*, Persian *namāz*) is called "worship" (*li-pai*). The mosque (*masjid*) is named "the temple of worship" (*li-pai ssu*) or "the temple of the pure and real" (*ch'ing-chen ssu*). In all these cases, the Arabic expressions are basic Koranic terms, but the Chinese words are unrecognizable as Islamic terminology except in the context of the Islamic writings.

The Islamic languages also have numerous theological and philosophical terms that are necessary for serious discussion of the religion, and translating these called for a good knowledge not only of Islamic thought but also of the Chinese intellectual tradition. The first principle of faith, *tawḥīd*, is often rendered as "returning to one" (*kuei-i*) or "practicing one" (*hsi-i*). God is frequently discussed in Islamic texts in terms of "essence and attributes" (*dhāt wa ṣifāt*), and for this pairing the Chinese ulama used standard Neo-Confucian pairings such as "root nature" (*pen-jan*) and "movement and quietude" (*tung-ching*), or "substance" (*t'i*) and "function" (*yung*). One of the goals of seeking knowledge is to discover the "reality" (*ḥaqīqa*) of things, and this term is often rendered by the extremely important Neo-Confucian term "principle" (*li*). The two basic worlds of the cosmos, often called the "world of the witnessed" (*ʿālam al-shahāda*) and the "world of the absent" (*ʿālam al-ghayb*), become the "world of color" (*yu-se chiai*) and the "colorless world" (*wu-se chiai*)—terms that in the context of Buddhism have usually been translated into English as the "world of forms" and the "formless world."[7]

Wang Tai-yü

In *Islam in Traditional China*, Donald Leslie writes that the first Chinese book on Islam known to have been written by a Muslim is *The Real Commentary on the True Teaching* (*Cheng-chiao chen-ch'üan*) by Wang Tai-yü.[8] Other historians agree that the *The Real Commentary* is one of the most basic works in the history of Chinese Islam, and that its author is one of the two most important leaders of Chinese-language Islam.[9]

Little is known of Wang Tai-yü's life. The modern editor of his works can come no closer to a date of birth than 1573–1619. Nonetheless, circa 1590 seems likely. At the end of an autobiographical note in *The Real Commentary*, Wang signs his name as *chen-hui lao-jen* (an old man of the real Hui). This suggests that at the time of finishing the book he was at least forty. Most likely he was about fifty, which was Confucius' age when he came to know the heavenly mandate. Liang I-chün, a disciple of Wang Tai-yü, wrote an introduction to *The Real Commentary* and put its date at 1642.[10] Thus we can assume that Wang was born about 1592, or at most ten years later. The fact that he did not start studying classical Chinese seriously until he was thirty makes the earlier date much more likely than the later.

It is worth noting here that Wang is often referred to in the later literature as "the old man of the real Hui," and in his conversations and dialogues compiled by his disciples he is also referred to by this title. The disciples, if not Wang himself, certainly had in view the corresponding Arabic and Persian terms for "old man," that is *shaykh* and *pīr*, both of which were employed to mean teacher and especially Sufi master. Rūmī reminds us that "The shaykh is the 'old man' through the intellect, not through whiteness of beard and head,"[11] so one might think that Wang's own use of the term "old man" does not refer to age. However, it is unlikely that a young man would call himself by this term in the Chinese context, or even in the traditional Islamic context.

The best guess at the year of Wang's death seems to be 1657–58. His disciple Ho Han-ching wrote an introduction to what appears to be a second edition of *The Real Commentary*, dating it 1657; in it he refers to Wang as still alive.[12] In the introduction to another of Wang's work, Ma Chung-hsin, one of his most famous disciples, refers to his teacher as "the late master Wang," and this is dated 1658.[13]

In introducing *The Real Commentary*, Wang tells us that his ancestor was an astronomer who had come to China from "Arabia" (*t'ien-fang*, more likely Persia) to bring a tribute to the emperor Kao three hundred years earlier, during the Ming Hung-wu era (1368–98). He then undertook to correct the details of the emperor's astronomy and to fix the mistakes of the calendars. "He surveyed high into the nine heavens and deep into the nine seas and stood aloof from previous works, without any mistakes." The emperor was pleased and thought that it was not possible to reach what he had reached if there was no true transmission of a true learning. Finally he bestowed upon him a Directorate of Astronomy, granted him a house, and exempted him from various obligations. "For three hundred years this mature learning has survived."[14]

Wang underwent the traditional training of a Muslim scholar in the Islamic languages. He is not specific, but he must have known both Persian and Arabic, if not a Turkic language as well. Sciences that he studied—because any Muslim scholar must study them— include Arabic grammar, Koran commentary, Hadith (sayings of the Prophet), jurisprudence, practical morality, and theology. He certainly also studied theoretical Sufism and perhaps Islamic philosophy.

Although Wang had immersed himself in Islamic learning, as a young man he did not have the ability to write proper Chinese—this despite the fact that he belonged to a Muslim family that had been established in China for three hundred years. He presumably had relatives who had become thoroughly Sinicized. This alone would have sensitized him to the difficulties of making Islamic teachings available to Muslims who were learned in Chinese but had no proper training in the Islamic languages. Moreover, his own social position did not allow him to be proud that he did not know Chinese—which might have been the case if his family had lived in some isolated part of China. He writes that he did not study Confucian learning in his childhood, and at the age of twenty his knowledge of Chinese was sufficient only for correspondence. At the age of thirty, he says, "I was so ashamed of my stupidity and smallness that I started to read [Chinese] books on metaphysics and history."[15] Given his role as a scholar serving the Muslim community, it is doubtful that he was ashamed before the non-Muslim Chinese. Most likely he means that he was not able to communicate properly with well-educated Muslims—that is, those who had gone through the standard Chinese educational system. One of his accomplishments seems precisely to be that he eventually mastered the intellectual arts of his time and was able to engage in discussions and debates with other Chinese scholars on their own level. When his student Liang writes in his introduction to *The Real Commentary*, "My teacher Wang Tai-yü had mastered the four teachings and had studied all the doctrines of the various schools,"[16] this does not seem to be too much of an exaggeration.

Chin Chi-t'ang, the first modern scholar to take a critical look at the Chinese sources on Islam, wrote a short biography of Wang that is reprinted in the 1987 edition of Wang's collected works. He tells us that Wang originally lived and taught in Nanjing.[17] When the soldiers of the newly established Ch'ing dynasty invaded the city in the year 1645, he went to Beijing. There he met a wealthy Muslim merchant named Ma Ssu-yüan, who offered him hospitality as a guest teacher. Ma was in the habit of holding sessions in which scholars of various traditions would gather and debate, and Wang soon became known as one of the most outstanding of these scholars. According to one anecdote, in 1650 the abbot of the Iron Mountain Buddhist monastery heard of Wang's prowess in debate and undertook to challenge him. He spent days debating Wang, but eventually had to admit the inferiority of his own understanding, and then he became Wang's disciple.[18] When Wang died, he was buried in the graveyard of his benefactor's family. In the year 1935, Wang's tomb was renewed and a new stele was erected.[19]

Three of Wang's works record his debates and conversations, which were gathered together by his disciples after his death. The longest of these works is called *The True Answers of the Very Real* (*Hsi-chen cheng-ta*). Published in 1658 by his disciple Wu Lien-ch'eng, it is a collection of some two hundred exchanges in the form of questions and answers. Some take the form of short or longer dialogues, and some are simply a single question along with Wang's answer. The questioners were Muslims, both scholars and commoners, as well as Taoists, Buddhists, and Confucians.

The other two collections of dialogues are presented as the *Appendix* (*fu-lu*) and the *Addendum* (*sheng-yü*) to *The True Answers*. The first of these, about three thousand characters long, adds thirty-six conversations in the same style as the main text, dealing mainly with Confucianism and Islam. The *Addendum* is a series of short questions from Buddhist monks with equally short answers in about four thousand characters. The latter text represents Wang as a skillful practitioner of Zen-style repartee, but it also presents him as sharply critical of Buddhist positions. Tazaka questions its authenticity, suggesting that it may have been written later and appended to the book as a way of making Wang appear more hostile to Buddhism than he actually was.

The Real Commentary is by far Wang's longest work. In it, he summarizes Islamic teachings in two volumes, each of which is divided into twenty chapters. The relatively scant attention that the work pays to Islamic practices suggests that Wang Tai-yü was not worried about the transmission of the Shariah. Presumably Muslims were being taught how to pray, fast, and prepare food in the proper way within the family. Instead, Wang is attempting to explain the logic of Islamic theological, cosmological, and psychological teachings, many of which might not have made sense to the Chinese mind, especially if offered without attention to the subtleties of Chinese thought. In cases where Wang does discuss practice, the issues are usually those that would go against Chinese customs, such as the prohibition of pork, wine, and gambling. Indeed, for the Chinese, the most striking characteristic of the followers of this foreign religion was precisely the fact that they refused to eat pork, that greatest of delicacies.

Wang depicts Islam in a way that makes it appear largely in agreement with Confucian ideas. He often quotes from the Chinese classics and sometimes employs Buddhist terminology to make his points. He is not uncritical of the three Chinese traditions, but it is probably fair to say that his criticisms do not transgress the degree of mutual criticism found among the three traditions themselves. The non-Muslim Chinese reader would not feel that Islam has too much to say that is very different from what was already available in Chinese learning. He would feel, however, that the Muslims are much more in agreement with the Confucians than with the Taoists and Buddhists.

This is not to suggest that all Muslim readers would have been happy with the way in which Wang was presenting Islam. In his introduction he remarks that certain scholars had read his manuscript and blamed him for quoting too much from the Chinese classics and going too deeply into Taoism and Buddhism. He agrees with his critics that everything can be found in the classical books of Islam, but he points out that Chinese speakers have no access to those books. Hence he has presented Islam in a way that those unfamiliar with its teachings can understand it.[20] Elsewhere he maintains that he cites Confucian sources only in those places where Islamic teachings are no different from those of Confucianism, such as in the cultivation of the personal life, regulating the family, and governing the country. Always, however, the foundation of the argument and the standard of judgment is the Koran.[21]

In his introduction to *The Real Commentary*, Wang's disciple Liang explains his own view of Confucianism, and this coincides more or less with what one can glean from the writings of Wang himself. It also coincides nicely with Erik Zürcher's points about the Chinese "cultural imperative," noted here in the introduction. Liang writes that if someone asks if the Tao of Confucianism is wrong, he will answer that it is not. On the level of everything under heaven, the Confucian way explicates the Five Relationships—ruler and minister, father and son, husband and wife, older brother and younger brother, and two friends. It also explains sincerity of will, correctness of heart, cultivation of the personal life, regulating the family, governing the country, and bringing peace to everything under heaven. It clarifies the principles of these relationships, and it exhausts the ways, such that nothing escapes from it. It is the totally correct middle way, and it avoids all extremes. Without these teachings, the way of heaven would not be perfect and the law of governing would not be complete, and because of them, the way of the Confucian teachers never changes. However, the teachers never speak of the origin of the world and the relationship between life and death. They talk about the middle, but not about the beginning and the end.[22]

In short, Liang tells us that the Confucian teachings fail to address the issue of creation on the one hand and eschatology on the other. Given that *maʿād* or the "return" to God is the third of the three principles of Islamic faith, this cannot but appear as a major lack in Muslim eyes. Moreover, discussion of the Return is invariably associated with discussion of the Origin (*mabdaʾ*). The Koran links the notion of returning to God with that of coming from him in numerous verses, and this sets the pattern for all subsequent discussions of Islam's third principle. Thus it seems that Chinese Muslims like Wang and Liang granted the correctness of traditional Confucian teachings on social relationships and cultivation of the personal life and the self, but they considered them lacking on the level of faith, where all three principles of the religion need to be addressed—*tawḥīd*, prophecy, and the return to God.

Practically nothing is known about Wang's training, but it is obvious from his writings that he was well grounded in theoretical Sufism. The research of Joseph Fletcher and others has shown that certain Sufi orders, especially the Naqshbandiyya, were active in China during this period, and there is no reason to suppose that the sophisticated theoretical doctrines of Sufism had not been brought along with the more practically oriented teachings.[23] The most obvious candidate for intellectual influence on Wang was the school of Ibn al-ʿArabī, which was flourishing throughout the Islamic world at this time and had several major representatives among the Naqshbandī masters. However, Wang almost never cites Arabic words or mentions names of Muslim scholars in his writings. At the present state of knowledge, it would be difficult to make anything more than circumstantial arguments for such influence.

Besides *The Real Commentary*, Wang wrote two longish treatises and several minor works. I referred to one of these treatises, *The Great Learning of the Pure and Real* (*Ch'ing-chen ta-hsüeh*), in the introduction. This work, whose title might also be translated as "The Principles of Islam," shows clearly the traces of Sufi theoretical teachings. As noted, the phrase "Great Learning" looks back to the Confucian classic by the same name. The expression "the Pure and Real" is a standard term by which Chinese Muslims refer to Islam—an expression that may have been coined by Wang himself.[24] The topic of the book is the first principle of Islam—*tawḥīd* or the assertion of God's unity—and the discussion is carried out in terms that are reminiscent of the school of Ibn al-ʿArabī, though Neo-Confucian thinking is far more obviously represented. We can conclude from this treatise that Wang found Neo-Confucian metaphysics sufficient to provide the basis for explicating the idea of *tawḥīd* along with the demands that it makes for cultivation of self and individual transformation. However, he does not deal with the second and third principles of faith, those of prophecy and the Return. For his teachings on these issues, one needs to refer to *The Real Commentary*.

Liu Chih

If anyone surpasses Wang Tai-yü in his influence on Chinese-language Islam, this would be Liu Chih, who was born about 1670, some dozen years after Wang's death.[25] He wrote the culminating work of his career in 1724; it is not known when he died. He tells us that his father was a scholar who deeply felt the lack of Islamic materials in Chinese. After a preliminary Islamic education, Liu began to study the Chinese classics at the age of fifteen, then devoted six years to Arabic and Islamic literature, three to Buddhism, and one to Taoism. He completed his education by studying 137 books from the "West." Most scholars have assumed that he means European books, and this is likely, given the fact that the famous Jesuit Matteo Ricci had arrived in China a century earlier, in 1601. He and his successors wrote many Chinese tracts on Christianity and Western knowledge in general. One Japanese scholar, however, thinks that this might mean Persian and Arabic books along with European books.[26]

Liu Chih turned his efforts toward making Islamic learning available in Chinese from the age of thirty-three, that is, around the year 1700. He says that he wrote several hundred manuscripts, of which he published only ten percent. Modern scholars have remarked that he is more sympathetic toward Confucianism than any other Chinese Muslim author. Like Wang, he saw no fundamental discrepancy between Islamic teachings on God and the world and the grand philosophical themes of Neo-Confucianism. Using the Neo-Confucian term *li*, he writes that the guiding "principle" of the Koran is similar to what motivated Confucius and

Mencius. This *li*, he says, "is the same *li* which exists everywhere under Heaven."[27] He seems to be expressing in Chinese terms the Koranic view that God has sent prophets to teach *tawḥīd* to all peoples.

Liu completed his first major work in 1704, calling it *T'ien-fang hsing-li*, a title that has usually been translated as *The Philosophy of Arabia*. *T'ien-fang* means literally "the direction of heaven," and is used both for Mecca, the direction of Muslim prayer, and for Arabia. *Hsing-li* means literally "nature and principle," but it refers specifically to Neo-Confucianism, which is typically called "the school of nature and principle" (*hsing-li hsüeh*). Thus, it would not be going too far to translate *T'ien-fang hsing-li* as "Islamic Neo-Confucianism." Like the title of Wang's *Great Learning of the Pure and the Real*, it points already to a synthesis of Islamic and Confucian teachings.

The *Philosophy of Arabia* is divided into six short books. The first book, which Liu Chih calls *pen-ching*, "the root classic," sets down the main ideas of the text in five chapters, for a total of about 2,000 characters. The five chapters are followed by ten diagrams that illustrate the metaphysical and cosmological relationships described in the chapters. Each of the five remaining books explains one of the five chapters in detail, and each employs twelve more diagrams to do so. The resulting seventy diagrams are reminiscent of those found in Arabic and Persian works of the school of Ibn al-ʿArabī from about the eighth/fourteenth century onward, but they also appear to be traditional Chinese depictions of the relationships among the three basic realities—heaven, earth, and the human being. This may be why a non-Muslim mandarin and Vice-Minister of the Board of Propriety could remark in a preface to the *Philosophy* that the Buddhists and Taoists had undermined the ancient Confucian doctrines. "Now, however, in this book of Liu Chih we can see once more the Way of the ancient sages. . . . Thus, although his book explains Islam, in truth it illuminates our Confucianism."[28]

If we do keep the translation *Philosophy of Arabia* for Liu Chih's *T'ien-fang hsing-li*, it needs to be kept in mind that the study of "Nature and the Principle" that he undertakes does not coincide with *falsafa* in the technical Islamic sense. His Neo-Confucian approach to things is much more congenial with the world view of later Sufism than with that of the Muslim philosophers. The fact that he had an eye on Sufi texts becomes completely clear in the first book, the "root classic," where he repeatedly mentions a number of Persian and Arabic works by name. These include Najm al-Dīn Rāzī's *Mirṣād al-ʿibād* (twenty-nine times), ʿAbd al-Raḥmān Jāmī's *Ashiʿʿat al-lamaʿāt* (fifteen times), ʿAzīz al-Dīn Nasafī's *Maqṣad-i aqṣā* (twelve times), and Jāmī's *Lawāʾiḥ* (eleven times).[29] These are four classic Sufi texts, the first three of which had been translated into Chinese some thirty or forty years earlier, and the last of which was later translated by Liu Chih himself. I will have more to say about them shortly.

Liu Chih completed his second major work, *[A Selection of the Important] Rules and Proprieties of Arabia* (*T'ien-fang tien-li [tse yao-chieh]*), in 1710; it deals in twenty sections with a variety of theoretical and practical teachings. He finished his third and last major work, a biography of Muhammad, in Nanjing in 1137/1724. This is the only long Chinese work on Islam to have been studied by modern scholars; it was partly translated into English in 1921, and also into Russian, French, and Japanese.[30] The article on Liu Chih in the *Encyclopaedia of Islam* calls it "undoubtedly Liu Chih's greatest work," but this seems a premature judgment, since greatness is not necessarily gauged by widespread appeal. The work is a relatively straightforward recounting of the historico-mythic origins of Islam in terms that agree with traditional Arabic and Persian texts and fit the rhetorical and religious needs of Chinese Muslims. Certainly a study of Liu Chih's methods in this book would tell us a great deal about how Islam was being taught to Chinese Muslims. But Liu Chih's two other major books, especially the *Philosophy*, are sophisticated attempts to harmonize Islamic metaphysical, cosmological, and spiritual teachings with the Chinese traditions. They are certainly more interesting for Chinese intellectual history, and either or both may have made a more important contribution to the permanent establishment of Islam in China.[31]

In both *Philosophy* and *Rules and Proprieties*, Liu Chih provides lists of the titles that he employed as his sources. There are altogether sixty-eight different titles, eighteen of which are used in both books. At least fifteen titles represent various Sufi schools of thought.[32] Although the exact identity of many of the titles has not yet been established, there do not seem to be any significant works pertaining to the fields of Kalam and Islamic philosophy. In other words, most of the works that provide theoretical explanations of the nature of things—God, the cosmos, the soul—belong to the Sufi tradition. It is clearly the Sufi works along with Neo-Confucianism that form the basis for Liu Chih's explanation of Islamic teachings.

Even more indicative of the Sufi context of Liu Chih's *Philosophy* is the actual text, which is a synthesis of the metaphysical and cosmological teachings of the just-mentioned Persian works presented in the language of Neo-Confucianism. The book seems to have been widely read well into the twentieth century, because it was republished twenty-five times between 1760 and 1939.[33] A brief summary of the contents of its first book can help provide a sense of the theoretical issues that occupied the minds of Muslim intellectuals.

Chapter one: The beginning of creation and transformation. The beginningless beginning is the origin of the ten thousand things. This is the Real Substance, which is the root nature of creation and transformation. It is the Real Being, the Uniquely One, and the Real Principle. Its knowledge and power pervade its root nature, and these two become manifest as the inward and outward of the subtle function. As the subtle function starts to move, yin and yang become separate, bringing about the manifestation of water and fire. Fire appears outwardly along with air, and then heaven and the stars become manifest. Water piles up inwardly along with earth, and then the earth and the oceans come into existence. Next the four elements bring forth the ten thousand things.

Chapter two: The separate endeavors of the ten thousand beings. The One Real overflows and transforms, and this results in the appearance of principle along with images. The principle is possessed by the Real's knowledge, and the images are seen because of its power. Knowledge pertains to the domain of before-heaven (the spiritual realm), and power spreads out in after-heaven (the earthly realm). The domain of before-heaven reveals itself through images, and the domain of after-heaven gives form to the principle. Knowledge and power become manifest in a great variety of human types, including four degrees of sagehood and various lesser degrees such as those of worthies, men of knowledge, modest servants, and good people. So also they appear in the various levels of creatures, including the three "children" (Chinese *tzu*, Arabic *muwalladāt*), which are the animals, plants, and inanimate things, and in the nine heavens, the four elements, and the four seasons.

Chapter three: How human nature and the human body come to be manifest. The essence of the seven elements (the four elements and the three children) turns outwardly and gives birth to the human ancestor. All the qualities and characteristics of the created things appear in human beings gradually, beginning month by month in the womb and extending to the stages of their gradual growth and development until they reach perfection.

Chapter four: The virtues preserved in the human body, heart, nature, and mandate. All virtues are gathered together in the heart. Seven virtues make the heart spiritual and clear. These are obedience, faithfulness, kindness, clear discernment, sincere reality, issuing concealment, and real appearance. The last of these is the first heart, or the real human heart that gave birth to all the levels of the descending arc of manifestation. The human task is to traverse the ascending arc. Thereby one can return to the real heart, complete the circle, and achieve the perfect form of human fullness, the state of the human ultimate.

Chapter five: How everything described in the first four chapters returns to the One. One is the root nature of all numbers, and the numbers are the subtle functions of the One. When substance (*t'i*) and function (*yung*) are undivided, this is the "Real One." When function manifests substance, this is the "Numerical One." When the function returns to the substance, this is the "Embodied One." Although there are three Ones, in fact each is the same One with a different description. The Real One gives rise to transformation, the Numerical One perfects transformation, and the Embodied One transforms the transformations. Each of the three Ones has in turn three levels, each of which has a variety of manifestations on the level of cosmic transformation, though all manifest the same Principle. The tiniest thing manifests the complete substance of the root nature, and each moment is everlasting and infinite. Heaven and the human being are undivided transformations, and all things and the "I" go back to the Real. The first act is the principle of reality, the present act is the guise of reality, and the seeing of the guise is the being of the reality. At this point the seed and the fruit are completed.

It should be noted here that Liu Chih's discussion of the "three Ones" in the fifth chapter has in view Wang Tai-yü's discussion of the same three Ones in the *Great Learning*, though the subdivisions of each One do not follow Wang's scheme.

The Arabic Translation of Liu Chih's *Philosophy*

Liu Chih's *Philosophy of Arabia* was highly esteemed by the Chinese ulama, so much so that one of them translated it into Arabic. This was Ma Lian-yüan, who was born around 1840 and died in 1903. He was a member of a famous scholarly family from Yunnan and played an active role in encouraging Islamic education in that province. He is said to have written about twenty books, mostly in Arabic and Persian. He published his translation of Liu's *Philosophy* in two stages. In 1898, he published the Chinese text of the root classic, along with an interlinear Arabic translation. This appeared in Yunnan with the Chinese title *Hsing-li wei-yen* ("The concealed words of the *Philosophy*") and the Arabic title *Laṭāʾif* ("Subtleties").[34]

Given that the text of *Laṭāʾif* is extremely dense, Ma no doubt had planned to provide a commentary on it from the beginning. However, it seems that he left China around the time that the book appeared, going first to Burma and ending up in Cawnpore in India. There he published his commentary (a book of 165 pages) during the last year of his life. He called it *Sharḥ-i laṭāʾif* ("The explanation of the 'subtleties'"). It seems to have had quite a readership, because it was republished in Cawnpore some twenty years later, and then published for a third time in Shanghai. In the text, Ma calls himself by his Arabic name Muḥammad Nūr al-Ḥaqq ibn al-Sayyid Luqmān.[35] He makes a good deal of use of Liu Chih's five books of commentary on the five chapters, but his explanation of the text is far too free to be called anything but a paraphrase of Liu Chih's own commentary.

Ma's *Laṭā'if* and *Sharḥ-i laṭā'if* present Liu Chih's teachings in Arabic terms that would be familiar to anyone versed in theoretical Sufism. At first glance, they seem to be more or less standard Sufi explanations of the nature of God's relationship with the cosmos and the soul. There is no overt trace of the Neo-Confucian world view that is so obvious in Liu Chih's original. However, careful study shows that the text depicts the Islamic universe in a way that is clearly reminiscent of Chinese thought. A unifying theme of the book is the balance that is established between two complementary divine attributes—knowledge and power—whose mutual activity brings the universe into existence. The original Chinese text demonstrates explicitly that Liu Chih had in mind the yin-yang complementarity that guides Chinese depictions of the nature of the universe.

In Ma's *Laṭā'if*, the first chapter is called "Explaining the descents of the macrocosm." In it he describes twelve descending levels of reality. The second chapter details all the kinds of existent things in the macrocosm, explaining how their diverse characteristics depend on the divine attributes that they manifest. Chapter three explains that the human being was created in twelve levels that coincide with the twelve levels of the macrocosm. Chapter four deals with the specific characteristics of human beings, especially the virtues and character traits that distinguish them from other creatures, and it also describes the various human types. The fifth and final chapter explains how human beings bring together all the characteristics and qualities of the universe and then, by means of their own all-comprehensive nature, return to the One from which the universe arose.

The manner in which Ma's Arabic text is infused with yin-yang thinking can be seen by any careful reader. Here it will suffice to analyze the argument of the first chapter, in which the pattern is set for the rest of the book. The chapter begins by dividing reality into three basic stages, which are God, heaven, and earth; or True Existence, the spiritual realm, and the corporeal realm. Each of these stages can be further subdivided. The first stage can be divided into three levels, which are God's Essence, his attributes, and his acts—though Ma also mentions many other well-known names for these levels. The second stage, also in three levels, pertains to the spiritual world. It includes the supreme Spirit (the First Intellect), the universal soul, and the universal intellect. As for the third stage, it covers the six levels of the corporeal world, beginning with the Dust (universal substance), moving down through the four elements, heaven and earth, and the three progeny (the three kingdoms); and ending with human beings.

The Chinese influence on this scheme begins to appear right at the beginning when the text explains how the divine attributes give rise to the divine acts. What is unusual is the focus on two divine attributes to the exclusion of others, these two being knowledge and power, or omniscience and omnipotence. The two join together to issue the creative "command" (*amr*), which is "Be" (*kun*), and this in turn gives rise to the first "being" (*kawn*), which is none other than the Spirit (the First Intellect).

The Spirit is a single created reality that displays the traces of knowledge and power. The dual aspect of its divine source appears in the two remaining levels of the spiritual world. The trace of knowledge gives rise to the universal soul, which is the spiritual reality of all possessors of spirits, meaning animals, humans, jinn, and angels. The trace of power gives rise to the universal intellect, which is the spiritual reality governing inanimate things, meaning celestial spheres, elements, minerals, and plants. In short, the cooperation of knowledge and power brings about two sorts of spiritual reality, one centered on awareness and the other on activity. Thus, the universal soul and the universal intellect are the yin and yang of the spiritual realm. A slight Taoist influence might be discerned here in the fact that yin, represented by knowledge and soul, stands higher on the scale of reality than yang, represented by power and intellect, though the standard Sufi schemes also place knowledge higher than power.

The text calls the first level of the corporeal world, which is the Dust (*habāʾ*) or universal substance, the "dregs" of soul and intellect. Since soul and intellect arise from the traces of knowledge and power, the dregs manifest these same two divine attributes. Within the Dust, the traces of these two attributes are differentiated into two forces, which the Chinese text calls yin and yang. In place of these two words, Ma introduces two rather strange Arabic words, *qarrānī* and *ḥarrānī*, which may be his own coinage. The meanings of the two terms are clear both from their derivation and from Ma's explanation of the text. They can be translated respectively as "frigid" and "fervid."

Ma explains that the divine power, which becomes manifest in the spiritual domain as intellect, demands the movement of creative activity, and this movement produces heat. In contrast, the divine knowledge, which becomes manifest in the spiritual domain as soul, demands stillness, or the fixity of the objects of knowledge within the knowing subject, and this stillness gives rise to cold. Thus, within the original, undifferentiated and chaotic Dust, some of the dust is fervid or yang and some frigid or yin; some is moving and some still. The fervid dust moves toward the outside, and the frigid dust settles down on the inside.

Having explained the movement of the frigid and fervid forces, Ma draws a diagram to illustrate his point. It consists of three concentric circles. The central circle, which represents movement toward the center, is labeled "frigid," and the outermost circle, which represents movement toward the periphery, is labeled "fervid." Ma then refers explicitly, for one of the few times in the text, to Chinese teachings. He provides the famous diagram of *tai-chi*, which represents yang on the right side and yin on the left, and he says that the circle of fervid and frigid provides a more adequate representation of the nature of things.

The differentiation of the Dust into fervid and frigid gives rise to a second level of bodily creation, which is fire and water, and these in turn produce the third level, that of the four elements. The elements, still under the influence of fervid and frigid, give rise to heaven (manifesting the fervid) and earth (the frigid), then to the three progeny, and finally to human beings. In each succeeding level, the interplay of forces becomes more complex, but Ma frequently refers back to the original divine duality of knowledge and power. So also, in the remaining four chapters he sometimes mentions the complementarity of the two divine attributes or that of frigid and fervid, to explain how creation and transformation bring about the differentiation of the universe in its entirety. In the last chapter, he illustrates how the same two forces are harnessed in the reverse movement, which reintegrates all things in the Real One through the activities of human beings.

Translations into Chinese

Few Islamic works are known for certain to have been translated into Chinese, and the Koran itself was not translated in its entirety until 1927.[36] The primary or secondary literature sometimes mentions that a given book is a translation, but these statements need to be treated with caution. Traditional Chinese authors spoke of translations rather loosely, and the authors of most of the secondary literature have been conversant with Chinese but unfamiliar with the Islamic languages. If a book is to be called a "translation," it should certainly have two characteristics. First, the original text should be available for comparison. Second, the work should follow the original text rather closely, not simply be inspired by it. Drawing the line here may not be easy, but some attempt should be made, and this cannot be done without having both texts available.

In trying to track down books with both of these characteristics, I have been able to discover only three works—three of the four Persian Sufi texts mentioned as having been translated into Chinese. Although I am reasonably certain that the fourth, *Maqṣad-i aqṣā*, was also translated, I have not seen the Chinese text and can judge only on the basis of a description made by Palladius in the nineteenth century.[37] The originals of these four works are all well enough known to be among the small number of Sufi books to have been translated at least partially into English.

The first, *Mirṣād al-ʿibād min al-mabdaʾ ila'l-maʿād* ("The path of God's servants from the origin to the return"), was written by Najm al-Dīn Rāzī (d. 654/1256), an important master of the Kubrawī Sufi order. It was translated as *Kuei-chen yao-tao* in the year 1670 by Wu Tzu-hsien, who is believed by some scholars to have been a student of Wang Tai-yü.[38] This is by far the longest of the four works, and the Persian text is deservedly the most famous and widely read. It can be considered, as its English translator puts it, "the summation of the historical elaboration of Sufism" down to the thirteenth century, when there was an extraordinary flowering of Sufi literature. It is a thorough exposition of right understanding, the second dimension of Islam, with the aim of inspiring Muslims to engage themselves in the third dimension, that of spiritual aspiration. It deals in a relatively systematic manner with the nature of human beings as the linchpin of cosmic existence and universal equilibrium. It describes the prophets as the guides to ultimate happiness and presents a detailed enumeration of the ascending levels of human perfection. It discusses the various modes of unveiling and spiritual vision that the travelers may witness in their journeys to God, and describes their final attainment to the Divine Presence. It explains that human beings have been given charge of fashioning their own souls during their sojourn in this world and that, in the next world, they will find themselves divided into four basic types, depending on the nature of the soul that they have achieved. A final section devotes eight chapters to explaining how various sorts of people should follow the path to God—kings, ministers, scholars, the wealthy, farmers, merchants, and craftsmen.

Among the qualities that have made *Mirṣād al-ʿibād* a classic are the clarity, fluency, and beauty of its prose. Although it deals with issues that remain abstruse in the hands of theologians and philosophers, it avoids technical discussions and uses the imagery and analogies of everyday language. The result has been an extraordinarily popular book, read throughout the eastern lands of Islam as a guide to all dimensions of the path to God. Although understanding the book does not demand training in the technical Islamic sciences, it does require a degree of knowledge of the tradition that would have made its translation into Chinese no easy task. On the whole, Wu Tzu-hsien is as faithful to the original as one could hope, and he is helped in his efforts by the nature of the text, rooted more in imagery than in technical discourse. Nonetheless, when the discussion enters areas that would be difficult for Chinese readers to understand without detailed commentary, he is not averse to dropping the passage.

The second of the four texts is *Maqṣad-i aqṣā* by the well-known Sufi ʿAzīz al-Dīn Nasafī (d. ca 700/1300), also a master of the Kubrawī order.

According to the description of the work given by Palladius, it was translated by She Yün-shan in 1679, less than ten years after *Mirṣād al-ʿibād*, as *Yen-chen ching*. According to other sources, it was translated under the name *Kuei-chen pi-yao* by P'o Na-ch'ih. It seems, however, that P'o Na-ch'ih is the pen-name of She Yün-shan, who was a disciple of Ch'ang Chih-mei (d. 1683), the author of a popular Persian grammar.[39] The Persian text presents us with a much shorter, more systematic, and drier explanation of the Sufi path and its relation with the Shariah and Ultimate Reality. It provides a straightforward exposition of many basic philosophical, cosmological, and psychological teachings, focusing mainly on the relation between God, the cosmos, and the perfect human being (*insān-i kāmil*). It is much more philosophical than *Mirṣād*, though written in relatively simple language. Chinese Muslims would have liked the clarity with which the text explains the basic elements of spiritual cultivation, but, lacking a copy of the Chinese, I cannot judge how the translator dealt with the text.

The third was *Ashiʿʿat al-lamaʿāt* ("The rays of *The flashes*") by Jāmī, a famous scholar who was a member of the Naqshbandī order. It is a commentary on *Lamaʿāt*, a Persian classic by Fakhr al-Dīn ʿIrāqī, a thirteenth-century Sufi of the school of Ibn al-ʿArabī. It was translated by P'o Na-chih, the same person who translated *Maqṣad-i aqṣā*, though it is not known to have been published before 1927. The book's cover gives the title as the Chinese transliteration of the word *Ashiʿʿat*, that is, *E-shen-erh-ting*. Inside the text, the name of the book is given as *Chao-yüan pi-chüeh* ("The mysterious secret of the original display").[40] Since the commentary moves forward phrase by phrase and sometimes word by word, it includes the whole text of ʿIrāqī's work, which is an exquisite disquisition on the metaphysics of love in mixed prose and poetry, and, in She's arrangement, *Lamaʿāt* is more clearly differentiated from the commentary than in Jāmī's original. The commentary itself unfolds the meaning of the text in a relatively dry and systematic manner, and She is rather free in making use of those parts of the commentary that would be relevant to Chinese readers and ignoring other parts. He is not as faithful to the original as Wu Tzu-hsien is to the text of *Mirṣād al-ʿibād*, but he seems to have made a serious attempt to stick to the literal meaning.

The fourth is the text translated here in part 6, *Lawāʾiḥ* ("Gleams"), also by Jāmī. It was translated into Chinese by Liu Chih as *Chen-ching chao-wei* ("Displaying the concealment of the real realm"). It is not clear when it was first published, but the 1925 edition has a preface dated 1751. Liu Chih is not as faithful as She to Jāmī's original text, and unlike him, he drops the poetry, which plays a significant role in the original.

We can now turn to a few examples of works that are called translations in the secondary literature without sufficient evidence. The earliest example is *Ssu-p'ien yao-tao* by Chang Shih-chung, which has a preface by Sha Chen-ch'ung dated 1653. Wang Chan-ch'ao, who wrote a second preface in 1872, says that the work is a translation, but he does not mention the original title or author. Other sources give it the Persian title *Chahār faṣl* ("Four chapters"). The four chapters deal with faith, the Real Lord and Islam, worship and its rules, and purification. The book was recorded by three students who attended lectures given by Chang, in which he commented on the original text. It quotes from *Mirṣād al-ʿibād* several times as well as a book called *ʿAqāʾid*. The book seems to be a paraphrase and commentary rather than a translation.[41]

A second example of a work that is claimed to be a translation is Liu Chih's most famous book, to which he gave both a Persian/Arabic and a Chinese title, *Tarjama-yi Muṣṭafā: T'ien-fang chih-sheng shih-lu* ("The translation of Muṣṭafā: The biography of the utmost sage of Arabia"). Leslie thinks that the main body of the text is in fact a translation of a fourteenth-century Persian work, *Tarjama-yi mawlūd-i Muṣṭafā*, by ʿAfīf ibn Muḥammad Kāzirūnī, which in turn is a translation from the Arabic original by ʿAfīf's father. A comparison of the Chinese text with one version of the original, however, shows that while Liu Chih retells many of the stories in ʿAfīf's work and follows the same general order, he also condenses the text drastically and adds material from other sources. In addition, he freely adapts the stories to fit the needs of Chinese narrative; among other things, his version places a far greater stress on the supernatural elements than does the original.[42]

In the nineteenth century, Lan Hsü Tzu-hsi wrote a book called *T'ien-fang cheng-hsüeh*. In a preface dated 1861, Wang Shou-ch'ien says that the book is translated from the language of T'ien-fang, but there is little evidence that it should in fact be called a translation. It consists of seven chapters dealing with cosmology, the Arabic alphabet, Koran and Hadith, human nature, the Real One, important Islamic teachings, and descriptions of "real persons." The last chapter is especially interesting. Beginning with Adam, it mentions a few of the prophets, describes Muhammad and some of his family and companions, praises two unnamed persons from the central Islamic lands, and concludes with accounts of two Chinese scholars, Wang Tai-yü and Ma Ming-lung, the latter being the author of *Jen-chi hsing-yü*, written in 1656. As the last "real person," the author describes his own mother.[43]

Ma Fu-chu, a nineteenth-century scholar who was executed for his alleged involvement in a rebellion in Yunnan, wrote about his extensive travels in the central Islamic lands and composed some twenty of his thirty-seven surviving works in Arabic. One of his Chinese works is *Han-i tao-hsing chiu-ching*, the original of which he himself had written in Persian.[44] He is also said to be the author of a short rhymed treatise on the Kaabah, which is available in an English translation and provides a fine example of the synthesis of Islamic and Chinese thinking.[45]

Among Ma's works said to be translations is one of the most significant works waiting to be studied in the context of Sufi writings. This is *Ta-hua tsung-kuei* ("The great transformation of all returning"), which is described as having been dictated and edited by Ma and written down by Ma Kai-k'o in 1865, when Ma Fu-chu was seventy-two years old.[46] It is offered as a translation of the "*Fuṣūṣ*," that is, the *Fuṣūṣ al-ḥikam* by Ibn al-ʿArabī, whose school of thought was already represented in Chinese by the two works of Jāmī. The *Fuṣūṣ* is the most famous text in Sufism and the work most often commented on. In the introduction to the Chinese work, Ma Kai-k'o states that the significance of the book is that, in contrast to the works of Wang Tai-yü and Liu Chih, it explains the nature of death and the resurrection. However, the Arabic *Fuṣūṣ* has little to say about these topics.

Ma also wrote a book called *Ssu-tien yao-hui*, which was published along with his study of the *Fuṣūṣ*. Two contemporary Chinese scholars claim that it is a translation,[47] but this seems unlikely. In the introduction, Ma An-li says that Ma Fu-chu studied many Arabic and Persian books on Islam, and then spent eight years writing the essence of these books in Chinese. The book itself consists of four chapters, dealing with these topics: (1) six warnings about the fountainhead of faith; (2) the essential meanings of the rituals and the endeavors; (3) an interpretation of the meaning of the hidden and the clear; and (4) a descriptive examination of the true and the false.

The Neo-Confucian Background

Those familiar with the Chinese intellectual tradition in general and Neo-Confucian teachings in particular will quickly recognize that many of the important discussions of Chinese-language Islam are old friends. However, those unfamiliar with this background may find useful a brief outline of some of the more important terms and concepts that have been assimilated by the Chinese ulama. Before looking at these, however, it is well to remember that Neo-Confucianism was a tradition of learning that was hardly static or monolithic.

The "Neo" in Neo-Confucianism refers to the fact that beginning in about the tenth century, there was a major revival of Confucian teachings, after centuries of relative neglect and strong rivalry from Buddhism and Taoism. Confucianism had itself been largely responsible for the shape Chinese civilization had taken, and Taoist and Buddhist teachings were formulated with it in view. Neo-Confucianism in turn assimilated a good many of the Taoist and Buddhist terms and concepts in its own formulations. The exact relationship among the three traditions is much debated by experts in Chinese intellectual history, but few would disagree with Wing-tsit Chan's statement that Neo-Confucianism represents "the full flowering of Chinese thought." He goes on to explain that "Its major topics of debate, especially in the Sung (960–1279) and Ming (1368–1644) periods, are the nature and principle (*li*) of man and things. (For this reason it is called the School of Nature and Principle, or *Hsing-li hsüeh*.)"[48]

The great thinkers of the Neo-Confucian tradition represent high points in the history of Chinese thought, much like the great figures of the Islamic tradition, such as Avicenna, Averroes, Ghazālī, Suhrawardī, Ibn al-ʿArabī, and Rūmī. Major authors included Ch'ang Tsai (d. 1077), Ch'eng Hao (d. 1085) and his brother Ch'eng I (d. 1107), Lu Hsiang-shan (d. 1193), Chu Hsi (d. 1200), and Wang Yang-ming (d. 1529), but there were dozens of other significant figures during the same period, not to mention Buddhist and Taoist teachers. There was a great deal of dialogue, debate, and disagreement among the Neo-Confucians themselves and between them and the Taoists and Buddhists. Indeed, one of the common criticisms that Neo-Confucians leveled at each other was that they had distorted the teachings of Confucius and Mencius by importing ideas from the other two traditions. In short, the Chinese tradition, much like the Islamic tradition that was flourishing at the same time, was highly diverse and dynamic.

Despite the diversity of perspectives represented by the Neo-Confucian masters, certain concepts and themes are constantly discussed and debated, and it is these that form the backdrop for the work of the Chinese ulama. Wing-tsit Chan, for example, declares that Neo-Confucian thought has three cardinal concepts—principle (*li*), nature (*hsing*), and destiny or mandate (*ming*). He adds that by the time of Chu Hsi, the greatest of the Neo-Confucians, six concepts had become central to the discussion. In addition to principle and nature were the Great Ultimate (*t'ai-chi*), vital-energy (or material force, *ch'i*), the investigation of things (*ko-wu*), and humanity (*jen*).[49] All these terms play significant roles in Chinese Islam.

The term *Tao* itself means, of course, "way," and the word is employed constantly in both Confucianism and Taoism with a variety of meanings depending on the context. As Ch'en Ch'un (d. 1223) remarks in his chapter on the word in his *Neo-Confucian Terms Explained*, "The general principle of Tao is the principle people should follow in their daily affairs and human relations."[50] Like other Neo-Confucians, Ch'en identifies the Tao with principle (*li*), though he does not neglect to point out the differences in nuance, as in his remark "The Way is that which can be followed forever, and principle is that which is forever unchanging."[51]

The term *t'ai-chi* or the Great Ultimate is typically paired with *wu-chi*, which can be translated as "the Ultimate of Nonbeing" or "the Non-Ultimate." This pairing becomes important to Neo-Confucian thinking at least from the time of *An Explanation of the Diagram of the Great Ultimate*, a brief but highly influential treatise by Chou Tun-i (d. 1073).[52] In the Taoist perspective, the Non-Ultimate represents a reality that is situated beyond all being, differentiation, and conceptualization. It is the Tao that cannot be named. In contrast, the Great Ultimate is the Tao that can be named. It is pure and undifferentiated being, carrying within itself the roots of all manifest reality. According to Chu Hsi's influential interpretation of these two terms, they designate a single reality, the Principle, but from two different points of view. As Wing-tsit Chan explains, "The Non-Ultimate is the state of reality before the appearance of forms whereas the Great Ultimate is the state after the appearance of forms."[53]

For Chu Hsi, the concept of the Great Ultimate is inextricably bound up with principle, an ancient term that had been made the center of Neo-Confucian thinking by the Ch'eng brothers. According to them, principle is "self-evident and self-sufficient, extending everywhere and governing all things. . . . It is many but essentially one, for all specific principles are but one principle. It is possessed by all people and all things. . . . It is universal truth, universal order, universal law. . . . [I]t is a universal process of creation and production."[54]

The Great Ultimate gives rise to the universe through movement (*tung*) and quietude (*ching*), which are designations for the two basic cosmic forces, yang and yin. As Chu Hsi writes,

> There is no other event in the universe except yin and yang succeeding each other in an unceasing cycle. This is called Change. However, for this movement and quietude, there must be the Principle that makes them possible. This is the Great Ultimate.[55]

Principle is often paired with vital-energy (or material force, *ch'i*). Vital-energy designates the subtle force that is differentiated first into yin and yang, then into the Five Agents (or elements). These are water, fire, wood, metal, and earth. Ch'en Ch'un writes, "Originally there was only one vital-energy. It is divided into yin and yang and further divided into the Five Agents. The two and five separate and combine in their own way as they operate, producing and reproducing throughout time without cease."[56]

For Chu Hsi, principle and vital-energy are two sides of the same reality. Principle is hidden, while vital-energy is manifest. Vital-energy determines the movement and quietude of everything that appears to human beings. In effect, the whole universe is vitally dynamic and ever-changing because of the principle that animates it. *Ch'i* manifests *li*.

To use another pair of terms well known both to Neo-Confucians and Buddhists, principle is the "substance" (*t'i*)—or, as some prefer to translate it, the "essence"—that underlies and infuses all things, while vital-energy is the "function" (*yung*) that becomes manifest in all things. Substance is one, functions are many. The myriad manifestations that appear in the world—the "ten thousand things"—well up from a single substance that undergirds them.

In human terms, a key synonym for both substance and principle is *hsin* or "heart," one of the most important expressions in all of Chinese thought. Many Sinologists, such as Chan, have translated this term as "mind," and others as "mind-and-heart." But to translate *hsin* as "mind" in the present context would lose sight of the fact that in Islamic thought, the "heart" (Arabic *qalb*, Persian *dil*) plays nearly the same role as *hsin* in Chinese thought. In the Koran and the Islamic tradition in general, the heart is the center of the human being and the root of awareness. The Koran associates all good with a healthy heart, and notably it makes the heart the locus of consciousness and intelligence (*ʿaql*). The Sufi tradition constantly discusses the necessity of purifying the heart so as to reach the special intimacy with God that only human beings can achieve.

In Islamic discourse, the whole enterprise of becoming truly human has to do with making the heart "wholesome" (*ṣāliḥ*). Remember here that the Koran calls the prophets and worthies the "wholesome" (*ṣāliḥūn*) and it repeatedly commands the doing of "wholesome deeds" (*ṣāliḥāt*). The Prophet said, "There is in the body a lump of flesh. When it is wholesome, the whole body is wholesome, and when it is corrupt, the whole body is corrupt. Indeed, it is the heart."[57] According to a hadith often cited in Sufi sources, God says, "My heaven embraces Me not, nor My earth, but the heart of My faithful, gentle, and meek servant does embrace Me." For both Islam and the Chinese tradition, then, the "heart" is the spiritual organ that is specific to the highest possibilities of human nature, especially the understanding of things as they truly are.

In Neo-Confucian terms, the process of refining human nature and aligning oneself with the Tao is associated with the idea of "cultivation" (*hsiu*), a word that can also be translated as repairing, regulating, refining, reforming, pruning. The first stage of cultivation of the self is "cultivation of the personal life," which is mentioned in the Confucian *Great Learning* between "regulating the family" and "making the heart true." The literal meaning of the term *personal life* here is "body" (*shen*), which is a general designation for "the four limbs and the one hundred bones." As we saw in the introduction, the *Great Learning* tells us, "Those who wished to govern their countries would first regulate their families. Those who wished to regulate their families would first cultivate their bodies. Those who wished to cultivate their bodies would first make their hearts true." The body here is the foundation for human consciousness and the basis for all human relationships. It must be trained to act correctly in all circumstances and to observe the propriety (*li*, Arabic *adab*) in every situation.

In short, "cultivation of the body" designates roughly the same domain as that denoted by the Arabic expression, *tahdhīb al-akhlāq*, or "refinement of character traits." *Tahdhīb* means to prune, clean, purify, polish, and refine. *Akhlāq*, the plural of *khuluq*, means "character traits" and is used technically to designate the science of ethics. Hence, "cultivation of the body" can be understood to mean refinement of moral and ethical character. In Islamic terms, it is to eliminate base character traits (*safsāf al-akhlāq*) and to acquire noble character traits (*makārim al-akhlāq*).

In Confucianism, the most important of the virtuous traits that need to be acquired are summed up as the Five Constants (*wu-ch'ang*), which are often listed as humanity (*jen*), righteousness (*i*), propriety (*li*), wisdom (*chih*), and faithfulness (*hsin*). One Neo-Confucian version says that they are "righteousness on the part of the father, love on the part of the mother, brotherliness on the part of the elder brother, respect on the part of the younger brother, and filial piety on the part of the son."[58] These are closely associated with the Three Bonds (*san-kang*) —the moral and ethical ties between ruler and minister, father and son, and husband and wife.

In Chu Hsi's way of looking at things, the heart can be said to have two sides. In terms of its substance or original nature, it is identical with principle. In terms of its function, it is principle mixed with vital-energy. In its substance, the heart is purely good, but in its function, it becomes involved with both good and evil. If people must undertake "the investigation of things," this is so that they may cultivate the body, train themselves in good character, and return to the original nature of the heart, which is identical with the substance of all things. Ultimately they will reach the principles of all things, and the principles of the things are in reality one principle, which is none other than the Great Ultimate. According to Wing-tsit Chan, Chu Hsi's central idea is encapsulated in his maxim, "The Great Ultimate is nothing other than principle."[59]

The first and most important of the Five Constants is *jen*. This term is impossible to translate, and among the many attempts that have been made are benevolence, perfect virtue, human-heartedness, love, benevolent love, goodness, altruism, co-humanity, and true manhood.[60] I use "humanity," following Wing-tsit Chan. In Confucianism it is the highest human good, and for Chu Hsi it is identical with the substance of the heart. To recover one's heart is to become truly human and truly humane. Humanity in this sense is the substance of all good and the wellspring of every virtue and beautiful human quality. Chu Hsi writes,

> In discussing the excellence of man's heart, [Mencius] said, "*Jen* is man's heart" [6A:11]. Both the substance and the function of the four moral qualities [*jen*, righteousness, propriety, and wisdom] are thus fully presented without mentioning them. For *jen* as constituting

> the Tao consists of the fact that the heart of Heaven and Earth, which produces things, is present in everything. . . . In the teachings (of Confucius, it is said), "Conquer oneself and return to propriety" [*Analects* 12:1]. This means that if we can overcome and eliminate selfishness and return to the Principle of Heaven, then the substance of this heart will be present everywhere and its function will always be operative.[61]

The differentiation that is referred to by the pairings "principle and vital-energy," or "substance and function," parallels the two domains that are mentioned in another ancient pair of terms—*ming* (destiny or mandate) and *hsing* (nature).[62] The first of these is typically associated with heaven and what comes down from heaven, and the second with what becomes established in the earth as a result of heavenly activity. Thus, for example, when Confucius tells us about the stages of his lifetime, he says that he came to know the "mandate of heaven" at the age of fifty (*Analects* 2:4). The exact meaning of this mandate was much debated in Chinese thought. Those inclined toward a more theistic view of things tended to look upon it as God's decree and commandment, while those who looked at things in more impersonal terms associated it with the natural order. Thus Chan tells us that "in religion it generally means fate or personal order of God, but in philosophy it is practically always understood as moral destiny, natural endowment, or moral order."[63]

In the Chinese Islamic texts, it seems best to translate the term *ming* as "mandate" rather than "destiny" or "fate." The same range of meanings is found in the Koranic term *amr*, usually translated as "command." The Islamic intellectual tradition divides God's command into two sorts. One sort of divine command, called the "engendering command" (*amr takwīnī*), pertains to the natural order. It is the command that brings about the existence of things. "His only command, when He desires a thing, is to say to it 'Be!', and it comes to be" (Koran 36:82). The other sort, called the "prescriptive command" (*amr taklīfī*), pertains to the human order and designates the moral and social commandments that God sends down through the prophets. Thus, in Islamic thinking, both natural laws and moral laws are God's "command," which is to say that they both have the same source and manifest the same principle. Reading the Chinese texts in Islamic terms, one might say that *ming*, like *amr*, refers to the divine command as embracing both the engendering and the prescriptive commands. However, scholars understand it to mean "mandate" when it refers to the moral order, and "destiny" or "fate" when it refers to the natural order.

The correlation between mandate and nature goes back at least to the *I Ching*, where it is used in the commentary on the first hexagram: "The way of the Creative works through change and transformation, so that each thing receives its true nature and destiny [mandate] and comes into permanent accord with the Great Harmony."[64] Chu Hsi provides a well-known Neo-Confucian formula when he tells us, "What is imparted by Heaven to all things is called mandate. What is received by them from Heaven is called nature."[65] Or again,

> Nature refers to what is stabilized, whereas mandate refers to what is operating. Mandate, for example, refers to water flowing, while nature refers to water contained in a bowl. A big bowl contains more water, while a small one contains less. The water in a clean bowl will be clear, whereas that in a dirty bowl will be turbid.[66]

One of the most vexing questions that arises here is why some bowls are large and some small, some clean and some dirty. In other words, what is it that causes the differentiation of the ten thousand things? And what is it that makes human beings uniquely able to achieve sagehood, and uniquely blameworthy if they fail to achieve it? All things, after all, follow heaven's mandate and their own natures, and as such they are what they must be. If this is so, why should human beings be criticized for being what they are? What is wrong if they simply live according to their own nature, which manifests the heavenly mandate? A basic Islamic answer to this question is simply to differentiate between the two commands, or the two "mandates." The engendering and creative command establishes nature, but the prescriptive command addresses human free will, which itself is given by nature. People will be held responsible for following the prescriptive command inasmuch as they are free. Of course, the question remains as to how free they are, and this was constantly debated. Chu Hsi and others frequently address these issues. In the following, Chu Hsi does so while answering the question, "Physical nature differs in the degree of purity. Does the nature bestowed by Heaven differ in degree of its completeness?"

> No, there is no difference in the degree of its completeness. It is like the light of the sun and the moon. In a clear, open field, it is seen in its entirely. Under a mat-shed, however, some of it is hidden and obstructed so that part of it is visible and part of it is not. What is impure is due to the impurity of vital-energy. The obstruction is due to the self, like the mat-shed obstructing itself. However, man possesses the principle that can penetrate this obstruction, whereas in birds and animals, though they also possess this nature, it is nevertheless restricted by their physical structure, which creates such a degree of obstruction as to be impenetrable.[67]

The basic Neo-Confucian perspective on things can be summarized as follows: One principle, which is the Tao or the Great Ultimate, gives rise to the infinite diversity that is called heaven, earth, and the ten thousand things. All things are constituted by the interplay of the vital-energies, yin and yang, which manifest the one Principle. The function of each thing is distinct, but, in the last analysis, the substance of all is the Great Ultimate. Things naturally flow according to the mandate of heaven, but the natures of things are such that some display heaven's characteristics more fully than others. In the case of human beings, nature has become obscured and needs to be purified and clarified. This is achieved by learning, which aims to recover the true heart, within which all the virtues are fully present. As Wang Yang-ming puts it,

> When the heart is free from the obscuration of selfish desires, it is the embodiment of the Principle of Heaven, which requires not an iota added from the outside. When this heart, which has become completely identical with the Principle of Heaven, is applied and arises to serve parents, there is filial piety; when it arises to serve the ruler, there is loyalty; when it rises to deal with friends or to govern the people, there are faithfulness and humanity. The main thing is for the heart to make an effort to get rid of selfish human desires and preserve the Principle of Heaven.[68]

2

The Works of Wang Tai-yü

It was said that Wang Tai-yü is the author of one long book, *The Real Commentary on the True Teaching*; two longish treatises, *The True Answers of the Very Real* and *The Great Learning of the Pure and Real*; and a few shorter works. The *Great Learning* is introduced and translated in parts three and four. What follows here is a description of three minor works not yet mentioned and a more detailed description of *The True Answers* and *The Real Commentary*, including translations of excerpts.

The excerpts in particular will show one characteristic of Wang's works that is probably shared by many of the Chinese writings. Those familiar with Islamic texts will be struck by the free translations of passages from the Koran. In many cases, one can only guess which Koranic verse he may have in mind. In addition, he does not always discriminate between the Koran and the Hadith. Sometimes he ascribes what are clearly hadiths to the Sage, and at other times he ascribes them to the Classic. Although I said in the previous chapter that Chinese authors call the Koran "the Classic," it will be clear in what follows that Wang sometimes calls Hadith "the Classic" as well. Indeed, other Islamic works can also be called by the same term.

I noted that the Chinese works rarely mention Arabic names, and even when they do, it is often difficult to decipher them. Wang mentions several in the *Real Commentary*, and I have given a few examples in the summaries. He seems to have a special interest in Abū Yazīd Basṭāmī (d. ca. 261/874), using the Persian form of his name, Bāyazīd (Ibn al-ʿArabī quotes from Abū Yazīd more than any figure after the Prophet).

One old edition of *The True Answers* includes all the short writings attributed to Wang.[1] Two of these, the *Appendix* (*fu-lu*) and the *Addendum* (*sheng-yü*), also found in the 1925 edition of the same book, were described earlier. Three more are as follows:

1. A five page essay discussing the word *hui-hui*, by which Muslims are called by non-Muslim Chinese. Wang explains that the Chinese use this term as an insult, but Muslims should be proud to call themselves by the name. He devotes Chapter 19 of *The Real Commentary* to the same word, but his treatment there is quite different.

2. A ten-part poem (each part consists of eight lines with seven characters each). In a short introduction Wang says that he enjoyed spending his leisure time visiting mountains, woods, and lakes, and that he composed the lines on those occasions.

3. Twelve eight-line poems that are titled respectively "recognition with body, life and death, nature and mandate, hindering self, true learning, tinged practice, manifestation and concealment, false loyalty, illusory filial piety, the common people's opinion, friendship, and the illusory path." The first of these titles is especially significant in that it is the same expression that Wang employs to describe the stage of human perfection in *The Great Learning* (p. 96). The first poem and the first two lines of the second are found in its "General Discussion" (pp. 104–5, 111).

The True Answers

The True Answers has about 25,000 characters, for a total of 32,000 if we include its *Appendix* and *Addendum*. It is a collection of exchanges in which Wang answers questions posed by a variety of people. It was compiled by Wang's disciple Wu Lien-ch'eng. The book resembles the compilations of sayings of Sufi masters that are especially common in India (the *malfūẓāt* literature). The topics of the exchanges range from highly sophisticated philosophical issues to everyday concerns of practice and ritual. As examples, the following exchanges can be cited:

A guest asked, "The language of the Lord—what kind of sound and what kind of script does it have?"

He answered, "The real word of the Lord does not belong to sound or script."

The guest asked, "How did the Honored Classic come to be?"

He answered, "It descended from heaven."

The guest said, "The Lord has no abiding place. How can it descend from heaven?"

He answered, "There are heavenly immortals in heaven, and sages live in this world. But the existence of the Lord has no abiding place at root." (p. 260)[2]

A guest asked, "What are life and death?"

He answered, "Life is also not life, and death is also not death."

He said, "Please give me one more word."

He answered, "Life is also not life, because it has death. Death is also not death, because it returns to life." (p. 261)

A guest [Taoist] asked, "For what reason did the Real Lord create heaven, earth, and the ten thousand things?"

Answer: "For human beings."

Question: "Why were human beings created?"

Answer: "When the Lord wanted to manifest His own utmost honor, He created human beings specifically. This is the general meaning."

Question: "The Lord is the most honored and the utmost great. Why should it be necessary for Him to manifest Himself?"

Answer: "If there were no heaven and earth, humans, and spirits, how could the Lord be the Lord of the ten thousand things? According to your statement, it is not necessary for the greatly honored to manifest himself. This would mean that it is possible for him to be a king without ministers and multitudes. Were there none of these people, who would make him a king?"[3] (p. 263)

A Taoist priest asked, "Which is prior, heaven or earth?"

He answered, "If you know the sequence of men and women, you will naturally know the priority and posteriority of heaven and earth." (p. 268)

A guest said, "The Classic says that the Real Lord created *tun-ya* [*dunyā*] (which translates as the 'earthly world'). He has never been looking and guarding it, because He dislikes it. If there were no looking and observation by the Lord, there would be places He did not reach."

Answer: "If you hate and dislike someone and say that you will not guard him, at root it means that you do not want to do it, not that you will never guard him."

The guest also said, "When the Real Lord hates and dislikes the *tun-ya*, why did He create it?"

Answer: "The *tun-ya* is the dregs of the ten thousand spirits, so it can surely be hated and disliked. There is also something to be taken from it. The Classic says, 'The Real Lord created and transformed the life and death of humans specifically to test whether or not they have loyalty and filial piety.'[4] If there were not this place, where would they be tested?" (pp. 273–74)

A guest asked, "In which place is the Real Lord?"

He answered, "Being in a place belongs to creation and transformation."

The guest said, "If something does not exist here, certainly its dwelling is outside heaven [and earth]. How can it not be in a place?"

He answered, "When yang is in harmony and moves with one movement and the ten thousand things flourish, do you say that spring is inside the things, or outside the things? Inside and outside can be argued only for you and me. How can you argue them for the Real Lord? Tell me, then—before there were heaven and earth, how many things are here and how many outside heaven?" (p. 274)

A guest asked, "At the time of animal sacrifice, why is the honored name of the Lord invoked?"

Answer: "The meaning is because of his origination. The proof of the Lord's creation and transformation is itself the proof of clearly witnessing the Lord. In people, this is to conquer the self and not to forget the Lord." (p. 277)

A guest asked, "In the Tao of the True Teaching, minister and son do not do obeisance to ruler and father. Is this propriety?"

Answer: "The obeisance and propriety of the minister and son toward ruler and father is not like obeisance and propriety toward the Real Lord. Between Lord and servant there is naturally a division and distinction of the utmost propriety. This is not 'obeisance.'" (p. 281)

A guest asked, "Is there anything useless in the heaven and earth?"

Answer: "If you reflect upon and observe your own body, you will awaken." (Appendix, p. 296)

A guest asked, "The life and death of birds and beasts—are their nature and mandate taken by the heavenly immortals or not?"

He answered, "The true meaning of life and death is in humans. Birds and beasts have no share in it. The Classic says, 'The Real Lord created and transformed life and death to test and examine among you people who will have deeds of loyalty.'[5] Because of this, in the beginning He issued the mandate to the heavenly immortals to take earth with which to create form, and in the end He issued the mandate to the heavenly immortals to take back the mandate and return [the earth] to the root.[6] All of this is unique to humans. The life and death of birds and beasts at root depend on the ebb and flow of humans. Their form is nothing but the collectedness and dispersion of vital-energy. When vital-energy is collected, form is perfected, and when form perishes, then it returns and is transformed to become vital-energy. In reality they are for the use of humans and they cannot be compared to eternal and everlasting humankind." (Appendix, pp. 298–99)

A monk asked, "Why is this temple of worship called 'Clean and Aware'?[7]

He answered: "When water is clean, fish appear."

He further asked: "What is water? What are fish?"

He answered: "The True Teaching and real people." (Addendum, p. 305)

A monk asked, "What is the Pure and Real?"

The old man said, "Neither increase nor decrease."

The monk clapped his hands and said, "Eating plenty of the meat of cows and sheep and sleeping with beautiful women—where is the Pure and Real?"

The old man said, "Still, do you not talk about dwelling in the earth and not being tainted? Let me ask you: Where does your body come from?"

The monk said, "The causes and conditions[8] of my parents."

The old man said, "The inside of the sack of skin is filled with pus and blood, the inside of the mother's belly is thoroughly defiled with filth. Where is your Pure and Real?"

The monk said, "This is the illusory body of false unity. What has it to do with the Pure and Real?"

The old man shouted and said, "Cows, sheep, women—how do you make mistakes in recognizing the Real?"

The monk said nothing.

The old man said, "Count out and record thirty whacks of the stick for your foolish saying."[9] (Addendum, p. 308)

A monk asked, "What is heart? What is Buddha? What is a thing?"

The old man answered: "The heart is not flesh, the Buddha is not a person, a thing is not a thing."

He also asked: "Apart from heart, apart from Buddha, and apart from thing, with which principle do we understand?"

The old man said: "No heart, no Buddha, no thing."

Weeping, the monk made obeisance and left. (Addendum, p. 309)

The Real Commentary on the True Teaching

Wang's *Real Commentary* contains about 82,000 characters—150 pages in its modern printed form. It consists of four sections divided into two books, each with twenty chapters. Its contents can be summarized as follows:

Book One

1. The Real One (*chen-i*). There are two levels of oneness: the Only-One, which is the Real Lord; and the Numerical One (*shu-i*), which is the origin of the universe. It is the latter that is referred to by such well-known sayings as "The Great Ultimate produces the two wings, and the two wings produce the four images" (*I Ching*); "The ten thousand dharmas return to One" (Buddhism); and "The Nameless is the beginning of heaven and earth, and the Named is the mother of the ten thousand things" (*Tao Te Ching* 1). The Real One is the Unique One, not the Numerical One.

2. The Original Beginning (*yüan-shih*). The Real Lord is the Original Being without beginning and the root origin of the Non-Ultimate (*wu-chi*), which is the beginning of all the subtle lights. The human ultimate (*jen-chi*) is the original source with beginning. Before creation, the surplus light of the Real Lord made manifest the original chief of the ten thousand sages, who is Muhammad, the root origin of the Non-Ultimate. There are two levels of being, the Original Being that is not related to the ten thousand things, and the Powerful Being or the "surplus light" that nourishes the ten thousand things.

Note that in these first two chapters Wang offers interpretations of the terms Great Ultimate and the Non-Ultimate, making both of them stand at the level of the Numerical One, which designates the function of the ultimate substance, which is the Real One. Thus he differs from the Taoists, who would put the Non-Ultimate at the highest level, beyond the Great Ultimate, and from Chu Hsi, who discusses the two Ultimates as two aspects of the same supreme Principle. In Chapter 6, Wang tells us that the substance of the Utmost Sage (*chih-sheng*) is the Non-Ultimate and his function the Great Ultimate. Thus he makes clear that the Utmost Sage is another designation for the Numerical One, a point to which he devotes the third chapter of his *Great Learning*.

In Islamic terms, what Wang seems to be saying is that the "Real One" refers to the divine Essence (*dhāt*), which cannot properly be designated by any name or attribute, while the "Numerical One" refers to the Divinity (*ulūhiyya*), the One God who gives rise to all multiplicity and who can be discussed in terms of names and attributes. Inasmuch as the Divinity embraces all possibilities and principles, it is called the "Reality of Realities" (*ḥaqīqat al-ḥaqāʾiq*). Inasmuch as it is the pattern (or logos) for all of creation, it is called the "Muhammadan Reality." If we think of God's attributes in negative terms, declaring him beyond all positive conceptions on our part, then he is called the "Non-Ultimate." If we think of them in positive terms as related to the universe, then he is called the "Great Ultimate." (For parallel discussions in *Lawāʾiḥ*, see Gleams 17 and 24).[10]

By "Human Ultimate" (*jen-chi*) Wang seems to mean the perfect human being, who is embodied most fully in Muhammad. The term goes back at least to Chou Tun-i's *Explanation of the Diagram of the Great Ultimate*. Wing-tsit Chan and Michael Kalton both translate the expression as "the ultimate standard for man." Chou Tun-i writes: "The sage settles these affairs by the Mean, truth, humanity, and righteousness, taking quietude as chief. Thus he establishes the Human Ultimate."[11]

3. Predetermination (*ch'ien-ting*). Freedom and predetermination are correlative realities of human existence. Establishing good and evil is predetermination, and making use of good and evil is freedom. Were there no predetermination, there would be no freedom, and without freedom, predetermination would not be manifest. Were there no differences, perfection would not become manifest, and were there no crookedness, the ultimate justice would not become clear.

4. Universal Compassion (*p'u-tz'u*). The Real Lord is the universal compassion of this world and the unique compassion of the afterworld. Whatever is needed by the ten thousand things is supplied by him without anything lacking. Everything is different and each thing has its own place. Worldly honor and abasement must be distinguished from real honor and abasement.

Here Wang has in view the common distinction drawn in Islamic texts between two varieties of divine mercy (*raḥma*), in keeping with the two names of mercy found in the formula of consecration, "In the name of God, the All-merciful, the Ever-merciful." A common distinction made between the two names is that the first designates a universal, all-embracing mercy from which nothing is excluded, and the second a more specific mercy that pertains to the afterlife.

5. The Real Solicitude (*chen-tz'u*). The real solicitude is *īmān* or "faith" (see the translation of this chapter on pp. 65–68).

6. The Real Sage (*chen-sheng*). Before heaven, earth, and the ten thousand things, God created the origin of the Utmost Sage, which is called the Non-Ultimate. The manifestation of the Non-Ultimate is called the Great Ultimate. The substance of the Great Ultimate is identical with the function of the Non-Ultimate. The Utmost Sage is prior to heaven and earth and is the fountainhead of the ten thousand things. Heaven and earth are like a great tree, and the ten thousand images are like its flowers. The true teaching of the Pure and Real has three important elements: the heavenly mandate, the heavenly principle, and sagely governing. The three are the taproot of the ten thousand deeds.

7. Resemblance to the Real (*ssu-chen*). In order to attain resemblance to the Real, one needs to observe the clear mandate and recognize the Real Lord, who transforms and produces everything. To do this one needs to know the relationship between the Real Lord and the universe. If you cannot recognize yourself, you cannot investigate things. If you cannot investigate things, you cannot exhaustively search for the principle. If you cannot exhaustively search for the principle, you cannot purify your nature and clarify your heart. Hence you cannot discern your origin. If you cannot discern your origin, you cannot know the Utmost Sage. How then will it be possible to serve the Real Lord?

8. Changing the Real (*i-chen*). Taoism and Buddhism, by emphasizing the principle of emptiness, fail to make the distinction between the Real One and the Numerical One—between the One that has nothing to do with the things and the One that is the beginning of all things.

9. Darkening the Real (*mei-chen*). Forgetting the distinction between Creator and creation often leads people to worship their own selves. Buddhist texts are full of passages that illustrate this point.

10. The Outstanding Differences (*chiung-i*). There are seven differences between Islam and other traditions. (1) The True Teaching

respects the unique and independent One. The other teachings respect the Numerical One. (2) The True Teaching differentiates between the Original Being and the newborn, which is what comes to be. The other teachings say that the ten thousand things are originally of one substance, but the names and forms are different. (3) The True Teaching holds that human beings are the noblest creatures, and heaven, earth, and the ten thousand things were created for their sake. Others say that heaven and earth are the great father and mother and are nobler than humans. (4) The True Teaching has preserved the clear mandate of the Real Lord for cultivating the Tao without change from ancient times. Other teachings follow self-nature, so their teaching authorities differ among themselves in each place. (5) The True Teaching is loyal to the Real only in respect of the one Lord. Other teachings worship a variety of buddhas and gods, since they are mixed and not one. (6) The True Teaching talks about both predetermination and freedom. Other teachings talk only about the principle of nature. (7) The True Teaching talks about the return to God. Other traditions talk about the rotating wheel.

11. Nature and Mandate (*hsing-ming*). There have been five basic Chinese theories on the subtle reality of human nature: It is good; it is evil; it is a mixture of good and evil; it is in three levels, which are good, evil, and what is between; and it is principle and vital-energy. At the present time, the most popular is Master Ch'eng's theory of the balance between principle and vital-energy—good pertains to principle, evil to vital-energy. From the Sung dynasty (960–1279) onward, people have the theory that the principle is the same, but the vital-energy is different. The *Hsing-li ta-ch'üan* says that nature is one, but vital-energy is different. The teaching of the Pure and Real says that nature is not the same, and that the vital-energy is also different. The before-heaven is the mandate, and the after-heaven is nature. Mandate is the seed and nature the fruit. Mandate is not nature, but it is inseparable from nature.

Hsing-li ta-ch'üan is "The Great Collection of Nature and Principle," a seventy-volume anthology of Neo-Confucian writings compiled by Hu Kuang and others in the year 1405. The Neo-Confucian theory is that of Ch'eng Hao. Chu Hsi has a "Treatise on Ch'eng Ming-tao's Discourse on the Nature" in which he writes, "Man's nature and mandate exist before physical form, while vital-energy exists after physical form. What exists before physical form is the one principle harmonious and undifferentiated, and is invariably good. What exists after physical form, however, is confused and mixed, and good and evil are thereby differentiated."[12]

The terms "before-heaven" (*hsien-t'ien*) and "after-heaven" (*hou-t'ien*) are Taoist expressions referring to the state of existence before this world and existence in this world. In Neo-Confucianism, the two terms are closely associated with Shao Yung (d. 1077), whose thought was commonly called the "learning of before-heaven."[13] Wang is clearly using before-heaven to designate the realm of reality that is preparatory to the appearance of this world. In Sufi texts it is often discussed as the "Arc of Descent" (*qaws al-nuzūl*), and in philosophical texts as the "Origin" (*mabda'*).

12. The Real Heart (*chen-hsin*). There are three kinds of heart—animal, human, and real—each of which has seven levels. These are desire, wisdom, humanity, seeing, enjoying, mystery, and the ultimate level. Worldly people have three levels: desire, wisdom, and humanity. Only true people have all seven levels. The real heart is the Koranic heart, about which God said (in the *ḥadīth qudsī*), "Heaven and earth encompasses Me not, but the heart of the true believer does encompass Me."

The seven levels are reminiscent of the seven ascending "subtleties" (*laṭā'if*) that are often discussed in later Sufism. A typical version has body, soul (*nafs*), spirit (*rūḥ*), heart (*qalb*), mystery (*sirr*), hidden (*khafī*), and most hidden (*akhfā*); another version has body, soul, heart, mystery, spirit, hidden, and Real (*ḥaqq*).

13. Life and Death (*sheng-ssu*). Life and death need to be defined in terms of being and nonbeing. There are three degrees of being—being without beginning or end, being with beginning and without end, and being with both beginning and end. Death should be understood in relation to three degrees of nature: living, aware, and spiritual. The death of the human body does not mean the death of the human spirit.

14. Human Level (*jen-p'in*). The mysterious pivot of the Human Ultimate encompasses the ten thousand images. It is one, but it is then transformed into two, which are husband and wife. "One" is the human, and "two" is humanity (*jen*). Thus, the Three Bonds and Five Constants are established on the humanity of husband and wife. Only the human being—not heaven or earth—was able to manifest the great ability of the Real Lord.

15. Husband and Wife (*fu-fu*). The Non-Ultimate is the beginning of husband and wife, and the Great Ultimate is the origin of the

ten thousand things. The Human Ultimate is the heart of the great human (i.e., Muhammad), and the human is the spirit of the ten thousand things. The Human Ultimate embodies the principle of the Non-Ultimate and follows the function of the Great Ultimate, undergoing transformation to become husband and wife. Without husband and wife, there would be no ruler and minister, no father and son. Hence marriage is the clear mandate of the Real Lord.

16. Immortals and Spirits (*hsien-shen*). Immortals are the heavenly immortals, and the spirits are the spirits and demons (*shen-kuei*). The immortals are made of light, which is yang without yin. They live in heaven, where there is no young or old, male or female, sleep, food or drink. Demons are pure yin; they live in the earth, and do evil. Only humans combine yin and yang completely, so the human spirit is half pure and half turbid. After death good human spirits go up to heaven and befriend the heavenly immortals, but evil human spirits go down to the earth and befriend the demons. Iblis disobeyed the Real Lord and claimed that he was better than the Human Ultimate because he was made of fire.

According to Wing-tsit Chan, the expression *shen-kuei* goes back to the Confucian Classics, and in popular religion it means "gods (who are good) and demons (who are not always good)." In the Neo-Confucian context, he thinks it can best be translated as "spiritual beings" or as "positive spiritual forces and negative spiritual forces."[14] The generally accepted Neo-Confucian understanding of the two is provided by a dictum of Ch'ang Tsai, who says that *shen* and *kuei* are the spontaneous activity of the two vital-energies, that is, yang and yin.[15] Chu Hsi, after drawing a circle on a desk and pointing to its center, said, "The Principle is like a circle . . . . All cases of vital-energy that is coming forth [from the center] belong to yang and are *shen*. All cases of vital-energy that is returning to its origin belong to yin and are *kuei*."[16] Although Wang clearly has the Neo-Confucian understanding in view, he also wants to correlate the concept with Islamic teachings, where "spirits and demons" are commonly discussed.

17. The True Teaching (*cheng-chiao*). The Classic says that the Tao of the True Teaching is nothing but loyalty and sincerity.[17] Followers of this teaching discuss the beginning so as to know the origin of themselves and the end so as to be awake to the final resting place of the body. They also discuss the law, all of which indicates the ultimate principle of becoming a perfect human being. The

origin of the True Teaching is that in the beginning, before the creation of the universe, the Real Lord was self-standing. He commanded the heavenly immortals to descend and to transmit to the human ancestor the clear mandate to represent Him, to open up the ultimate Tao, and to establish the proper Bonds and Constants.

18. The True Learning (*cheng-hsüeh*). The Sage said, "Both the male and the female of the True Teaching have the clear mandate to learn and practice."[18] Learning is not useless learning, it must be learning along with deeds. Learning without deeds is like a flower without fruit.[19] Deeds without learning are like a house without a gate. The true learning has three kinds: the great learning, which is returning to the Real; the middle learning, which is clarifying the heart; and the constant learning, which is cultivating the self.

19. Muslims (*hui-hui*, literally, "returning of returning"). The Hui-Hui are the mirror of the Pure and the Real, while heaven and earth are their model. *Hui* has two kinds: the returning of the body and the returning of the heart. The returning of the body is of two kinds: "coming back" and "going away." The returning of the heart is also of two kinds: that of the true heart and that of no-heart. The returning of the true heart is to awaken to the original beginning of oneself. The returning of no-heart is to manifest the fountainhead of the mandate and to gain the Non-Ultimate. Embodying the Non-Ultimate and recognizing the Real Lord is the ultimate station of returning.

The term *no-heart* (*wu-hsin*) comes from a Taoist background and was also used by the Buddhists. Chan translates it as "no deliberate mind of one's own" or "no mind of one's own," and, in a Buddhist context, as "the non-being of the mind." As he explains in his discussion of the Neo-Taoism of Wang Pi (d. 249) and Kuo Hsiang (d. 312), the Taoist sage rises beyond all distinctions and contradictions while remaining in the midst of human affairs. "In dealing with things he has 'no deliberate mind of his own' (*wu-hsin*) but responds to them spontaneously without any discrimination." The Neo-Confucian Ch'eng Hao identifies the no-heart with the heart of heaven and earth. Thus he writes, "The constant principle of Heaven and Earth is that their mind is in all things, and yet they have no mind of their own." The Buddhist Chi-tsang (d. 623) writes that it means "that one should not have any deliberate mind toward the myriad things."[20] Wang seems to have the no-heart in view when he discusses "no-self" (*wu-chi*) as the third and highest stage of embodying the One (*Great Learning* IV 3; cf. Liu Chih's translation of *Lawāʾiḥ*, Gleams 8–10).

20. Bearing Witness (*tso-cheng*). To recognize the Lord, you first must say, "I bear witness." This is because, in order to recognize the Lord, you must first recognize yourself.[21] Bearing witness (i.e., the Shahadah) is the call to awakening from the drunken dream of the ancients and the moderns.

Book Two

1. The Five Constants (*wu-ch'ang*). The Five Constants (i.e., Islam's Five Pillars) are remembrance (the Shahadah), giving (alms tax, *zakāt*), worship (daily prayer, *ṣalāt*), abstention (fasting during Ramadan), and gathering (the hajj).

This relatively long chapter describes briefly the basic activities involved in Muslim observance and explains the meaning behind the actions. Note that here Wang appropriates the expression Five Constants for the Five Pillars, whereas earlier, in Chapter 14, he had used the expression in the standard Confucian sense.

2. Real Loyalty (*chen-chung*). Honoring the Unique One, the Lord without twoness, is called "real loyalty." The term *one* refers to three things—the Unique One, which is the Real Lord; the Numerical One, which is the seed, and Practicing One, which is the act of the real human being. When people recognize the Lord, their heart is made true. When a heart is made true, this brings about real loyalty. The ten thousand good things all issue forth from this loyalty.

The three "ones" are the topic of Wang's *Great Learning*, though there he calls the last of them the "Embodied One" (*t'i-i*) instead of "Practicing One" (*hsi-i*). In the Confucian writings, "loyalty" (*chung*) is often paired with "faithfulness" (*hsin*), as in *Analects* 1:8, "Hold loyalty and faithfulness as first principles." Wang employs this pairing twice in the *Great Learning*. The Neo-Confucians frequently discussed the relationship between the two terms. According to Ch'eng Hao, "Loyalty issues from the self with a spontaneous exertion to the utmost, and faithfulness is following things without any deviation."[22]

3. Utmost Filial Piety (*chih-hsiao*). The necessity to worship the Lord and to be filial toward one's parents is the utmost filial piety. Those who have real loyalty are sure to have filial piety, and those who practice filial piety are surely loyal. When loyalty and

filial piety are both complete, they perfect the True Teaching. As the Classic says, "The joy of the Real Lord is entrusted to the joy of parents and children."[23] Filial piety has three levels: body, heart, and mandate. Nourishing only the parents' bodies is not filial piety—the same nourishment is given to dogs and horses. The filial piety of the heart's will is constant filial piety, but it is not the ultimate filial piety. Acts such as worshiping five times a day, giving alms, and helping the poor are the filial piety of nature and mandate. The utmost filial piety is to worship the Lord.

4. Listening to the Mandate (*t'ing-ming*). Those who listen to the mandate do not follow their own nature, but rather conquer themselves and their selfish hearts. Listening to the mandate is the Tao of heaven, and conquering the self is the Tao of human beings. These two ways are the two sides of the human heart. They should be followed on the levels of intention, word, body, and property.

We have already met the expression "conquering the self" in a quotation from Chu Hsi and in a passage quoted from *The True Answers*. Note that it is drawn from the *Analects* (12:1), where Confucius defines humanity (*jen*) as "conquering the self and returning to propriety." Wang discusses the term frequently, both in this work and in the *Great Learning*. Liu Chih, in his translation of *Lawāʾiḥ* (Gleam 8), uses it to express the general Sufi idea of exerting efforts on the path to God, and then, in the next Gleam, he uses it to translate the important term *fanāʾ* or "annihilation." Annihilation designates the purification of the self and the elimination of the constricting limitations of ignorance and forgetfulness; or the transformation of blameworthy character traits into praiseworthy character traits. It is usually paired with "subsistence" (*baqāʾ*), which is the actualization of the divine attributes in whose image the human being was created. The Koranic source of the pairing is the verse, "Everything upon the earth [and pertaining to the bodily side of things] is *annihilated*, and there *subsists* the face [i.e., the manifestation] of God, Possessor of Majesty and Generous Giving" (55:27).

5. The Chief Leader (*shou-ling*). The Prophet said, "You are like a shepherd, and each of you will be asked how you handled your task."[24] The body is like a country; hearing, seeing, and speaking are its ministers; the four limbs and the one hundred bones are its people; and the heart is its leader. If the heart is true, the body is true, and if the heart is crooked, the body is crooked.[25] The public way among human beings is the scale of the Real Lord.

6. The Way of Friendship (*yu-tao*). What you enjoy, give to your friend, and what you do not want, keep for yourself. The Heavenly Classic is your first ancestor, and true people are all your brothers. The Bonds and Constants of the True Teaching are the Tao of brothers, friends, families, and neighbors.

7. Taking and Putting Away (*ch'ü-she*). Everything is perishing except the Real Lord (cf. Koran 28:88). The Real Lord is the Original Being that exists eternally. He creates the ten thousand things, and the ten thousand things interchange between being and nonbeing, coming and going, life and death. Moment by moment they are renewed as different beings. Knowing self produces modesty, which is the fountainhead of all good things and is no-self. Not knowing self produces arrogance, which is the taproot of all evil. It is to know only one's own being and not the being of the Lord. Bāyazīd said, "Purity and modesty are deeds of endeavor, and I did them for only three days. On the first day I put away the wealth and nobility of the lodging place, which is this world. On the second day, I put away the glory of the eternal abode, which is the next world. On the third day I put away myself, which is no-I."[26] When you must put away but you do not, this is called "stinginess." When you must not put away but you do, this is called "foolishness." When you must take but you do not, this is called "perversion." When you must not take but you do, this is called "greed." When taking and putting away are not clear, there is corruption.

8. Providing Beforehand (*yü-pei*). The Classic says that you must die before you die.[27] This world is where one cultivates the seed of the return to the Origin. If you do not make provision beforehand, how can you sail against the wind and the waves? If you do not have endeavor, how can you reach the boundless Heavenly Country? Profit, loss, and the consequences of good and evil deeds occur on three levels—body, wealth, and name.

9. The Observation of Time (*ch'a-shih*). The human body has the subtlety of seeing, hearing, listening, and speaking, all of which are controlled by the principle of the true heart. If the heart principle is not clear, one cannot govern the eyes, ears, nose, tongue, and the hundred bones. There are many mistakes in what is seen with the eyes, but there will be no fault in what is observed by the principle. To cultivate the heart principle one must increase

virtues such as real knowledge, humility, frugality, modesty, patience, faithfulness, and nobility. In sum, one needs to conquer oneself, because although the form is the same in having self and not having self, the gap is that between good and evil.

10. Reflecting and Awakening (*ts'an-wu*). The Classic says, "Why do you not reflect upon what is in yourself?" (Koran 6:50). The Sage said, "You can reflect upon the internal or external solicitude and mercy of the Real Lord, but you cannot reflect upon the root nature of the Real Lord."[28] Mercy has three sorts: external, internal, and real. The external mercy is heaven, earth, and the ten thousand things, which are for the use of humans. The internal mercy is body, life, and the power to pursue the principles of affairs. The real mercy is the teachings and rulings of the true Tao, which guide the deluded on the path. Only when you follow the true Tao and cause the human level to advance will you not betray the three mercies.

11. Profit and Name (*li-ming*). People who drown in the ocean of profit and name are those whose words and deeds do not arise from the root heart, but rather sometimes for the sake of name, and sometimes for profit. Thus they become hypocrites. They are human in form but not in reality. Bāyazīd said, "Repentance for mistakes and errors occurs once in a lifetime, but why should repentance for the virtue of endeavor stop at a thousand times?"

12. Comparing the Measures (*chiao-liang*). The Classic says, "He who comes closest to the utmost nobility of the Lord is most in comparing the measures."[29] In cultivating the Tao of the True Teaching, it is not possible to exhaust one's efforts. You should not lack one of them, but the beginner should maintain three levels and ten items. The three levels are sincerity and faithfulness of the heart, constant remembrance [of God] with the tongue [i.e., the practice of *dhikr*], and obedient deeds with the body. The ten items are modesty of eating and drinking, modesty of speech, modesty of sleep, repentance of mistakes, seclusion in silence, contentment with poverty, being at ease with one's allotment; the patience of (1) cultivating the Tao, (2) seeing the Tao, and (3) gaining the Tao; submissiveness, and being pleased to follow.

13. Animal Sacrifice (*tsai-sheng*). The animal sacrifice at Mecca during the hajj is important because it is the cause of nearness to the Lord and makes possible sailing across the boundless ocean of fire. The saying of Confucius, "O Tz'u, you love the sheep, I love

the ceremony" (*Analects* 3:17), lets us know that the name of the sacrifice remains, but the reality is lost. There are two levels of "animal"—internal and external. Sacrifice of the internal animal is to surrender self-nature and to embody the person of the sage at every moment. Sacrifice of the external animal is not neglecting the ancient code, observing the rulings of the sage, and restricting oneself to the wise and clear.

14. Meat and Vegetables (*hun-su*). It is not good to eat only vegetables or only meat. Once a worthy visited Bāyazīd. He wanted to enter the room, but the room was transformed into an ocean. Bāyazīd entered the ocean and invited the guest to come swim with him. The guest replied that he could not. Bāyazīd said, "You cannot because what you eat is not refined and clean. How can you ford this pure and clean ocean?" This indicates that the worthy was partial to eating vegetables. Once a worthy visited Rābiʿa, who was sitting among birds and animals, but they all ran away. He asked why they fled, and she asked him what he had eaten that day. When he replied that he had eaten meat, she said, "When you want to eat their meat, how is it possible for them not to run away from you?" This indicates that the worthy was partial to eating meat.[30] Some meats are not permitted, and on certain occasions, no meat is permitted.

15. Gambling and Drinking (*po-yin*). The True Teaching prohibits both gambling and drinking wine because these perplex people's hearts, which then swing and become irresolute. Then the devil takes advantage of them and seduces them. The devil's seduction follows what people desire. The Classic says, "Wine is the key to all evils."[31]

16. Interest and Hoarding (*li-ku*). Interest and hoarding are acts against the clear mandate and betray the great mercy of the Lord. Both are strictly prohibited by the Pure and Real. When the mandate is with the people, there is a day's life and a day's body. When there is a day's body, there is a day's nourishment. Thus it is said, "It is not that people die young or have a long life, but when one's emolument is exhausted, one dies."

17. Wind and Water (*feng-shui*, i.e., geomancy). Attempting by human power to choose auspicious sites for burning the dead and giving profit to the living is ignorance, especially when people do not know good and evil, which are the root of yin and yang, nor the heart-ground, which is the fountainhead of *feng-shui*. Good

thinking nourishes peaceful winds and timely rains, and evil thinking causes ill situations like hail and dense fog. *Feng-shui* is not in the mountains and rivers, but in the human body. Coffins are not used in Islamic burial because the origin of humans is the earth, so they should return to it naturally; and when the blood and flesh of humans is buried in the ground, it is transformed into earth and purified.

18. True Mandate (*cheng-ming*). The mandate one receives returns to the Real, going away and not coming back. In the Tao of the Pure and Real, death is the true mandate. When a person is born, this is called a "descent." It is the beginning of entering into the drunken dream of the floating life. When a person goes away, this is called an "ascent," and it transcends the deluded illusion of empty death.

19. This World (*chin-shih*). Life in the earthly world is one act [of a drama].[32] Everyone has four enemies: self-nature, devils, deluded people, and the earthly world. The earthly world is a big theater. Fame, wealth, nobility, the ten thousand things, and the ten thousand affairs are the puppets. The chief devil is dressed up as an actor. Deluded people rush to watch the drama. Self-nature is for you to sit together with others. But, a true human is simply a passing guest in the theater. The Classic says, "People in the world are traveling merchants, and whatever they possess is borrowed or rented."[33] Whatever is borrowed will certainly return to the Original Lord.

20. The Afterworld (*hou-shih*). Human beings experience three worlds: the original beginning, which is the time of the seed; the present, which is the time of the sprouting; and the return, which is the perfecting of the fruit. The Classic says, "This world is the field of the afterworld."[34] Those who cultivate flowers reap flowers, and those who plant thorns reap thorns.

Adam and Eve: From Chapter Two of the *Real Commentary*

Chapter Two of the *Real Commentary*, "The Original Beginning," starts with a discussion of the Real Lord, the Non-Ultimate, and the Great Ultimate. Toward the middle of the chapter, Wang describes in some detail the stages of creation, arranged in terms of the six days mentioned in the Koran. At the end of this discussion and before the conclusion of the chapter, he describes the creation of Adam on the sixth day. He begins his account with what can be recognized as allusions to various hadiths according to which God sent an angel to gather the earth for Adam's clay from the four corners of the earth and then molded the clay with his own two hands, after which he let it sit for forty days. Wang also alludes to the Koranic verse, "Surely a day with your Lord is as a thousand years of your counting" (22:47). He then answers an objection that Chinese readers could be presumed to make.

> On the sixth day [of creation], at the time of the monkey, for the first time the Real Lord commanded the heavenly immortals to bring the soil of the five directions. He created the form and body of A-tan, the human ancestor, and this is the form and body that people have had from ancient times until now. The body was perfected in forty days. Hence, from the creation of heaven, earth, and the ten thousand things to the end [of Adam's creation], it took forty-six days. This is the time scale of the everlasting world, where every day is one thousand years of our time.
>
> Someone may say that the whole is one world. Why should there be different lengths of time like this? I would reply as follows: If a worldly prince seeks to become an immortal, he will be transformed into a crane, and then the length of time will be different. Like a crane, who lives a thousand years, he will not himself have awareness of the length. So also a mayfly, which is born in the morning and dies in the evening, does not itself know the shortness. In the same way, as long as the saltiness of the sea does not penetrate the freshness of the river, the things in salt water are not aware of the saltiness, and the things in fresh water are not aware of the freshness. How can any of these transcend salt and fresh, long and short, so as not to be bound by the restraints of the conditions before the eyes?[35]

Wang now turns to the next stage of Adam's creation, when God blew of his own breath into Adam's clay. However, Wang apparently does not feel that this sort of anthropomorphic imagery is appropriate for his readers, even if it is found in the Koran.

> At the time when the human ancestor's body was perfectly completed, his original real nature was still with the Real Lord. The two fountainheads that are life and wisdom wandered until they combined naturally in the body. After that, the four limbs and the one hundred bones, the eyes, the ears, the nose, and the tongue, all started to move with spiritual illumination.

Wang now turns to the Koranic account according to which God taught Adam all the names and commanded the angels to prostrate themselves before him. However, he presents the events in a different order, and then he draws both social and metaphysical conclusions:

> The Lord showed solicitude to the ancestor with caps and robes and He made him ascend the throne. He issued the mandate to the heavenly immortals to prostrate themselves before him all together, and He made them rise up and carry him around the heavenly spheres, and all of them obeyed the mandate. Then the Real Lord showed solicitude to the human ancestor by giving him great wisdom and real knowledge, so he penetrated thoroughly into the principle of heaven and earth and the nature of all ten thousand things. In this way, every name of each kind of thing was established. However, when the human ancestor remembered that the origin is pure and clean, and when he also considered that the body belongs originally to muddy dirt, he naturally became modest, and pride was not born in him.
>
> When the human ancestor was sleeping deeply, the Real Lord created his wife from his left rib and named her "Hao-wa" [Arabic Ḥawwā].[36] The reason for the intimacy of husband and wife is that originally they are of one body. Hence they should love and respect each other. The wife appeared from the husband, and the husband is the origin of the wife, so she should listen to his commands.
>
> Thus you should know that the ancestor of human beings is one body, and this body was transformed into man and woman. From this we come to know the yin and the yang of the Great Ultimate, the life and the wisdom of the Non-Ultimate, the mercy and the severity of the Real Lord, the highest and the lowest, and the subtleness of the Original Beginning without end. Human beings are endowed with everything. If one fails to grasp this principle, one's whole life will be a drunken dream, and that would be a great pity.

Wang now turns to explaining the reason for Adam's fall and the entrance into the earth. He tells the story of his temptation by Satan, but he then points out that there is a great wisdom in the fall. In this he is following many Muslim commentators, who saw the entrance into the earth as simply the next stage in the development of human perfection, not the punishment for sin, and certainly not something to be regretted.

> Then the Real Lord gave the mandate to these two that they should live in the heavenly country forever and enjoy complete bliss everlastingly. However, a tree of wheat had grown up there, another name for which was "the tree of causes and conditions."[37] The Lord forbade them to take from this tree. Unexpectedly, the leader of the devils and his followers came up stealthily to the heavenly country and seduced them to eat from the tree. At this time

they just happened to become confused for a moment, and finally they were influenced by the devil's seduction and "they disobeyed the contract" with the Lord. Although this name is strong, in reality it was unavoidable that they would hit the target. At its root, this harmed them, but then it was turned into an advantage. Here there was a secret that could not be known by the devil.

At this time the couple's caps and robes fell off and they became naked, so they covered their bodies with the leaves of the fig tree of the upper world. They did not look at each other, and they fell to the earthly world.

Next Wang explains why it is that human existence should begin as a fall. Here again he seems to be addressing questions that would be foremost in the minds of traditional Chinese readers. He answers first by telling of the objection made to Adam's creation by the angels, according to the Koranic verse, "And when your Lord said to the angels, 'I am placing in the earth a vicegerent,' they said, 'What, will you place therein one who will work corruption and shed blood?'" (2:30). Wang explains, in terms that can easily be found in Arabic and Persian texts, that this objection had to do with the fact that Adam was a compound being, made of the four elements.

Someone may say that human beings are the most spiritual and the most noble of all things. Why should they fall into trouble like this at the very beginning? I would reply that there are two reasons for this.

At the time of the creation of human beings, the heavenly immortals and the various spirits did not know the reason for their creation. Because of this, the Real Lord issued a proclamation, saying, "Truly I want to create human beings to represent Me in the world of existence." The heavenly immortals protested and said, "Their body is earth, water, fire, and air. These four contrary agents were gathered together and became the body. They will insult and violate each other. They will perhaps cause disorder in the future." The chief spirit said, "These human beings have desires, and seducing them is very easy," so all despised the human beings. Hence the Real Lord issued another proclamation and said, "Indeed, I know affairs that you certainly do not know" [2:30].

The first reason for the descent of the human ancestors was that the heavenly country might become the place of ultimate happiness and complete bliss for good people. From ancient times to the present, tens of thousands of people have all been endowed with the one body of the human ancestor, and they combine with the two kinds—good and evil. If the ancestors had not descended and had not grown up here, good and evil would not have become divided. Moving to this earthly world is to live among good and evil. After that, people follow their own kind. Good people go up, but evil people descend further.

The second reason for the descent was so that the Real Lord could reject the protest of the heavenly immortals and shame the empty effort of the devils, because at root the Real Lord desired noble people. By making people suffer, He made them reach this situation. The human ancestors knew rightly the kindness and compassion of the Real Lord. At the beginning they woke up to their own disobedience and became more modest and humble.

The ancestors became upset at the heavenly immortals' protest and they guarded themselves against the devils' deception. They obeyed the clear mandate and they conquered the selfishness of their selves. They entrusted their bodies and lives loyally to the Real Lord, and from the lowest they ascended again to the highest. Naturally, the protest of the immortals and the deception of the devil died down and dissipated. The Real Lord's mysterious contrivance was bright and uniquely brilliant. When we look at this, we see that although the name is "falling into trouble," in reality this was an increase in completion.

After having told the rest of the story, including the fall, Adam's repentance, his acceptance by God, and the manner in which God taught lessons to the devils, Wang reaches the final moral, a good example of Neo-Confucian Islamic thinking:

> When you reflect and look at this situation, you will certainly come to know that the Non-Ultimate is the seed, the Great Ultimate is the tree, and the human ultimate is the fruit. The seed is the fruit, the tree is concealed in the fruit, and the fruit is concealed in the tree, which embraces comprehensively and penetrates thoroughly. Everything is complete. The Classic says, "Those who are attached to the words and separated from the substance merely talk about the principle."[38] This is all because the selfishness of the self has not yet been purified and the eyes of the heart have not yet been opened. How could a breast filled with dregs reach the Original Beginning of the great transformation?!

The Real Solicitude

The following is a translation of the full text of chapter five of *The Real Commentary*, which deals with the central Islamic concept of *īmān*, which is normally translated into English as "faith." The term is typically contrasted with *islām* or "submission," which means in this context submission to the will of God by following the practices set down in the Shariah. When *īmān* and *islām* are looked upon as complementary, *īmān* embraces not only the idea of belief and conviction, but also firm and steady commitment to the objects of faith, which are most briefly, the "unseen" (*ghayb*), and in more detail, God, the angels, the scriptures, the prophets, the Last Day, and the "measuring out" of good and evil. As pointed out earlier, faith demands knowledge of the objects in which one has faith. From the scholars' attempts to clarify the nature of faith's objects has arisen the whole enterprise of Islamic theorizing about God, prophecy, the soul, and the Last Day.

That *īmān* should be a "solicitude" is implied by many Koranic verses that assert that people will not have faith until God allows them to have it. "Those against whom thy Lord's word is realized will not have faith, though every sign come to them" (10:96). An often cited saying attributed to the Prophet tells us that *īmān* is a light "that God casts into the heart of whomsoever He will."

Wang's definition of the word *īmān* is especially worthy of note. He says at the outset that it means "the fountainhead of clear virtue" (*ming-te chih yüan*). The term "virtue" (*te*) has special resonance in Chinese thought. As Wing-tsit Chan explains, it means the power of the Tao when it becomes particularized through the good character and moral excellence of individuals.[39] The most famous example of its use is in the title of Lao Tzu's *Tao Te Ching*. The expression "clear virtue" is found already in the ancient classic, the *Book of Odes*, as in the lines, "The Lord on High said to King Wen: 'I cherish your clear virtue.'"[40] The most significant usage in the Neo-Confucian context is probably found in the *Great Learning*, which lays down "clarifying the clear virtue" as the first of the three items involved in learning. In his own version of the *Great Learning*, Wang places "knowing the fountainhead of clear virtue" next to discrimination of the Real One from the Numerical One, that is, next to the discernment that is established by the Shahadah, the most basic teaching of Islam.

The "real solicitude" is called *i-ma-na*. (This Arabic word translates as "the fountainhead of clear virtue.") It is the Real Lord's movement and quietude showing solicitude to human beings.

Hence, with this solicitude, people finally come to recognize the Real Lord correctly and properly. Thus it is called "the real solicitude." It is not a reward for effort.

The signs of the real solicitude are three: fear and dread, hope and expectation, and real happiness. If you have fear and dread, you will not go against the Lord, and if you do not go against the Lord, you will escape and stay apart from the Earth Prohibited. If you have hope and expectation, your deeds will be in obedience, and if your deeds are in obedience, you will ascend to the Heavenly Country. If you have real happiness, you will know that there is only the Lord and forget altogether the ten thousand things.

Generally, those who gain these signs see gold and jade as mud and sand, wealth and nobility as dreamlike things, life and death as identical. Gain and loss do not surprise them. Each of these signs has an essential comfort that is not comparable with the small happiness of fame and profit. This is what is called "seeing the large and forgetting the small."

Heaven, earth, and the ten thousand things, wealth and nobility, and success and fame are made for the sake of human beings and they all are called the "solicitudes of mercy." However, these are always changing and altering, and in the twinkling of an eye they become a dream. How could this be the real solicitude?

The Classic says, "Indeed the life of *tun-ya* is one act of a drama."[41] (The Arabic word *tun-ya* translates as the "earthly world.") This is what I meant. When you carefully reflect upon all the details, only one affair—*i-ma-na*—always is and exists eternally. It neither decreases nor increases. It is the ultimate equilibrium and the ultimate truth. It transcends the ten thousand beings and transforms all evils into surrender to it. Indeed, it is the real solicitude.

The real solicitude is prior to heaven and earth, and it is the ancestral teacher of the Human Ultimate. It is the rule of being in the world and the axis of the true Tao. Thus, when there is the real solicitude, there is real knowledge. When there is real knowledge, there is the fixed principle. From ancient times to the present the fixed principle is not two, and the far and the near are one.

But this [fixed principle] is not what is now called "the Tao." Why? Because each people is endowed with numerous different levels, and the natures are not one. Therefore Confucius said *ju* ["the learned"], Lao Tzu said *Tao*, Buddha said *shih* ["freedom"]. Each made right what he thought was right. The differences in the Tao are not less than ten thousand fragments, because all of them depended upon their own natures.

Moreover, these masters acted in accordance with teachings of their own natures from the beginning. They still have a jumbled dispute over right and wrong, and they compete with each other. The ordinary people are widely in confusion and perplexity, and they do not know what to follow. How could they be settled in one?

If heaven is not settled, the sun and the moon will move in disturbance. If the earth is not settled, oceans and rivers will overflow. If people are not settled, right and wrong will be reversed. When we look at this, the situation is like someone who crosses a vast ocean. If he does not have a compass, he cannot possibly escape delusion and confusion.

There are three meanings for real solicitude: following the One [*shun-i*], recognizing the One [*jen-i*], and becoming the One [*ch'eng-i*]. "Following the One" is at the time of receiving the mandate while existing before heaven.[42] It is the seed. "Recognizing the One" is at the time of obeying the mandate while existing in this world. It is nurture. "Becoming the One" is at the time of returning to the mandate while existing in the next world. It is the fruit.

Thus it has been said, "If you want to discern the real seed of the before-heaven, it is each sprout before your eyes." If there is no seed, how can life sprout forth? If you do not add to the nurture, how can you perfect the fruit? This is only the nature of the principle.

You should know that heaven, earth, and the ten thousand things; the sun, the moon, and the stars, were at root all set up to plant this one grain of the real solicitude. Whoever does not have this real solicitude is as a mirror without light. If a mirror does not have light, how can it be a mirror? If heaven and earth did not have people, they would be a mirror-stand without a mirror. If a mirror-stand does not have a mirror, what good is it?

This is enough to see that the creation of heaven, earth, and the ten thousand things is all for the sake of human beings.

The creation of humans and spirits is at root for the sake of receiving this ultimate treasure of the real solicitude. If people clearly understand the honor and nobility of their own body and obtain surely the ultimate treasure of the body, then they will know that this body reaches everywhere in heaven and earth. It subtly unites being and nonbeing, and nothing whatsoever is lacking from it. But unfortunately, people in the world abandoned and put aside the ultimate treasure of their own body without knowing how to be at ease with it. Instead, they toil laboriously toward "flowers in the sky" outside the body.[43] Truly this is a life in drunkenness and a death in dreaming. The Classic says, "People in the world are deep in sleep, and after death they become aware."[44] However, when they reach this station their regret will have no effect. Whoever talks about his dreams is certainly awake; whoever knows his own mistakes will surely move on to good.

However, in order for *i-ma-na* to become manifest as such, there must be evidence, which is called the "real solicitude" and "borrowing-and-lending." Whoever gains the real solicitude will be as if guarding a chain of jade jewelry while walking, stopping, sitting, and lying down, or, as if he is facing a great enemy and is afraid of loss. Borrowing-and-lending is like borrowing something from someone else. You cannot be without worry that you will make a mistake and lose the thing.

Whoever talks without the root thinking is following his own nature, or seeking fame, or looking for profit, or fearing people's admonitions, or wanting their help. He is like someone who walks along with someone else who is carrying a torch in the dark night. When the two arrive at a dividing path, the one without the torch is left in darkness. How can he walk further?

Whoever knows that the real solicitude is the ultimate treasure will take cleanness of the heart as root, and sincerity of intention as foremost. He will protect and assist the real solicitude without cease, and with virtuous deeds he will make it stand in gravity and seriousness. If the heart is not purified, there is no place to receive and contain it. If the intention is not sincere, there is no place to nourish and produce it. If there is no protection and assistance, it is not possible to gain perfection. If there are no virtuous deeds, how can there be any evidence? You must follow the sequence to observe and guard it. Then it may be that you will not lose it.

3

Wang Tai-yü's *Great Learning*

The Great Learning of the Pure and Real is the shortest of Wang's three longer treatises—about 13,000 characters, or twenty-two pages in its modern printed form. The Confucian *Great Learning* was originally a one-page chapter in the *Book of Rites*, which is traditionally considered to be by Confucius, though the *Great Learning* itself is sometimes attributed to Confucius's grandson Tzu-ssu. Chu Hsi, the most important of the Neo-Confucian scholars, specified it and three others as the "Four Books," the most basic of the Confucian classics. The other three are the *Doctrine of the Mean* (also from the *Book of Rites*), the *Analects* of Confucius, and the *Book of Mencius*.

Wing-tsit Chan's English translation of the text and commentary of the *Great Learning* takes up less than ten pages. Chan points out that the work has played a far more important role than its short size would suggest.[1] Its principal point is to designate and differentiate "the internal and the external, the fundamental and the secondary, and the first and the last. . . . No other Confucian Classic has presented this idea so clearly and so forcefully."[2] It is this distinguishing of levels that is the basic theme of Wang's Islamic version of the *Great Learning*.

In Chu Hsi's arrangement, the commentary on the *Great Learning* has ten chapters, and it sums up all of Confucian learning in "three items" and "eight steps." The three items are clarifying clear virtue, loving the people, and abiding in the utmost good. The eight steps are investigation of things, extension of knowledge, sincerity of intention, trueness of heart, cultivation of the body, regulation of the family, governing the country, and bringing peace to everything under heaven.[3]

Wang's *Great Learning* contains an introduction, three main parts, and a long conclusion that is called the "general discussion." Each of the three parts is divided into three chapters, giving a total of eleven sections. The "general discussion" takes up more than one-third of the book.

The Chinese Background

In comparing the Confucian and Islamic *Great Learnings*, the first thing that strikes the reader is the social orientation of the Confucian work and the theological orientation of the Islamic work. This is hardly surprising given the central status that has been accorded to the Confucian work and Wang's intention to provide a work of corresponding import for Islam. No doubt Islam has its own social teachings that are, in many ways, just as fundamental and as detailed as those of Confucianism. Nonetheless, the first principle of Islam remains *tawḥīd* as voiced in the first half of Shahadah—"There is no god but God"—and all of Islamic teachings begin and end with discussions of God. The Shariah legislates social injunctions in order to enact God's will, and anything other than God must remain secondary in Muslim eyes.

As already mentioned, Liang I-chün's introduction to *The Real Commentary* praises the basic Confucian teachings but criticizes them for dealing only with the middle, not the beginning and the end. Of the Confucian teachings that Liang enumerates as agreeing with Islam, six are taken word for word from the eight steps mentioned in the Confucian *Great Learning*: (3) sincerity of the intention, (4) trueness of heart, (5) cultivation of the body, (6) regulation of the family, (7) governing of the country, and (8) bringing peace to everything under heaven. It is obvious, moreover, that the "three items" and the other two steps—clarifying the clear virtue, loving the people, abiding in the utmost good, investigation of things, and extension of knowledge—are frequently discussed in the Islamic texts, though not always in so many words. We have already seen that Wang defines *īmān* or faith as "the fountainhead of clear virtue."

In brief, Wang's use of the title *Great Learning* should be understood as his affirmation of the fundamental correctness of the Confucian teachings as far as they go. What he adds to them, however, is a thorough discussion of principles that underlie "the beginning and the end," which are utterly essential to the Islamic teachings.

As noted earlier, Wang devotes chapter eighteen of the first part of his *Real Commentary* to "true learning" (*cheng-hsüeh*). There he divides true learning into three sorts—great, middle, and constant. Although he uses the term "great learning," he defines it as returning to the Real. He says that the "middle learning" is to clarify the heart, and the "constant learning" is to cultivate the self. Thus it would seem that what the Confucians call the "great learning" belongs in his view to the domain of the middle and constant learnings, but not to the true great learning.

At the beginning of the *Great Learning*, Wang says, "The true foundation of the great learning is the word that bears witness." He certainly has in mind the Shahadah, which in Arabic means precisely "bearing witness," and which is sometimes called simply *al-kalima*, "the word." He goes on to explain that what needs to be understood before all else is the distinction between the Real One, which is God in himself, and the Numerical One, which is the first principle of creation. In other words, one must distinguish the One that is eternally transcendent and, in Koranic terms, "independent of the worlds" (*ghanī ʿan al-ʿālamīn*) from the One that manifests itself through and in the universe, the One to which all the divine names refer.

The distinction between these two Ones can hardly be more basic to Wang's understanding of what differentiates the "True Teaching" from other schools of Chinese thought. The issue is intimately bound up with the discussion of transcendence and immanence that has been much debated among modern scholars of the Chinese tradition. On one side, Sinologists who have read the Chinese texts with a background in certain strands of Western thinking, Christianity in particular, have had no difficulty seeing many of the discussions of Tao, or of the Great Ultimate and the Non-Ultimate, as assertions of transcendence. Other scholars, claiming to be unbiased by the Christian background, maintain that the idea of transcendence is foreign to the Chinese tradition. For their part, the Chinese ulama saw references to "transcendence" throughout the classical teachings of the three traditions. However, by and large they felt that it was not emphasized sufficiently, and this was one of the correctives that Islamic thinking had to offer.

It needs to be kept in mind that "transcendence" and "immanence" are problematic terms in this discussion, given that they have specific connotations and nuances in the Western tradition and no exact equivalents in the Islamic languages, much less the Chinese tradition. The closest pair of technical terms in Arabic is *tanzīh* or "assertion of incomparability" and *tashbīh* or "assertion of similarity." In *The Tao of Islam*, I have illustrated in some detail how the later Islamic thinkers—precisely those whose schools of thought can be seen to be reflected in the writings of the Chinese ulama—employed these terms in a complementary fashion. The basic position of the Muslim thinkers was that God in his Essence was totally independent of the worlds, completely inaccessible to his creation, and utterly incomparable with anything known to any created thing. However, inasmuch as God discloses his own being and attributes in the universe and the soul, his names and attributes can be known. Thus God is declared incomparable in his Essence, while the things of the universe are acknowledged to be similar to him inasmuch as they are brought into existence by him. The modalities in which he brings them into existence are discernible in creation through the *āyāt* or "signs," a Koranic term that designates both the phenomena of the natural world and the normative teachings of all the prophets. In other words, God's "signs" manifest the heavenly mandate in both the natural order and the human order.

Wang's insistence that the first discernment is the most important—that is, the discernment between the Real One and the Numerical One—underscores two things. One is that this distinction between God in his Essence and God as designated by the names and attributes is utterly essential to Islamic theology (even if the terms of the discussion are not completely clarified in the earliest centuries of the Islamic era). Second is that Wang felt that his Chinese audience would have difficulty making this distinction, because the Chinese traditions fail to do so. But neither Wang nor any of the other Chinese ulama whose works I have read would go so far as to claim that the Chinese had no understanding of God's essential incomparability with creation, his "transcendence." They surely had the understanding, but they did not differentiate clearly enough between two basic levels of transcendence.

The fact that Wang's discussion employs terminology drawn largely from Neo-Confucianism shows that he felt it to be the most adequate of the Chinese traditions to explain the nature of things. He does not explicitly criticize Neo-Confucian metaphysics, though he does criticize, in the *Great Learning* and elsewhere, Buddhist and Taoist concepts, and these critiques are in fact quite similar to those made by the Neo-Confucians. For Wang, ideas like "emptiness" and "voidness" are inadequate to convey the notion of God's simultaneous incomparability and similarity, his transcendence and immanence.

Although it is too early in my research to attempt to specify all the ways in which Wang and other ulama highlighted the Islamic idea of God's incomparability in Chinese terms, it may be useful to stress in this context the importance of the word *chen*. I am translating the term as "real," though it may also be translated as true, genuine, unfeigned, authentic. It has already been noted that the word is employed in the expression "Pure and Real" that is commonly used to designate Islamic teachings. God is given names such as "Real Lord" and "Real One." The Koran can be called the "Real Classic." Wang uses the word in the titles of all three of his longer works. Eight of the forty chapters of his *Real Commentary* employ the term in their titles, and it is mentioned frequently in his writings. Liu Chih's translation of *Lawā'iḥ* also uses the word often. A word count of the two works translated in the present book would show it to be among the most commonly used of technical terms, if not the most common.

The word *chen* does not play any special role in Neo-Confucian thought, but it was used in significant senses by both Taoists and Buddhists. They use the term in the same sort of meaning and with the same heavy significance that Confucians give to the term *ch'eng* or "sincerity." In Buddhism the "Real I" is the self that dwells in Nirvana, and the "Real Principle" designates the ultimate suchness. In Taoism the "Real One" refers to the Tao and the "Real Realm" to the place of the heavenly immortals (the latter term is incorporated by Liu Chih into his title of the translation of *Lawāʾiḥ—Displaying the Concealment of the Real Realm*). In Chuang Tzu's writings, the term *chen* by itself is used to designate a transcendent principle. He cites a poem addressed to a true Taoist master: "You have gone back to the Real, but I remain a man" (6:13). Elsewhere he suggests what he means:

> Do not let the human make the heavenly perish, and do not let purposefulness make the mandate perish. Do not sacrifice [heavenly] gain to fame. Carefully guard [the Tao] and do not lose it—this is what we call "going back to the Real." (17:9)

Still another passage from Chuang Tzu can help us understand the flavor of the term in the Chinese context. He is recounting how Confucius was instructed by a Taoist sage:

> Confucius looked shamefaced and said, "Please, may I ask what you mean by 'the Real'?"
>
> The visitor said, "By 'the Real' I mean refinement and sincerity in their highest degree. He who lacks refinement and sincerity cannot move others. . . . When a man has the Real within himself, his spirit may move externally. That is why the Real is to be considered noble! . . . Propriety is what is made by the common people of the world; the Real is what is received from Heaven. By nature it is self-so, and it cannot be changed. Therefore the sage rules himself by heaven, considers the Real noble, and does not adhere to the common. The stupid man does the opposite of this. (Book 31)

The constant use of the term *real* in the Islamic texts helps add a taste of Buddhism and Taoism, but the basic metaphysical and cosmological positions are much closer to those of Neo-Confucianism. Like the Neo-Confucians, the Muslims assert the reality of an ultimate Principle in positive terms, but, much more than those texts, they insist on the ultimate incomparability and transcendence of the Principle. The term *real* serves as a reminder of the fundamental discernment offered by the Shahadah. "There is no god but God" means there is nothing real (*ḥaqq*) except the truly Real (*al-ḥaqq*)—one of the most commonly used divine names in the Islamic languages. Thus true reality belongs only to "the Real One, the Real Lord, the Real Being, the Real Principle, the Real Substance"—all of which are Chinese Islamic names of God that will be encountered repeatedly in the translated texts.

The Islamic Concepts

Throughout the *Great Learning*, the heart of Wang's discussion remains the concept of unity. This stress is perfectly consonant with the utterly central role that *tawḥīd*, the first principle of Islamic faith, plays in all theoretical elaborations of Islamic metaphysics, cosmology, and psychology. Wang looks at God in terms of three basic levels, which he calls the "Real One" (*chen-i*), the "Numerical One" (*shu-i*), and the "Embodied One" (*t'i-i*). In Islamic terms, these can perhaps best be understood in terms of the teachings of the school of Ibn al-ʿArabī. Then they can be said to correspond with God in himself or the "Essence" (*dhāt*), the Divinity (*ulūhiyya*), and the perfect human being (*al-insān al-kāmil*). Having explained the interrelationship of these three basic levels of unity, Wang embarks on a "General Discussion" that speaks of various ways in which these fundamental topics can be understood and applied.

The basic issue in all discussions of *tawḥīd* is how God, who is One, is related to creation, which is many. All Muslim thinkers maintain that God is One and that creation in all its endless multiplicity derives from him. At the same time, much of Islamic theorizing on *tawḥīd* focuses precisely on how the many can derive from the One without compromising the One's unity. This focus on explaining how the many arise from the One fits in nicely with what Wing-tsit Chan calls "the fundamental Neo-Confucian tenet, that substance is one but its manifestations are many."[4]

Although Ibn al-ʿArabī and his followers address the issue of the One and the many with an enormous variety of terms and from numerous perspectives, it may be fair to say that their basic teaching can be summarized as follows: The absolute and incomparable One is unknown to anything other than itself. But, inasmuch as he makes himself known through creation and scripture, we come to know that he is the God and Creator of the universe. In this respect he can be called the "Divinity," or God inasmuch as he is named by a diversity of names. On the basis of God's own knowledge of his infinite reality and the never-ending repercussions demanded by that reality, he brings the many into existence.

Human beings are unique in creation. Or rather, "perfect" human beings are unique, because they alone among all creatures are the image of the total range of God's self-knowledge. They alone are able to bring the many back to the One, and they achieve this through self-discipline and purification of the heart. In realizing the unity that is latent within themselves, the perfect human beings retain all the individual distinctiveness that had been gained through the manifestation of the many. In other words, when they come fully to actualize the One, they bring together in a comprehensive, differentiated, and unified whole all the manyness that had been present potentially in the divine knowledge and that had become manifest actually through the multiplicity of the universe.

One can express this perspective in Wang's terms by saying that the "Real One" knows in itself the principle of all manyness. This principle of manyness is called the "Numerical One," because it gives rise to the multiplicity of the universe just as the number one gives rise to all the numbers. But the universe can only reach the fullness of its possibilities through being brought back to the One from which it arose. This is the function of human beings, who, among all creatures, are uniquely qualified to be the "Embodied One."

In the introduction, Wang explains the necessity for coming to know the reality of oneness. Each of the three main parts has a short introduction and three chapters. The three chapters of the first part, which deal with the Real One or God in himself, are called "the root nature" (*pen-jan*), "the root allotment" (*pen-fen*), and "the root act" (*pen-wei*). These seem to correspond with the Arabic theological terms *dhāt* (essence), *ṣifāt* (attributes), and *afʿāl* (acts). The root nature of the Real One is Eternal Being without beginning and end. It does not belong to yin and yang and does not have any opposite. Its root allotment is the "movement and quietude" of its root nature, that is, its names and attributes, which are often discussed in Islamic texts as active and receptive, or majestic and beautiful.[5] Its root act is the diffusion of the Unique One, a diffusion that remains at the level of subtlety and formlessness. In other words, its root act is to differentiate heaven, earth, and the ten thousand things without becoming sullied by the limitations of creation.

The three chapters of the second part, on the Numerical One, are called "the originally honored" (*yüan-hsün*), "the representative" (*tai-li*), and "the scribe" (*tai-shu*). By "numerical one," Wang presumably has in mind the Arabic term *wāḥid* or "one," which is commonly contrasted with the term *aḥad*, which also means one. *Wāḥid* is employed to designate a oneness that is the origin of all multiplicity, while *aḥad* is used to refer to the unique and incomparable unity of the divine Essence, which has no relationship with the universe.[6] Wang explains that the Numerical One is the "Originally Honored" inasmuch as it is the Utmost Sage (*chih-sheng*), who is the great source of nature and mandate. This expression probably refers to the literal meaning of the name Muhammad, which is "praised" or "honored." As we saw in chapter six of Wang's *Real Commentary*, by the "Utmost Sage" he seems to have in mind the Muhammadan Reality, which is also called the "Reality of Realities." This is God inasmuch as he embraces in himself in unitary fashion all the realities and principles that give rise to the infinitely diverse universe.

Thus the Muhammadan Reality is God inasmuch as human beings are created in his image, or "upon His form" (*ʿalā ṣūratih*).

In the second chapter of this part, Wang explains that the Numerical One is the Representative, which is the origin of human beings, the heavenly immortals (angels), and the spirits and demons (jinn). It is the first level in the creative transformation that gives rise to the universe.

The third chapter of this part tells us that the Numerical One is the Scribe, which is the root of heaven and earth, the mother of the ten thousand things, and the ocean of images. Here Wang probably has in view the First Intellect, called in Koranic language the "Supreme Pen," and often identified with the Muhammadan Reality.

The third main part of the book addresses the stages of achieving the perfections of human embodiment (*t'i*) in terms of three degrees, which Wang calls "recognition with knowledge" (*chih-jen*) or "knowing one" (*chih-i*), "recognition with seeing" (*chien-jen*) or "seeing one" (*chien-i*), and "recognition with continuity" (*hsü-jen*) or "unmixed one" (*shun-i*). He may have in mind the well-known Sufi triad *ʿilm al-yaqīn* (knowledge of certainty), *ʿayn al-yaqīn* (eye of certainty), and *ḥaqq al-yaqīn* (truth or reality of certainty).

In the third part Wang mentions Arabic words for only the second time in the text. All are well-known terms derived from the same root as the word *wāḥid*, "one." He calls recognition with knowledge "*tawḥīd*," which he translates as "practicing one" (*hsi-i*); it is achieved through knowing the universe. Recognition with seeing is *ittiḥād* (unification, or the internalization of unity), a term that he translates as "self-one" (*tzu-i*), which is achieved through knowing self. He identifies recognition with continuity with *waḥda* (unity or oneness), which he translates as "unmixed one;" it is achieving unity through the One itself.

The stress of this part on achieving ultimate unity in the body is perfectly in harmony both with Islamic and Confucian teachings. On the Islamic side, the importance of bodily activity as the ground for all spiritual awakening becomes manifest graphically in the most basic praxis of Islam, the ritual prayer (*ṣalāt*) with its diversity of bodily movements, preceded by rites of bodily purification. The supreme significance of this specific bodily act is best summarized in the prophetic maxim, "The *ṣalāt* is the believer's spiritual ascent [*miʿrāj*]." On the Confucian side, Tu Weiming remarks as follows: "When Mencius defines the sage (who has attained the highest moral excellence in the human community) as the person who has brought the bodily form to fruition, he assumes that the body is where the deepest human spirituality dwells."[7]

In Neo-Confucian terms, Wang's outline of three ascending stages of human embodiment can be read as a description of the process whereby, in the well-known expression of Ch'eng Hao, the man of true humanity (*jen*) "forms one body with heaven, earth, and the ten thousand things."[8] But, as Wang Yang-ming reminds us, the realization of this oneness in its fullness takes place in the human heart, the highest spiritual organ. "At bottom heaven, earth, the ten thousand things, and man form one body. The point at which this unity manifests in its most refined and excellent form is the clear intelligence of the human heart."[9] Wang Yang-ming, in fact, defines the whole Confucian ethic as outlined in the *Great Learning* in terms of clarifying the clear virtue (which, as we saw, Wang Tai-yü associates with "faith," *īmān*) and achieving this one body:

> The various steps from the investigation of things and the extension of knowledge to bringing peace to everything under heaven are nothing but clarifying the clear virtue. Even loving the people is also a matter of clarifying the clear virtue. The clear virtue is the virtue of the heart; it is humanity [*jen*]. The man of *jen* regards heaven, earth, and the ten thousand things as one body. If a single thing is deprived of its place, it means that my *jen* is not yet demonstrated to the fullest extent.[10]

In describing the three stages of achieving proper embodiment, Wang tells us that at the first stage, the seekers recognize the benefit of enlightenment and sagehood. At the second stage, they are able to transcend causal connections and personal experiences and depend upon their own true self. At the third stage, constant recognition of the Real allows them to overcome all selfish ideas and personal opinions, to return to the source of the clear virtue, and to depend upon no-self (*wu-chi*). "No-self" seems to be the stage that is achieved by "conquering self," discussed earlier (p. 56). As such it correlates with Sufi expressions like "annihilation" (*fanā*ʾ), "the Station of No Station" (*maqām lā maqām*), and "selflessness" (*bī-khwudī*).[11]

In the last section of the *Great Learning*, the "General Discussion," Wang applies the teachings of the first ten sections to a variety of contexts. This section represents a significant change in voice, and some scholars, notably Tazaka, have claimed that it was added by another hand (for his arguments, see below). For one thing, the last section takes on a rather polemical tone that is lacking in the first ten. Tazaka's arguments against its authenticity need to be taken seriously, but I incline to accept the passage as representing Wang's teachings, since there are several parallels with passages from Wang's other works. Even if we do conclude that it was revised or added by another hand, it was accepted by the Chinese Muslims as part of the text, so it deserves to be considered as the tradition has received it.

The Text

The Great Learning of the Pure and Real has been published at least ten times, but the date of its first publication is not known, and it is not clear when it was written. Even the question of its authorship cannot be decided with complete certainty. Wang's two other major works are both ascribed to him explicitly in their printed texts, but at least some of the title pages of the *Great Learning* tell us that it was "commented" on by "the old man of the real Hui," that is, by Wang, and "commentary" does not suggest authorship.[12] In contrast to the other two works, the *Great Learning* has no preface or introduction providing information on Wang's life or the year of the book's original publication.

Even if we accept Wang's authorship as given, we still need to consider Tazaka's argument that the "General Discussion" does not belong to the main text. He makes three points. First, since the text is modeled on the Confucian *Great Learning*, it should have the same ten-fold structure, but it does not unless the General Discussion is dropped. Second, Isaac Mason described the 1918 edition of *The Great Learning* as having forty-four pages, which corresponds with the length of the first part of the 1921 edition, but the General Discussion adds another twenty-six pages.[13] Third, the 1852 introduction to the text by Yang Tsan-hsün (the "introduction" translated here) says clearly that Master Hsieh Sheng-wu requested the Ahung of the temple, Master Wang Shou-ch'ien, to collect the essential contents of Wang's *Great Learning of the Pure and Real* and Liu Chih's *Interpretation of the Five Endeavors* (*Wu-kung shi-i*) and to unite them as one book. The Ahung did this and named the book *A Summary of the Important Points for Enlightening the Young* (*Ch'i-meng yao-lüeh*). If the printed text is identical with this *Summary of the Important Points*, then Wang's *Great Learning* would be the first half of the book, and the "General Discussion" would be taken from Liu Chih.[14]

One can respond to Tazaka's arguments as follows: (1) It is true that we can look at the text as having ten sections in the pattern of the Confucian *Great Learning*, but Wang may simply have added an eleventh section, the "General Discussion," as a sort of complement to or commentary on the first half. After all, the Confucian text has been commented on by many of the great Neo-Confucians. (2) If the "General Discussion" was in fact left out of the 1918 edition, this does not prove that Wang was not the author, nor does it prove that the publishers of that edition thought he was not the author, since the last section may have been dropped for some other reason. It is perhaps significant here that Chin Chi-t'ang, in his discussion of the *Great Learning*, mentions four different editions and says nothing about the "General Discussion" being left out of any of them.[15] But Chin does say that he thinks the "General Discussion" is meant to extend the discussion so that its application to a number of different domains will be obvious to the reader. (3) Tazaka himself notes in answer to the third argument that the "General Discussion" has no resemblance to Liu Chih's *Interpretation of the Five Endeavors*, whether in style or content.[16] So, the introduction that says the Ahung put together Wang's work with that of Liu Chih's does not stand up to what we know about Liu Chih's work. That the Ahung had some hand in editing the work may be true, but there is no evidence that he employed Liu Chih's work in doing so.

In my first reading of Wang's *Great Learning*, I inclined toward Tazaka's position, especially because of the change in style and the polemical nature of some parts of the text. But a closer reading of the text and much discussion with Tu Weiming have led me to the position that it does in fact represent an integral part of the treatise. Among the evidence that can be offered for considering the "General Discussion" authentic is the similarity of several of the passages to discussions in the *Real Commentary* and the *True Answers*.

What I had first considered a rather too polemical approach toward Buddhism and Taoism does in fact correspond with arguments offered in Wang's other works. Moreover, these are the same sorts of arguments that are offered by the Neo-Confucian scholars in their attacks on the other two traditions. In fact, then, we can read these polemical passages as Wang's attempt to show that Islam largely agrees with Neo-Confucianism's interpretation of the world and its criticisms of Taoism and Buddhism.

The translation is based on the edition of 1921, which I have collated with the edition of 1987 and an undated edition from the Tenri University library in Japan. There are no significant differences among the three editions.[17]

The identity of the author of the preface, who calls himself "A Rustic of the Pure and Real" (Ch'ing-chen Pi-jen), is unknown. However, we do have at least one more work by the same author. At the end of the 1827 edition of Wang's *True Answers of the Very Real* (*Hsi-chen cheng-ta*), which also contains his already mentioned poetry, eight additional eight-line poems are attributed to the Rustic, and he explains his reasons for writing the poems in some detail. The topics he covers in the poetry as well as some of the expressions are quite close to various passages in the "General Discussion." This may suggest that he was influenced by Wang's work, or that he himself had a hand in composing the final version.[18]

4

The Great Learning of the Pure and Real

by The Old Man of the Real Hui

Preface

by

A Rustic of the Pure and Real

Reflecting upon this *Great Learning*, [we see that] the principle of righteousness is refined and detailed. It reaches directly to the root origin, specifically clarifying the Real One, manifesting the light of the clarity of the true Tao, and stamping out the mistakes and errors of the heretics. In its quietude, it rests in the bosom; in its function, it fills the universe. It penetrates fine dust, yet it is not tiny; it encloses heaven and earth, yet it is not vast.[1] It clears away and removes colors and guises, and it splits and dissolves emptiness and nonbeing. This is because it fully returns at root to the fountainhead of clear virtue, guiding and leading the return to the path of the Real. Thus may you escape and depart from the ocean of illusion and go back again to the other shore. Compare this to the wide Tao that gives rise to the great code of the Constants of the Bonds and Relationships.[2] Can that be better than this?

If you want to have an explication of the Pure and the Real so as to open up this original subtleness, but you lack the right person, you will not be able to do so. It will not be proper to receive it, and you cannot receive it. Only when you obtain the right person can you widen this path. Why? If you do not have the person, but there is explanation, this is like adding makeup to a jade-like face—it obscures the root color. It is not that someone does not exhaust his heart [in trying to explain the Tao], only that, compared to [the Tao], his ability and power stop short. He should not offer, but he does offer, like a puppet in brocade garments—

the outside is glorious and beautiful, but the inside is at root an empty corpse. If there is no working and handling, how will the puppet move by itself? If you want to hook the fish in the bottom of the pond with the sea-turtle's food, not only will the hook not be taken, but also the fish will be frightened and run away.

If a city of only ten houses still has someone with loyalty and faithfulness, will not ten thousand districts of a hundred *li* have a worthy companion? In general, a man of clarity is clear by himself, and a man of darkness is dark by himself. What a pity that men of real knowledge and firm opinions are few, but there are many reckless people who follow the waves and the flows. They do not discriminate between right and wrong. They use ears in place of eyes. You should observe the matter that everyone likes, and you should observe the matter that everyone hates, because the causes [for like and hate] issue from these people.

Nonetheless, we can expect that there be a true and profound person who embodies remembrance, loyalty, and sincerity, who reflects upon and seeks the ultimate Tao, and who clarifies the heart and breast. The broadness of his vision will mold the opinions of the common people and sweep away baseless views. He will follow the steps of the real transmission, and then obtain only the truth. If he polishes and sharpens in the same way, he will know the evidence and clarity of the ultimately great. He will suddenly awaken to the ancient record of his own self. Probably, he will not betray the author's earnest concern to elucidate fully the ultimate Tao of the Pure and Real.

Introduction

by

The Student Yang Tsan-hsün

Humans are born into quietude, which is the oneness of the undifferentiated state. They are the spirit of the ten thousand things, maintain the essence of the two vital-energies, and contain the refinement of the Five Agents. Purity and clarity exist in their selves along with real truth without falsehood. Human nature is good, and it can be so without learning. But self-nature is changed by practice, or perhaps it will gradually run to the realm of confusion and turbidity and all at once darken its origin. Endeavoring not and rebelling, it brings about transgression, or else it sinks and changes into the condition of emptiness and falsehood, more and more losing its great substance. Thus it abandons the truth, and in this it does not transform its crookedness. Yet it wants to start each day with endeavor and to obey respectfully the mandate and command of the Real Lord and the customs and patterns of the Utmost Sage. Without learning, how can it enter into this?

Those among us suitable for learning obey only the ultimate of the Five Constants, and they follow what should be of the Five Affairs. Thereby they infer and seek out the origin of the One Thread,[3] and they explain and open up the principle of the Unique One. So, once there is learning, there is teaching. With it, it is possible to give rise to endeavor and establish obligations that are not heavy.

Masters Wang Tai-yü and Liu I-chai [Chih] are the forerunners of the awareness of the Tao. They translated the refined meanings of the Classics of Arabia and wrote *The Interpretation of the Five Endeavors* and *The Great Learning of the Pure and Real*. Both books go back and forth over the examples and similatives, earnestly narrate the details, and open up and illuminate the essential substance of the Five Classics, the Five Basics, and the root fountainhead of the Real One without twoness. With untiring diligence, they provide thought that opens up the young and instructs them in wakefulness.

However, these books are still divided into two books. If they are not looked upon as united, those who want the learning have no way to find the sequence of earning endeavor, and those who want to examine endeavor cannot obtain the goal of the true learning.

Thereupon, Master Hsieh Sheng-wu requested the Ahung of the temple, Master Wang Shou-ch'ien, to collect the refined contents of both books and unite them into one book. He named this book *A Summary of the Important Points of Instructing the Young* (*Ch'i-meng yao-lüeh*). He asked me to write a preface. I accepted and read the book. I became aware of refined, concealed, deep, and broad language—none other than the principle of the flat and easy, the simple and common.[4] When one puts one's thoughts into this, propriety will increase the display of reverence and respect by the fasting heart and the fasting intention, and giving alms will surely become more abundant.

The higher [goal] is to assist in transforming the kingdom's foundation and to return with others to the beginning of human life. The lower is to carry on traditions, instruct the later generations, and then to be safe in the great Tao.

Learning is the refined and subtle, endeavor is returning to what is intimate and close—hopefully to the root of the clean and the pure. Without confusion of the will, the cultivation of the real advancement will greatly flourish. This is the basis for truly nourishing the young.

I brought together the essential points of the book and made it a preface.

Respectfully noted in the second year of the Hsien-Feng [era] of the Great Ch'ing [dynasty], *jen-tz'u* [1852], summer, the fourth month, on a lucky day, in the state of Chen.

SYNOPSIS: COMPREHENSIVE STATEMENT

The true foundation of the great learning is the word that bears witness. It especially clarifies the principle of the utmost greatness of the Real Lord and His [chief] servant, and it also clarifies the difference between the Real One and the Numerical One.

Therefore, first I clarify that the unique and independent One is the Real Lord who created heaven, earth, and the ten thousand things. However, He is not related to heaven, earth, and the ten thousand things. He is the Original Being without beginning.

As for the Numerical One, it is the original beginning of heaven, earth, and the ten thousand things, so it can represent heaven, earth, and the ten thousand things. Since it is the original beginning, it is designated as "the chief servant;" and since it is the representative, it is designated as "the utmost sage" or "the special envoy." This is the original foundation, but with a beginning, because it comes into being by receiving the mandate.

The most important thing in the Pure and Real is that you divide clearly between the Real Lord and the Chief Servant. Only then can you be sure to witness the Unique One and the Numerical One. What we call the Real Lord is the Unique One, the All-Powerful Being, and there is nothing that does not accord with His will. The Chief Servant is the Numerical One that receives the mandate, and it is not at all independent.

However, you cannot compare this with ruler and minister, father and son, because these [relationships] are occasional and nominal and cannot stand by themselves in reality. Why? Sometimes a son may be wiser than his father, or a minister may become the ruler by a turn of fortune. The success and failure of a nation or a family come and go, because the causes are all of the same kind. As for nature and mandate, life and death, worthiness and stupidity, untimely death and longevity, old age and youth, beauty and ugliness—all these are most important for the human body. A ruler or a father cannot be their means, for heaven must cover and earth must carry. So, what about the things outside the body?

You should know that the scale and measure of the universe are to clothe and feed the ten thousand living things, but there is only the Real Lord, the Unique One, who comprehensively embraces everything from the beginning of the universe to its end. If you take the propriety that pertains to the Bonds and Relationships among one kind and apply it to the utmost greatness between the Lord and the servant, this would be a major confusion relative to the Pure and Real.

So, when the Lord and the servant are clearly separated and the Real One and the Numerical One are established, then only can the fountainhead of clear virtue be known. When the fountainhead of clear virtue is known, the clear virtue will be clarified. When the clear virtue is clarified, there will be real knowledge. When there is real knowledge, the self will be known. When the self is known, the heart will be made true. When the heart is made true, intentions will be sincere. When intentions are sincere, words will be firm. When words are firm, the body will be cultivated. When the body is cultivated, the family will be regulated. When the family is regulated, the country will be governed.[5]

If the country is not governed, it is because the family is not regulated. If the family is not regulated, it is because the body is not cultivated. If the body is not cultivated, it is because the words are not one. If the words are not one, it is because the intention is not sincere. If the intention is not sincere, it is because the heart is not true. If the heart is not true, it is because the self is not known. If the self is not known, it is because knowledge is not real. If knowledge is not real, it is because the clear virtue has not been clarified. If the clear virtue is not clarified, it is because the fountainhead of clear virtue is not known. If the fountainhead of clear virtue is not known, it is because the Real One is not discriminated from the Numerical One. If the Real One is not discriminated from the Numerical One, it is because the principle of the utmost greatness of the Lord and the [Chief] Servant has not become clear. When the principle of the utmost greatness of the Lord and the Servant has not become clear, ten thousand good deeds may be done, but they are not worthy of mention. Why? When the taproot of the deed is not pure, its branches and twigs cannot be pure.

This book points directly at the fountainhead and clarifies its great root. Thus, true people under heaven will not make mistakes upon reaching the crossroads, and they will not be perplexed when facing the doubtful. There will be things that they take as witness.

You should know that the ultimately great and true concern is why only human beings can have witnessing. This is because in the beginning, when the Real Lord showed this important trust to the heaven, the earth, the oceans, the mountains, and all beings and things, all were fearful and did not dare to accept it. This was because they belonged to division, so it was impossible for them to combine the beings. Only the Human Ultimate accepted this great responsibility.[6] Its color and subtlety are both complete,[7] its spirit is beyond the ten thousand levels, and its strength is provided with all the conditions.

However, this utmost principle is possessed only by the true heart. If the heart is crooked, this principle cannot be received. Why? Those who have made their hearts true are able to complete this heavy trust because they do not know their own being—they know only the Lord's being. All the conditions are only its guardians. It is like jade inside stone, so naturally applications of propriety are all obtained. Those who do not have true hearts betray this heavy trust, because they do not know the Lord's being. They know only their own being and that all the conditions are their root substance. This is no different from a shell without a pearl. Although such people are human, they are so only in external appearance. They are nothing but name and color. How can they bear witness to the Real One?

The Classic says: "The Real Lord witnesses Himself; there is no being except the being of the Real Lord."[8] It also says: "Indeed, the Real Lord witnesses Himself in the ten thousand things, all of them."[9] How can we know the matter as such? This is like a ruler over a country or an elder in a household—if there were two, then the country and the household would certainly be in a confusion.[10] The vastness and the greatness of heaven and earth, the rising and setting of the sun and the moon, the brightness and darkness of day and night, the coming and going of the four seasons, the shape of the forms of the ten thousand things, the blooming and withering of trees and grasses—from ancient times until now, nothing has altered or changed. All these are the very proof that the Real Lord is the Unique One.[11]

That to which the human alone bears witness, in contrast to all other beings, is intimately connected to him because he is the fruit of the ten thousand things, the highest and the noblest, and he transcends the ten thousand conditions. This [relationship between the Real Lord and the human being] is like the relationship between a beautiful woman and a mirror. No matter how much makeup and ornament she puts on, the mirror will not be united with her. Does a mirror use its own light to cast a reflection? This is the meaning found in the saying of the sage, "Indeed the Real Lord created human beings and then manifested himself in them."[12]

In the beginning, the Human Ancestor said, "I bear witness that there is no other thing; there is only the Real Lord, who is the only one, the peerless. I also bear witness that the utmost sage"— Mu-han-me-te [Muhammad] (who is called "sage" out of respect)—"is the chief servant of the Real Lord and His special envoy."[13] The first cause for the human ancestor's *t'ao-po* [*tawba*] (which translates as "repentance") goes back to the Utmost Sage's inciting his awareness; only then did he wake up.[14]

This is why "The true foundation of the great learning is the word that bears witness."[15] At the beginning of creation, it was at root the chief summit of the true teaching.

The pivot of the Real One and the Numerical One is wholly provided in the "I" that bears witness. Know that the "I" of form and color is the "I" that divides and distinguishes between "I" and "the people." This is an illusory "I" that is not the "I" of bearing witness. The "I" that bears witness is the "I" whom the Real Lord entrusted, and it is the real "I." Other than this entrusted "I," at root there is no "I" at all.

A worthy said, "No human can say that the Real Lord is the only one; only the Real Lord is able to speak about His only-one-ness."[16] Why? The "I" of before-heaven has neither color nor guise. [1] It bears witness to the root nature of the Real Lord. [2] Its seeing and hearing, listening and speaking, spirit and clarity, life and knowledge, bear witness to the movement and quietude of the Real Lord. [3] The "I" of after-heaven combines principle and vital-energy. With form and spirit on One Thread, it bears witness to the activity of the Real Lord.

There is nothing greater than bearing witness to the evidence of the Real Lord. Outside of these three witnessings, if you try to think about the guise of the "I," is there anything? If there is something, it can only be flawed by the tinge of the newborn. What we call "the 'I' that divides and distinguishes between 'I' and 'the people'" is not the "'I' that bears witness."

Someone asked: What did the Real Lord witness in self, and what did the human ancestor's "I" witness? The answer is that the Real Lord witnessed in self His great "power" when He created heaven and earth, and He witnessed in self His own "completeness" when He created the Human Ultimate.

Heaven and earth are like a painter's painting, and the human ultimate is like a beautiful woman's mirror. Were there no heaven and earth, there would be no manifestation of His great power, and were there no human ultimate, there would be no manifestation of His completeness. This is the meaning of the Real Lord's witnessing in self.

When you see heaven and earth, this is enough to witness the Real Lord's great power, and when you reflect upon yourself, this is enough to witness the Real Lord's completeness. If there is no painter, there is no painting, and if there is no beautiful woman, why is there a mirror? This is the meaning of the "I"'s witnessing the Lord through the things.

The Lord's witnessing self is His witnessing that His powerful mandate makes things into being and nonbeing, but the "I"'s bearing witness is witnessing that by receiving the mandate, it has a beginning and an end.

The difference between having been created and creating is as clear as black and white. If a painting is considered the same as the painter or the mirror the same as the beautiful woman, this is terrible ignorance and delusion. A poet said:

> The Real Lord shows mercy, but no one would know it
>   if life and death did not suddenly deceive each other.
> Trying to think of the ten thousand affairs, who is capable of
>   oneness?
>   Why should we dwell in drunkenness and dreams?

Their ignorance and madness is all because they do not know the unique-oneness of the Real Lord. If this principle does not become clear, loyalty will not be real loyalty, and filial piety will not be real filial piety. Even if they do their best to be loyal or filial, they will not be awake as to why they must be so. This is a pity.

If you want loyalty and filial piety in their innermost fountainhead, you must reflect upon where you have come from so that you may wake up to that through which substance and function stand. The human being is the most refined among forms and spirits. Heaven, earth, and the ten thousand spirituals exist only for the sake of human beings. The original meaning of the creation of human beings is at root to recognize the unique-oneness of the Real Lord, to manifest the original pivot of movement and quietude, and to represent the subtle function of being and nonbeing.

Receiving these greatest of mercies, people do not delve into the origin of their nature and mandate, life and death. They think only of the importance of the mercy and righteousness of their ruler and their parents, but this has nothing to do with the most great Real Lord, who created ruler and parents, nature and mandate, life and death. Unfortunately, the people of the world do not discriminate the One from the unreal, and their hearts are in doubt concerning this and that. They are blind to the real mercy of the Original Being, and they worship emptiness, nonbeing, and idols. Their bodies stand at a thousand crossroads and their hearts divide into ten thousand branches. Humanity, wisdom, loyalty, and uprightness are obscured and wasted. This is surely a pity.

The endeavor of witnessing the One is indeed the chief task. In discriminating the One, there are three levels: the One that is unique and independent, the One that is the root of numbers, and the One that is recognized with the body. The unique and independent One is the Lord of heaven, earth, and the ten thousand things; the One that is the root of numbers is the seed of heaven, earth, and the ten thousand things; and the One that is recognized with the body is the fruit of heaven, earth, and the ten thousand things.

THE REAL ONE

The Main Topic

If you are to become a perfect human and the root cause of the ten thousand sorts of good, the most important thing is that you must first know that the unique and independent One is the Real Lord, and that at root He has nothing to do with the ten thousand things.

There are three levels of bearing witness: the Root Nature, the Root Allotment, and the Root Act. If you make a small mistake and error, the principle will not be penetrated, and you will not belong to the Pure and Real.

In order for you to clarify your heart, recognize the Real Lord, cultivate your body, and widen the Tao, you must first enter the true teaching of the Pure and Real. Then you must hope to see the Tao and a clear worthy. Why? If there is a true teaching but no true person, this is like the sun shining on the blind. How can they divide white from black? If there are true people but no true teaching, this is like those with clear vision walking in the dark. How can they follow the trace of a true path?

I am afraid that those who do not discriminate between true and false take only wrong ideas as ideas. They may emulate the words and deeds of a teacher, but this is like a brush and ink. The new learner's empty heart will be like the white bamboo on which the brush moves when listening to the teacher. Once the bamboo is filled with writing, if something is not correct, how can it be made white again? Therefore, to inquire after the Tao and to follow the teacher are the most important things—not at all something to be trifled with. You should never be careless in this, and you should not simply act to your own liking.

CHAPTER ONE

The Root Nature

What we call the "Root Nature" is the Beginningless Original Being, the Endless Eternal. It does not belong to yin and yang, and at root It has no opposite. It is the Unique One, the Most Honored, and there is nothing other than It—no time and space, no form and guise, no defilement and obstruction, no near and far. It has no spouse, and nothing can be compared to it, nor can anyone describe "how." Its powerful mandate brings about being and nonbeing, yet It Itself does not fall into being and nonbeing. It creates the ten thousand things, yet It is not of the same kind as the ten thousand things. Nothing at all is similar to It.[17] This is the Root Nature of the Real Lord's Original Being.

CHAPTER TWO

The Root Allotment

What we call the "Root Allotment" is the movement and quietude of the Root Nature. Although It is the Everlastingly Guarded and the Undifferentiated One, Its principle becomes manifest in different ways. This means that the Real One has nothing to do with the Numerical One; originally It is One, and thus It is always the Unique One.

The Real Being does not fall into being and nonbeing. Originally It is Being, so It transcends everything and is everlasting Being. It is the original living, without life; the whole of it is living, so it is never not-living. It is the original knowledge, without heart; It is the penetrating knowledge, so there is nothing that It does not know. It is the original power, without help; It is powerful originally, so there is nothing that It cannot do. It is the original looking, without eye; It looks without obstacle, so there is nothing upon which It does not look. It is the original hearing, without ear; It hears without direction, so there is nothing that It does not hear. It is the original speech, without tongue; It speaks without restraint, so there is nothing that It does not say. Everything accords with Its will, without thinking; wants accord with Its will, so there is nothing that does not accord with it. It is eternal, without planning; It is the original eternity, so It will never be non-eternal.[18]

All these are the movement and quietude of the Root Nature. Although the quietude is without change and has no movement, and the movement is ceaseless and never stops, if we talk about the quietude, the pivot always becomes manifest, and if we talk about the movement, the trace will not be seen. The reason we speak of movement and quietude together is that the two are truly in the midst of the Root Nature's acting and making.

Know that before the being of heaven and earth, the Real Lord wanted to manifest His own original power. So, with His original knowledge, He prearranged the ten thousand things for appropriate use, along with their beginnings and their ends, their insides and their outsides, with nothing surplus or lacking, and with no change or alteration. So, nothing is outside the wanting and acting of His knowledge and power. It is not that His knowledge and power constrict the ten thousand things, only that the ten thousand things cannot transgress these two. The Classic says that the Real Lord is the Original Being, the Unique One, and at root nothing was with Him.[19] Afterward, He mentioned and recorded the ten thousand things according to His own will. This is predetermination by the Real Lord's movement and quietude.

CHAPTER THREE
The Root Act

What we call the "Root Act" is the surplus of the unique and independent One, possessing all the subtlety of the formless. It is the Powerful Being, and it can be compared to an inkwell. The pure essences of the ten thousand spirituals and the ornaments of heaven and earth all depend on this Powerful Being. Afterward, with the pen of the representative, It started to put forth the principles contained in the inkwell. Before the pen's putting forth, these principles are neither the same as nor separable from the Real One. If you try to divide them, they do not come apart, and if you try to unite them, they still have differences. In [the inkwell] the pivot of protection and nourishment is stored, and the signs of doing according to will are already manifest, though only the Lord knows and sees this. This is the bounded realm of the Real Lord's root act.

There are six names for this bounded realm: the One Root of the Real Foundation, the Head of the Four Oceans, the Root Act, the Transforming Fountainhead, the Powerful Being, and the Surplus Light.

Someone may say: The Real Lord is spontaneous, all-penetrating, and complete perfection. How can it be said that He has a surplus? If there is a surplus, this means that the original being of the Real Lord has some defect.

I will reply: The Unique One and Most Honored is the Original Being and has no opposite. He issues universal compassion by Himself, and when He wants to make the ten thousand things, He commands the mandate to be or not to be according to His own convenience. Just then, the substance and function become divided for the first time, since these issue forth from the Original Being. It is the Powerful Being, so we call it the "surplus light." The substance and function are inseparable, and they have no defects whatsoever.

What we call the "Powerful Being" is the being of powerful issuing forth. The power of the Original One gives it oneness, the power of the Original Being gives it being, the power of the Original Life gives it life, the power of the Original Knowledge gives it knowledge, the power of the Original Power gives it power, the power of the Original Looking gives it looking, the power of the Original Hearing gives it hearing, the power of the Original Speech gives it speech. Therefore, in the midst of the Original Being and in the midst of the Powerful Being, the principles of the things start to arise.

The Original Being is beginningless and endless, without inside or outside, but the Powerful Being has the power to begin and the power to end, the power to be outside and the power to be inside. This is the meaning of the relationship [between the two]. A poet said,

> Why is fire preserved
>   inside water,
> But outside water,
>   self-burning disappears?
> The same heat is clearly divided
>   inside and outside.
> Still, you must examine thoroughly—
>   how is it preserved, how does it disappear?

This meaning clarifies especially why the Real Lord has no peer.

Afterward, with His original knowledge, He prearranged the origin of mankind, the spirits and immortals, and the foundations of guarding all the conditions. At this moment, He commanded all the subtleties to be raised and possessed by the Powerful Being, and through this activity, the guises and colors became perfect and complete. The ten thousand affairs and the ten thousand things are not original beings at root; each receives the mandate from the Root Nature of the Real Lord's protection and nourishment, which is the movement and quietude of the Root Act.

THE NUMERICAL ONE

The Topic

What we call the Numerical One is the one root of the ten thousand different things and the chief summit of the Powerful Being. It also is called by different names—the Chief Servant, the Originally Honored, the Special Envoy, the Representative, the Great Pen, the Original Beginning, the Chief Mandate, the Great Wisdom, the Ocean of Nature, the Human Ultimate, the Great Father, the Fountainhead of the Tao, the Great Root, the Light of Clarity, the Spiritual Taproot, the Utmost Sage. The names are different, but the principle is one at root. It is within the Powerful Being, accepts the mandate, and becomes manifest. It is the root origin of the ten thousand things and thereby carries ten thousand principles. It is the Non-Ultimate. There are three levels of bearing witness to it: as the Originally Honored, the Representative, and the Scribe.

CHAPTER ONE
The Originally Honored

What we call "the Originally Honored" is the general designation for the Utmost Sage, and it is the great fountainhead of nature and mandate. It is like an ocean—receiving all the rivers, it never overflows, and pouring into all the rivers, it never becomes exhausted. Neither this nor that, it keeps the great harmony, and it is called "the seed of all beings." It is what the Taoists say— "the Gate of All Subtlety," and "The Nameless is the beginning of heaven and earth."[20] It represents the root nature of the Real Lord's protecting and nourishing.

CHAPTER TWO
The Representative

What we call "the Representative" is the opening and issuing forth of the ten thousand spirituals. Its nature at origin is unmixedly limpid, its vital-energy at root weightlessly pure. It is not related to colors and beings. The origin of humankind, the heavenly immortals, the spirits and demons, the foundation of heaven, earth, and the ten thousand things—all begin at this time. There is nothing that does not depend on its mandate and command, which is the issuing disclosure. It represents the movement and quietude of the Real Lord's activity, such as the powerful mandate of being and nonbeing, life and death, nobility and meanness, safety and danger, gain and loss.

Know that the movement and quietude of the Root Nature is everlastingly guarded in the Real One, and it has nothing to do with any of the beings. However, the movement and quietude of the activity becomes manifest in the ten thousand things, and thus we bear witness. This is all because it issues forth from the Powerful Being, which is the creation and transformation of the chief forerunner.

CHAPTER THREE
The Scribe

What we call "the Scribe" is the surplus of the Pure Essence, and it is the naturally issuing disclosure to the outside. It also is called by different names—the Function of the Numerical One, the Bond of the Ten Thousand Forms, the Taproot of Heaven and Earth, the Mother of the Ten Thousand Things, the Scribe, the Ocean of Images. This is the Great Ultimate. At this moment the vital-energy becomes prosperous while the principle stays concealed. It is what the Taoists say—"The Named is the mother of the ten thousand things."[21] The Great Ultimate transforms and enacts yin and yang. If we speak of these two together, they are heaven and earth. If we speak of them as separate, they are sun and moon, stars and constellations, earth, water, fire, and air.

Yin and yang transform and enact the ten thousand forms, even though the ten thousand forms are not the same as yin and yang. Why? Heaven and earth are like the trunk of a great tree. That of it outside the six directions is the original taproot of yin and yang. By nature the original taproot does not change. That of it inside the six directions is the leaves and flowers of the tree. By nature the leaves and flowers wither and fall. When yin and yang are united, they produce the ten thousand things. When they scatter, each keeps to its own nature.

These are like creatures in water and on land, things that fly and walk, trees and grasses, metals and jewels, and so on—but human beings are not like them. The heavenly immortals and the spirits and demons come forth afterwards. Why? Because human beings are the original taproot of yin and yang. Coming forth from the formless, they are prior to all beings. Opening up in the after-heaven, they comprehensively embrace the beginning and end of all beings. They are the fruit of the ten thousand things, and like fruit, they are produced ceaselessly. Although they have a beginning, they have no end and they are preserved and do not decay. If you take ripe fruit, it still produces new life after its use. In the coming and going of the fruit, there is never any repetition, nor is the former fruit recognized in the latter.

The most important point here is the distinction between the true and the false, and you should know about it. In general, the tree's root is perfected in the fruit. Heaven and earth are completed in the ability of the human being who follows the mandate, establishes the ultimate, and binds together the beginning and the end. This is the "great perfection," and this is the bounded realm of representing the activity of the Real Lord, the Sole Mover. For this reason, we call [the Numerical One] "the Chief Servant" or "the Special Envoy."

We call it "the Chief Servant" because it is the originally honored among the ten thousand things, and everything follows its being. [We call it] "the Special Envoy" because it is the representative of the humans, the spirits, and the ten thousand things, and all things depend on its being brought forth. It is the great bond above the Three Bonds and the great relationship above the Five Relationships. Therefore the Classic says that the inkwell of the Powerful Being carries His mercy and severity; the intimate pen of the Non-Ultimate manifests the nature and mandate of all things; the scribe of the Great Ultimate transforms and enacts yin and yang; and the ten thousand images are sketches of yin and yang.[22] All these manifest the bounded realm of the root act.

THE EMBODIED ONE

The Topic

What we call "the oneness of recognition with body" is the human level, and it also is called by many names: the Heart of the Ten Thousand Spirituals, the Fruit of the Ten Thousand Images, the Furnace of Alchemy, the Gate of Life and Death, the Precious Mirror, the Great Perfection. This level is the Real Lord's original pivot in His ancient archive.

The Embodied One is provided with both form and spirit, the highest and the lowest. There is nothing that it does not cover or carry.[23] It indeed is the most complete of the ten thousand kinds of things.

Before heaven, the chief mandate is called "the Real Nature," and it embodies the subtlety of the Real One. After heaven, the bodily mandate is called "the Root Nature," and it embodies the principle of the Non-Ultimate. Yin and yang united as one are called "the Disposition of Form"; this embodies the function of the Great Ultimate. Hearing, seeing, speaking, walking, stopping, taking, giving, and the hundred bones of the body all listen to this one nature. Therefore, through the oneness of the appropriate body, the oneness of the root of numbers can be witnessed. After that, along with the Numerical One, and only then, can the oneness of the Unique and the Independent be witnessed. Advancing step by step to arrive there, no one will go astray. A poet said,

> One ink-slab, two pools, the great pen stretches out—
> one, yet two, then all return to one.
> The Creative, the Receptive, man, woman, all are like this—
> track down the trace, ascend the hall, then enter the room![24]

The Classic says, "He who recognizes himself will be able to witness the Utmost Sage, then recognize the Real Lord."[25]

There are three levels of bearing witness: recognition with knowledge, recognition with seeing, and recognition with continuity. Recognition with knowledge is called "clear penetration," recognition with seeing is called "intimate connection," and recognition with continuity is called "unity in union."

CHAPTER ONE

Recognition with Knowledge

What we call "recognition with knowledge" is to inquire about and to imitate what the sages and worthies reflected upon and witnessed. It is to infer in detail from the Real Classic of the True Teaching while one looks at things, thoughts, and feelings. So, it is to embody the Real Lord while depending on all the conditions. Thus, heaven is high and earth abundant, water is cold and fire hot, wind moves and the earth is in repose, sun and moon come and go, stars and constellations turn and revolve, the four seasons change and alternate, day and night are rolled up and unfolded, metal and stone alter and transform, grasses and trees show fragrant faces; water creatures, flyers, and land-walkers are all of different kinds, not equal in hardness and softness. If there are too many, they give no benefit; if there are too few, this is not complete. Everything has been most suitable and without change from ancient times to the present. If some small thing is not exactly as it should be, naturally it is not safe and sound. Other than the Real Lord, who can keep on creating things in this arrangement of utmost subtlety?[26]

This is "attaining one from ten thousand." It is like the time of the blossoms and the leaves. What a pity that there is so little time! This stage is called *t'ao-hei-te [tawḥīd]* (which means "practicing one"). When you reach this station, only then can you trace the activity of the Real Lord, though it is not possible to grasp everything.

This truly depends on learning. After learning, you can know; after knowing, you can be faithful; after being faithful, you can be sincere; and after being sincere, you can be loyal. If you are loyal, you will surely not waver. It is not that you have what is seen; it is rather that you have not the slightest doubt. Only when you stand firm without moving can you witness the Real Lord. If you enact real knowledge, you will not be perplexed.

CHAPTER TWO

Recognition with Seeing

What we call "recognition with seeing" is transcending all the conditions so that you experience yourself intimately and, while depending on the body, you recognize the Real Lord with the body. He is the root cause for the transformation of the human ancestor into man and woman, who are the embodied images of the Great Ultimate and of yin and yang. He comprehensively embraces the pivot of heaven and earth and thoroughly penetrates the subtlety of being and nonbeing. He contains nature and mandate, knowledge and power, each of them bright and lively; sight, hearing, listening, and speech, each in its utmost refinement. In relation to the universe, He is like the most great and the original pivot. Other than the Real Lord, who can abide through himself? Even the worldly affairs in front of the eyes, such as endeavor and reputation, wealth and nobility, gain and loss, safety and danger—no one is capable of keeping these. How much less the greatest things, like life and death!

If you have an astonished awaking, such that you turn your intention and return your heart, this is the beginning discrimination between the newborn and the Original Being and the clear division between the Lord and the servant, none of this depending on your own self. This is "attaining one from two." Even though the subtle clarity is manifest, unity in union has not yet been reached. This stage is called *i-t'i-ha-te* [*ittiḥād*] (which means "self-one"). When you arrive at this station, you will begin to reach the movement and quietude of activity.

You should know that the propriety and righteousness of the constants of the Bonds—such as loyalty toward the ruler and filial piety toward parents—give rewards simply for the unplanned meetings of the floating life, even though you ignore your own self-being. If you act the same toward the Creator and Transformer of nature and mandate and of life and death, who also gives the eternal abode at the bodies' Return, how can you not receive recompense for sincere intention and loyal uprightness?

Nonetheless, if you do reach the utmost ultimate of longing [for the Real Lord], union will occur only sometimes. This is like someone drunk and without self, but now and again he is sober. A poet said,

> If he becomes drunk
> 	and unawake in his saying and doing,
> this is because wine attacks
> 	the form and spirit.
> The shining light of stars and moon
> 	never fades away
> but quickly it is gathered up
> 	by the greatest light.

When you reach this degree and site, this is like the time between the blossom's opening and the fruit's ripening. Between self and no-self, you have to be very cautious about severe rain and strong wind. It is important to preserve and protect the heart. Only then can you suddenly set aside the obstacles of self. Then you will see without witnessing, but this is not two. If you encounter an opportunity like this, at that moment you can witness the Real Lord untinged by the ten thousand conditions. This is intimate connection without break.

CHAPTER THREE
Recognition with Continuity

What we call "recognition with continuity" is conquering entirely both crooked selfishness and opinions of self, returning completely to the fountainhead of clear virtue, and recognizing the Real Lord with body while depending on no-self. Our selves' origin has a beginning and an end, and it comes and goes. The Real Lord at root does not arise or become exhausted, and He has no place. If by means of the human level, which has a beginning and end, you wish to delve into the Real Lord, who is without arising and exhaustion, this is impossible to achieve. It is like attempting to unite by force water and fire or a square and a circle. No matter how much you can delve into the principle and investigate the things through seeing, hearing, knowledge, and power, you cannot penetrate the Original Being. To do that, self-being must be completely molded. Only then will you gain the subtle clarity of the immediate manifestation of the Root Nature's movement and quietude. From this moment, everything will become clear, and you will know through the knowledge of the Lord, see through the sight of the Lord, and speak with the tongue of the Lord.[27] This is "one from one," and it is called *wa-ha-te-te* [*waḥdat*] (which means unmixed one).

When you reach this ultimate level, you will be neither the same nor separable. At this level, nothing at all is independent and everything is with the Lord, and this is "unity in union." This is because the inward and outward[28] of after-heaven combine in essence, and the origin of before-heaven discloses uniquely. The wind will be calm and the water placid, the sun high and the clouds scattered. Although you have form and spirit, yet their movement and quietude is one. You can witness the Real Lord only with a pure and clean no-self, and this is with mutual continuity and undifferentiated togetherness. A worthy said, "All the created newborn things mutually continue in the Original Being, and no trace of the self's selfishness and the newly born remains."[29] This is the meaning of this station.

The Utmost Sage said, "I am with the Real Lord and recognize the Real Lord with the body. If it were not through the Real Lord, it would be impossible to recognize the Real Lord."[30]

When you reach this station, only then does the fruit become perfect and the human being perfect. In this station all things will be settled in one and not change, and this is "no-bearing-witness."

At this moment you will know that the Non-Ultimate belongs to the before-heaven and it is the time of the first planting of the seed. Since this is from the above to the below, it is called "descending." This is the original seed, and it is the beginning of no-bearing-witness. The Human

Ultimate belongs to the after-heaven, and it is the time of cultivation. Since this is from the below to the above, it is called "ascending." This is the root cause for producing fruit.

A tree is hidden in a seed, and the fruits become manifest according to the tree. In the final analysis, the fruit is the seed and they are not two, but in fact, there has been an increase in profit. If the seeds do not [sprout and blossom with] fine color and good scent, this will betray the occasion for growth.

The reason why heaven and earth, the ten thousand affairs, and the ten thousand things are produced is specifically for the sake of bringing together this one great cause and condition. The human level is the only being who received this heavy responsibility. In fact, you should overcome the hardships of the ten thousand beings and experience the one hundred thousand dangers. Only then can you gain the perfect, complete, true fruit. This is the highest, above which there is no thing and no place, and there is no more witnessing.

Know that there are three levels of perfect fruit. The human ancestor is the fruit of the ten thousand things, the sages are the fruit of human beings, and the Utmost Sage, Mu-han-me-te, is the fruit of all the sages. Only when you reach this ultimate level will the root nature of the Real Lord become manifest.

It is sad that the people of the world are drowning in this ocean of pain and betraying this heavy Trust. Compared to the other kinds [of creatures], surely they show no difference.

GENERAL DISCUSSION

In addition to explaining the creative transformation, the "three ones" also deal with the gates of teaching nature and mandate, life and death, emptiness and nonbeing, and so on.

In order to be human, the most essential thing is to know correctly that among "unmixed one," "seeing one," and "knowing one," there are distinctions similar to the high and the low of human character traits. The distance among them is no less than that between heaven and earth. If you do not fully understand this, it is not a trifling matter.

Among the Real One, the Numerical One, and the Embodied One, there is the utmost, great distinction found among [1] Lord, [2] Chief Servant, and [3] sages and worthies. It is still necessary to observe it more.

The concealed fineness in reflecting upon this is that the root of the ten thousand differences is One Being. Outside this Powerful Being, there is no other being at all. If there were other beings, how could it be one? Lamentably, the people of the world are all caught up by the branch-tips of the ten thousand images and they are blind to the Real One's Being. There are some people who discuss it, but they have not yet been correctly directed, so they still end up unfocused and disoriented.

Only true people with clear eyes will see luminously into the Chief Taproot, and thus they will return to the Original Lord. However, the Original Lord and the Chief Taproot should be separated and clearly divided. Why? The Real One is unique, independent, and peerless; hence it is the Original Lord. The Numerical One is the Chief Taproot of the ten thousand things. Therefore it is designated as the "Great Father." Were there no Real One, how could there be a Numerical One? Although this is the Numerical One of the Non-Ultimate, it is not the Original Lord; in reality it is rooted in the Powerful Being of the Original Lord.

The Real One and Powerful Being are like the root substance of light and the shining of light. The root substance of light is such that when you go near it, you will be transformed. If you share in the shining of light, you will become capacious.

So, the One that has no sameness is called "Real One," and that which has a sameness that does not obstruct is called "Powerful Being." The

One that possesses all the principles is called "Numerical One." The Powerful Being is not differentiated from the Real One and the Numerical One. The Powerful Being is rooted in the Real One, and the Numerical One is manifest in the Powerful Being.

The Numerical One is like the clear brightness of the shining. The "shining" is similar to the majestic solemnity of imperial guards; although it is possible for attendants to go near, they are in awe and dread. The "clear brightness" is like the administrators on behalf of the king. They indeed constantly have the same place in dealing with him, and they are comfortable and relaxed. They increase their human level and have no deficiency or lack. This is the distinction between the Powerful Being and the Numerical One. If we talk about these as divisions, the root is one; if we speak of unity, they are not of the same class.

All the other subtleties and all the forms are at root the Non-Ultimate and the Great Ultimate. The long-flowing life-water does not change or alter at root, and it is translucent and pure. This is all because the Original Being is all-penetrating. As for the stagnant water of pond and pool, certainly it has both purity and muddiness, so it alters and transforms, and all this restricts and obstructs the newborn.

At origin the creative transformation clarifies the complete act of substance and function. Even more do nature and mandate manifest the root nature and the movement and quietude. Life and death discriminate the Original Being from the newborn. The Tao of teaching points to the correct path of returning to the Real. Emptiness and nonbeing are the illusory ocean without shore. People must depend upon the wise master who takes charge of the tiller. He looks up to observe the images of heaven, and looks down to see the compass. Only then will he gain a favorable tide and a smooth crossing. Otherwise, they will capsize and drown.

You should know that the creative transformation of the ten thousand things is like a beautiful heart designing a game. At root, this is simply to test human beings' looking and observing.[31] And you should know that the creative transformation is not the same as designing a game; but without designing the game, the creative transformation will not become manifest. Designing the game is not the same as looking and observing; but without looking and observing, what is the purpose of designing the game? The ability to look is not the same as the clear brightness; but without the clear brightness, how can there be looking? The clear brightness is not the same as the shining; but without the shining, how can there be the clear brightness? The shining is not the same as the sun; but without the sun, how will there be shining? In general, all the levels rely on this clarity; otherwise, nothing at all has the ability to act. It is said,

All the beings and the ten thousand spirituals
exist together in the universe,
but if there is no sun,
all quickly turn to delusion.
Alas! Without the sun,
they are already deluded.

Without the Lord, can anything have its own being? This is why the Classic says, "The Real Lord has created the form and spirit of you people; He has also created affairs and things for your own use."[32]

But the ten thousand completenesses are not all of the same class, and this allows people to choose. The sages, the wise, the ordinary, and the stupid—all have existence in this same activity. Although people's bodies, spirits, affairs, and things are prearranged by the Real Lord prior to their being, when these reach the Non-Ultimate, they start to interpenetrate and they issue disclosures. There is nothing that does not come out in the creative transformation, but all this depends on each person's self-desire in will and thought.

Someone said that painting is specifically for drawing beautiful faces and not for drawing ugly demeanor. But why should this be so? I say that whatever can be beautiful can certainly be ugly. If not so, it would not be complete.[33]

Someone also said that beauty and ugliness have already come out in the painting. Why do you still discuss the thing's beauty and ugliness? I say that the causes of good and evil all come out in the creative transformation of the Real Lord, and the choice of whether to go beyond, or not to reach, exists at root only in people's self-satisfaction. "Things have roots and branches," affairs have befores and afters; knowing the central and moderate, you will surely not be perplexed.[34]

You should know that all humans are rooted in the clear virtue.[35] Before they see the things that they desire, they all want to emulate the sages and worthies. Once they see what they like, only then do they know the real truth of choosing and leaving aside.

In general, after there are human talents, there will be an examination. After the examination, there will be reward and punishment. Reward and punishment come out according to mercy and severity. Mercy is applied for the high wisdom, but severity is inflicted for the low stupidity. This is the principle of nature. Why? Because those who are high have already been united in union and have gained their pleasure, but those who are low oppose and disobey the mandate, thus encountering its wrath. Therefore, pleasure comes from the origin; wrath is caused to be issued after, not that it comes into being later. Thus it is known of pleasure and wrath that each has its own beginning. At root they are not of one principle, but both pleasure and wrath have being from the beginning.

You must reflect carefully upon the concealed details, and you should not read them carelessly with a coarse heart.

Moreover, movement and quietude has two divisions—how is it possible for Lord and servant to be the same and undifferentiated? If you make a small mistake and error, you will fall forever into the path of delusion. This would indeed be lamentable. It is said in a poem,

> The ocean is pure and clean in its origin
> demanding the wind.
> The waves support
> the turtles and dragons.
> The waves of universal compassion subside
> and compassion alone arises.
> You should know that the fish and creatures of water
> will be preserved forever.

It is also said,

> The ocean manifests the rivers and lakes,
> but the ocean remains as it always was.
> The origin of the rivers and lakes
> is divided at root from the clear ocean.
> Stop doubting—
> this ocean is rivers and lakes,
> rivers are rivers and lakes,
> but the ocean is by itself the ocean.[36]

Even if water reflects bamboo's shadow, these two substances are not related. The wind plays with the flower's fragrance—they are together, but not the same. This is the meaning.

You should know that among the Real One, the Powerful Being, and the Numerical One, there is a subtlety in representing substance and function. Power is to Being as clarity is to light. The Utmost Sage, who is the Numerical One, is like an ancient mirror, and each of the sages and groups of worthies are attendants in waiting. The various heavens and worlds are the makeup stand. Although the Real Lord manifests His complete levels, entrusting something special to the Human Ultimate, yet high and low among them are not the same class.

As for the heretical teachings and wrong Taos, they should not be looked upon in the guise of one body, because they are deluded at the fountainhead and rebel against the root. They recognize nature as their lord. Even though they are human in form, they are not human in reality. Thus the poet says,

> Life and death are all caused
> by a unique and independent honor.

Other than the Utmost Great
who has any power?
They fall and become deluded in the path
only because of self-satisfaction,
and they suddenly forget
the Original One and the first covenant.
If you gain once more the oneness of
recognition with body,
then the principles will all be possessed
within this body.[37]

The real nature is the light of clarity, the true heart is the mirror, the bodily governing is the makeup stand, and the ten thousand things are the officials in waiting. These are the patterns and models of the Numerical One, but they have no share of the beautiful woman. Therefore it is said, "The beautiful woman is unique and distinctive. But whose face does she have? She has a desire to manifest her beautiful shape and is waiting to put on her colors. When the makeup stand is provided with the artful effects for a likable game, the light of clarity starts to appear on the precious mirror."

There are some who dream drunkenly and think foolishly that the beautiful woman is the mirror's light. Oh, how could they say such a thing—that the beautiful woman and the mirror's light come from the same crucible in the furnace of smelting! That they will enter together into the mold and receive an equal polishing! Who is the creator of the furnace and who perfects the mirror?

Suppose someone among men proclaims himself to be of equal honor with the son of heaven, without regard to propriety. Can this crime be forgiven? So much more is the case if someone desires to be one body with the Real Lord, who has created and transformed heaven, earth, humans, and spirits.

Moreover, according to the people, "You are you, I am I." The more closely they follow their hearts, the more opinions are diverse. Is this only for the human species? Even the tiny flying and swimming things, the animals, and the plants have a share. But the lord of emptiness and nonbeing says, "You are I, I am you." Thus they say, "Green bamboo and yellow flowers, all have this nature. Every family, every place, is the same Buddha." If this indeed is the case, life and death, stopping and penetration, safety and danger, gain and loss—certainly all depend on oneself. If this is not so, what possibly could be the foundation? If these people were not ultimately stupid and deluded, what would give birth to such foolishness?

Thus the Classic says, "The Real Lord manifested His great power when He created heaven and the earth. Heaven and the earth have no power. He wanted to manifest Himself, and He created the Human Ultimate."[38]

The Human Ultimate does not belong to self. Thus it is said, "Those who recognize themselves can then recognize the Real Lord of themselves."[39] By depending on this body, it will be possible to witness Him.

You must know that without darkness you cannot awaken to the light of clarity. Without life and death, how will you know the Real Being? If you can understand life and death thoroughly, then life also is not life, because there is death; death also is not death, because there is coming back to life.[40] When you transcend these two gates, there will no longer be life or death.

Everything controlled by life and death is a sentient being. Depending on their nature and mandate, all have been established and stand. What does not fall into life and death is the Real One, the Beginningless Beginning, the Original Being.

The before-heaven is the mandate, the after-heaven is nature. The mandate is not nature, but it is inseparable from nature. The mandate is the seed that descends, and nature is the fruit that ascends. Although they share one body, they are different in reality.

When you reach this point, only then will you know for certain that the without-beginning is called "Lord," and the with-beginning is called "human." Therefore, only the forms and spirits that have already received the mandate will be able to manifest and disclose the Real Lord, who has the power to create life and death. This is the utmost, great distinction [between Lord and human].

If you desire to be loyal and upright without two, to see nature, to clarify the heart, and to be united in union with the Original Being—all of which is necessary for the Garden of the True Teaching—then you will be able to complete the true fruit. If you look still more at the precious mirror of the Real Person, you will be able to issue forth and disclose the real shining that naturally and thoroughly illumines the complete levels.

If the mirror suddenly encounters dense fog, naturally it will be darkened. If flowers and fruits encounter a violent wind, they will wither and fall. Would this not be to disobey and betray the Original Lord who perfected the creation? For this reason the Classic says, "The Real Lord did not create humans and spirits for themselves. Rather, the creation of the humans and spirits is for the sake of recognizing the Lord at the origin."[41] It is also said in the sermon of the Utmost Sage, "Do you not see this kind of people? In the end they make their own nature into their own lord."[42]

In the True Teaching are the clear mandate of the Real Lord and the real transmission of the Utmost Sage. These are the guides to the fountainhead of virtue, and both are the great roots of making the heart true and cultivating the body. You cannot lack either of them.

Heretics have the illusion and foolishness of various evils. They are tainted by the evil custom of deluded people and the stupidity and madness of self-nature. All of these are the deep taproot of darkening the heart and forgetting the root. If you have any of them, you will be unlucky.

You should know that at root, square and compass are for making rectangles and circles in a certain fashion. What does not follow this fashion is because of the misuse of square and compass. The misuse of square and compass is due to the artisan's stupidity, so the artisan's stupidity damages the varieties of wood. Once they are affected, they will become useless things. How lamentable![43]

As for worldly endeavor, name, and wealth; and worldly nobility, wives, children, and social relationships, in the True Teaching there are methods for true people to guard against them and resist them. When people encounter heretics, they can use these as weapons with which to assault and attack stupidity and delusion. Why is this so? When true people gain them, they honor and venerate the Great Root, and, basing themselves on worldly conditions, they escape and depart from the ocean of suffering. Their body returns toward the everlasting abode, until finally they become a buoyant ship for crossing back. Thereby they ascend to the Heavenly Gate.

When stupid and deluded people gain these things, they embody them fully, and this strikes a deep taproot in them. They take charge of themselves and foolishly think about transcending and escaping life and death, and they wander about according to their own intentions. They take so much delight in these that they forget about returning, and they turn them into sharp weapons for rebelliousness and deviation. They are mixed up and not one, and loyalty and filial piety are both injured. Thereby they go down degraded to the Earth Prohibited.

If there were no teaching the Tao by the Pure and Real and if there were no true people making clear indications, who could cross the ocean of illusion and search for the Real? Who could turn his body toward the further shore? The endeavor of following the mandate and returning to the Real will hang down eternally.

If you encounter the stupidity and madness of self-nature, it will be difficult to avoid the dangers and obstacles of wave and wind. Like the drunken and dreaming, you will come and go all in delusion, and your transgressions will be immeasurable. You must turn your intention and return your heart. You must leave the lake of dragons and the den of tigers. You must quickly arrange the baggage for what comes after the body. You must keep and protect virtuous karma[44] in the present. Hopefully, you will not lose your humanity. The Classic says, "Creation of this life and death is at root for the sake of experiencing who are the loyal and faithful among you."[45]

When you reflect upon the meaning of this Classic, you must immediately turn your head, which is resting in a sleepy state. Originally, nature and mandate are all the untainted mercy of the Real Lord's special solicitude. He also gives covering and carrying to heaven and earth, nourishment to the ten thousand things, and the gateway to life and death. What the teaching of the Pure and Real indicates, such as polishing, is all to complete that great affair. It is necessary to reflect carefully upon the concealed details, so that it may be possible for you to make some provision for yourself. This is not like the righteousness of a ruler and the loyalty of the minister, or the father's compassion and the child's filial piety. The need for those reciprocal relationships cannot be compared to this.

You ought to think where you have come from and where you will be returning in the end. Sometimes this will be because of receiving the mandate of life and death, and sometimes you can do things according to your own intention. The only fear is that the great limit [death] is at hand. Profit and name will fade like a dream, mercy and sympathy will be scattered around like a drama's end. Only then will you know that the ten thousand affairs are all empty. There exists only the karma of one body. When the stupid and deluded reach this place, they sorrow and regret. Even if they weep blood, what profit will that have?

How is it possible to break beforehand [the dream of kingship and realize that one lives only with] yellow millet?[46] How can one wake up at present to the fact that the things of dust are void and meaningless? In order to escape from worldly conditions, you need to have one heart that is pure and clean so as to reflect upon the Real Being properly. Most of all, you should avoid emptiness and nonbeing.

This so-called "emptiness" is to regard heaven and earth, mountains and rivers, and everything that has being as "flowers in the sky" before gazing eyes; they emerge and disappear naturally, with no declaration of lordship.

It is said in the "Learning of the Principle" [i.e., Neo-Confucianism], "The Great Void cannot but have vital-energy, vital-energy cannot but be collected to become the ten thousand things, the ten thousand things cannot but scatter to become vital-energy, and vital-energy cannot but be transformed to become the Great Void."[47] It is also said, "Ice melts and bubbles disperse, and yet they are originally water." It is also said, "The calm waves, the placid water—all of them form one ocean." All of these are similar to "flowers in the sky."

The ground of this is that [the Buddha] is at root the king of Emptiness, who manifested his body according to his own intention and then explained the dharma. Why did he rely on the causes and conditions, which are father and mother? This does not tally with the pattern and fashion of "flowers in the sky." If he comes and goes by the gateway of production [the womb], how can he be the Lord-Ruler of the ten thousand spirituals? If his life and death are the same as theirs, why should he say, "I alone am honored"?[48] Defiling himself and then cleansing himself is no different from cutting one's flesh for injured parents and then curing oneself.[49] If you make images and then sweep them away, how is this different from destroying a strong wall and then building it up again? The bonds and relationships are so different from the usual that lords and parents must pay respect [to ministers and children].[50]

He abandoned the body and he avoided killing, and his heart inclined toward preserving and nourishing all the animals. The yang was alone, the yin was alone, and he intended and desired to abolish the human species. Since he rebelled against the creative transformation, he reversed the order of honor and meanness. For fifty years, he lived alone all over the world with the birds and the beasts. If a wise man reflects on all the details, he will come to know this Tao [of theirs].

Those [Taoists] who are called "the men of nonbeing" take voidness and nonbeing as the Tao. This is like scattering chaff and blinding the eyes, while wanting the six directions to change their sites.[51] Why? Because everyone under heaven regards the Real Being as noble, and voidness and nonbeing as lowly. You must know that the Original Being without beginning is the most honored and real, the most spiritual and clear. But they take as its match the vaguest voidness and nonbeing, which is the most obscure and obstinate and the most lowly and mean. How can this be called "true awareness"? Moreover, the sages and spirits of the world cannot regard nonbeing as being. How then can a man of voidness and nonbeing regard voidness and nonbeing as being?

People like Buddha and Lao Tzu are the ancestors of emptiness and nonbeing. Before they were born, at root there were no Buddha and Lao Tzu. Afterward, they surely depended on their parents for their birth, for nothing comes into being from emptiness and nonbeing. Heaven, earth, and the ten thousand things are all like this—they dwell in undifferentiated nonbeing before becoming things. There must be the one—the most honored Original Being, the Real Lord — who transforms and produces them.

They take no-acting, no-intending, and no-arguing as the teaching. But when you look at their writings and established teachings—are these not acting? To desire people to follow them—is this not intending? To argue about the named principles under heaven—is this not arguing? Their own acts contradict each other, yet they desire to be the masters of the ten thousand generations. This is wrong.

Humans are more spiritual than the ten thousand things because of heart, intention, and desire to act. They have the power to pursue propriety and righteousness and to make skillful arguments for right and wrong. Those who gain the truth will return to the Real, but those who lose the truth will fall down. How is it possible that the followers of the heretical principles do not know propriety and righteousness and do not apprehend right and wrong? They are neither blamed for losing these, nor praised for gaining them, and their ability is non-wisdom.

Still, there are things that are wholly without heart and intention, without desire, and without act—such as metal, stone, grass, and trees. This means that if a sharp sword injures someone, the injured person does not blunt the blade. If a falling stone strikes someone, the struck person does not attack its hardness. If a thorn pricks someone, the pricked person does not break the thorn. These things have no intention for good and evil, so people's joy and anger are not aimed at these bodies, which have no knowledge and awareness.

By reflecting on this, we see that the teaching of these Taos is that they want to turn the noblest of the spiritual under heaven into the meanest of the ignorant. The human species turns around and becomes a different species. Even worse, they transform human beings into trees and stones, and then call them "utmost persons." Is this enough to witness that all real beings are based originally on what is called "emptiness" and "nonbeing"? Thus it is said,

> Those who do not understand right and wrong
>   are indeed a different kind.
> Only by establishing the division between true and false
>   will you begin to be human.
> The honored ones transcend the ten thousand levels
>   because of the ability of wisdom.
> Insulting the Tao in ignorance
>   is like imitating the darkness of things.

This bears witness to that. Ah! Hiding and concealing the Real Lord of humans and spirits, and sweeping away the scale and measure of the creative transformation! If something like this could be the Tao, there could be a country without a ruler and a household without a head.

Moreover, if no one makes the houses, rooms, porches, and all the tiny vessels and things, it will certainly be impossible for these to come to be by themselves. The greatness of heaven and earth and the manyness of the ten thousand things—how could they come to be by themselves? When one looks at this, this is truly [like the proverb says]: "A foolish person talking about his dream."

Someone said: If the Real Lord is the most impartial and the most compassionate, this indicates that even the deluded will return to the truth. Furthermore, He transforms and produces all these people who perplex and confuse the people of the world. Why?

I say: In the floating life, which is a moment's twinkling of the eye, people desire to catch the real bliss of the immeasurable. Were there not the wind and waves of name and profit and the dangerous passes of the heretics, how could the great honor of the True Teaching be constructed and the great procedure of returning to the Real be established? With these dangers, people will be instructed and opened up to the hidden ambush of wicked evil, but without the dangers, the real sincerity of loyalty and faithfulness will not become manifest. Good and evil are clearly divided on this basis, and reward and punishment make their hearts and wills obedient. If this is not the utmost impartiality and the utmost compassion, then what is it?

The True Teaching is like the clinic of a famous physician. Everyone who enters will be made comfortable and healthy. But the wrong path is like a house of plague. If a person goes near, it will be difficult to escape poisonous infection. How can one not be careful? You must know where these two beginnings will lead you. Perhaps some people who have fallen mistakenly into the crooked path will wake up to the foolishness of their unfocused self-estimation when they listen to this discussion

This collection, which at root pertains to the Pure and Real, is a means to point in the right direction, but it resembles a dust mote in the sky and a drop in the ocean. If you gain the true awareness, you will be fit for the basis of leading to guidance. If you are fixed on heretical teachings, you will have no place for this teaching. You will become like people who shout in hunger in the midst of rice and who cry out in thirst while standing in water. If that is the case, I am afraid that these few pages will not be able to relieve you. Let a poem bear witness:

Recognizing the Lord is originally
    relying on the recognition of oneself.
Even if you witness yourself,
    you must further reflect and delve.
The beginning and end of heaven and earth
    will enter your weighing and measuring.
Humans' and spirits' production and extinction
    will be within your grasp.
You will fully penetrate the finest dust
    and not be small and thin.
You will comprehensively embrace the universe
    and not be huge and vast.
You will go greatly beyond the two ultimates
    and become unique and independent.
You will not fall to emptiness and nonbeing
    which are the same as having a form.

Another poem says,

Without beginning, without match,
He alone is honored.
The power overshadows heaven and earth,
buddhas, immortals, and gods.
He perfects things to which no artisan
can make anything similar.
The Original Lord of transformation and production
is the root of the different productions.
If you awaken to the subtle origin
of going beyond the universe,
Then you will know that sounds and colors
are nothing but varieties of forms.
The ocean's drop and the sky's dust mote
are like instructions urging.
Boasting of small wisdom,
they act with vast reality.

5

Liu Chih's Translation of *Lawā'iḥ*

ʿAbd al-Raḥmān Jāmī (817–898/1414–1492) is one of the most famous scholars of the later period in the eastern lands of Islam. He is the author of over fifty works in a variety of fields, such as Arabic grammar, Persian grammar, the Prophet's life, Sufi theory and practice, music, and the literary device known as the "riddle" (*muʿammā*). His account of the great Sufis of the past, *Nafaḥāt al-uns* ("The outbreathings of intimacy"), has been an enormously influential hagiography wherever Persian has been known, as well as an important source of information for scholars. He has been considered the last of the great Persian poets. He showed his poetical skills not only in the quatrains that he interspersed throughout many of his prose works, such as *Lawā'iḥ* ("Gleams") but also in seven *mathnawī*s and a large *dīwān*, consisting mainly of ghazals. He was a member of the Naqshbandī Order, a disciple first of Saʿd al-Dīn Kāshgharī (d. 860/1456) and then of perhaps the most politically influential of all the Naqshbandī shaykhs, ʿUbayd Allāh Aḥrār (d. 895/1490).

The important role that the Naqshbandī Order played in Chinese Islam has been described by Joseph Fletcher, Françoise Aubin, and others. Given this role, it is tempting to suggest that Jāmī's Naqshbandī connection was the primary factor that led the Chinese Muslims to translate two of his works, thus giving him and his order a half-share of the four Sufi works translated before the nineteenth century (the other two being by Kubrawī shaykhs). However, this would be to ignore the fact that engagement with Sufi intellectual teachings—as opposed to practical teachings—had little to do with affiliation with specific Sufi orders. Relatively few Sufis, no matter what their affiliation, concerned themselves with the theoretical elaboration of metaphysical, theological, cosmological, and psychological issues, because relatively few people were intellectually inclined. This is a human reality that remains true today, whatever sort of "intellectual" issues we may be discussing. However this may be, from about the eighth/fourteenth century, those Muslims who did concern themselves with theoretical issues could not have avoided exposure to the teachings of Ibn al-ʿArabī and his followers,[1] and from the ninth/fifteenth century, Jāmī was probably the most widely read of the authors representing this school of thought in the sphere of Persian cultural influence, which extended from Turkey to China and Indonesia.

Jāmī's immersion in the school of Ibn al-ʿArabī can be judged by the contents of his theoretical works. His first book in this field was *Naqd al-nuṣūṣ fī sharḥ naqsh al-fuṣūṣ* ("Selected texts to explain the 'Imprint of the *Fuṣūṣ*'"), which he completed at the age of forty-six in the year 863/1459. This 250-page work of mixed Arabic and Persian prose is a commentary on Ibn al-ʿArabī's 10-page précis of his own most famous and widely read work, *Fuṣūṣ al-ḥikam*.[2] In a long introduction and in detailed explanations of the words and sentences of the treatise, Jāmī quotes and sometimes translates into Persian many passages from major authors in this school of thought, especially Ṣadr al-Dīn Qūnawī, Qūnawī's disciples Mu'ayyid al-Dīn Jandī and Saʿīd al-Dīn Farghānī, Jandī's student ʿAbd al-Razzāq Kāshānī, and Kāshānī's student Dāwūd al-Qayṣarī. Jandī, Kāshānī, and Qayṣarī are the authors of the most influential of the more than one hundred commentaries on the *Fuṣūṣ*. Jāmī's *Naqd al-nuṣūṣ* is as much a scholar's collection of favorite passages as a commentary. Although his skill at translating technical Arabic discussions into fluent Persian is already obvious in this work, for the most part he prefers to keep the original Arabic. It is a difficult book and could only have been studied by advanced students, but it was extremely popular, as shown by the large number of copies found in manuscript libraries throughout the Islamic world.

Jāmī completed his last book, an Arabic commentary on the *Fuṣūṣ al-ḥikam*, in 896/1491, a year and a half before his death. It covers some of the same ground as *Naqd al-nuṣūṣ*, but is much more wide ranging, given the variety of topics covered in the *Fuṣūṣ* itself. The work shows Jāmī at the height of his intellectual powers. Among all the commentaries on this seminal work, it is probably Jāmī's that keeps the best balance between careful attention to the nuances of the text and detailed exposition of the theoretical background. It was widely known in the Arabic speaking countries, and was published in Egypt along with the commentary of al-Nābulusī one hundred years ago.

Between *Naqd al-nuṣūṣ* and the commentary on the *Fuṣūṣ* itself, Jāmī wrote five medium-length Persian works explicating the teachings of Ibn al-ʿArabī's school of thought. These include (in order of completion): (1) *Sharḥ-i rubāʿiyyāt* ("Explanation of the quatrains"), a collection of his own quatrains with commentary. Several passages are translated from Arabic texts found in *Naqd al-nuṣūṣ*, and Jāmī's prose style has not yet reached its maturity. (2) *Sharḥ-i baʿḍī az abyāt-i qaṣīda-yi tāʾiyya-yi fāriḍiyya*

("An explanation of a few verses of Ibn al-Fāriḍ's *qaṣīda* rhyming in *tā'*"), an explanation of 75 of the 750 verses of the famous *Poem of the Way* by the Egyptian saint Ibn al-Fāriḍ (d. 632/1235). (3) *Lawā'iḥ*, completed about 870/1465. (4) *Lawāmi'* ("The flashes," dated 883/1478), a commentary on Ibn al-Fāriḍ's forty-verse wine poem. (5) *Ashi''at al-lama'āt* ("The gleams of the flashes," dated 886/1481), the already-mentioned commentary on 'Irāqī's *Lama'āt*, the first of Jāmī's works to be translated into Chinese. Also in 886/1481, Jāmī completed *al-Durrat al-fākhira fī taḥqīq madhhab al-ṣūfiyya wa'l-mutakallimīn wa'l-ḥukamā'*, "The precious pearl: Verifying the positions of the Sufis, the Kalam authorities, and the philosophers." This is an Arabic work that compares the views of the three intellectual schools on eleven specific theological issues, explaining why, in each case, the views of theoretical Sufism (i.e., the school of Ibn al-'Arabī) are to be preferred.[3]

Of all Jāmī's Persian works on Ibn al-'Arabī's school of thought, only *Lawā'iḥ* is not a commentary on a specific work. In terms of attractive style and balance of poetry and prose, it is the most successful, and indeed it was the most widely read. It is a fine summary of what Jāmī considered Ibn al-'Arabī's key teachings, and the topics that it covers are representative of the themes that he discusses in all of his theoretical writings and much of his poetry as well.[4] Nonetheless, Jāmī wrote *Lawā'iḥ* with full attention toward the works of his predecessors. He is not simply being humble when he says in the introduction that the texts he is presenting were unveiled to the secret hearts of "the lords of gnosis and the masters of tasting," meaning the great Sufis of earlier times. He continues by saying, "the author has no share save the post of translator, and no portion but the trade of speaker." In other words *Lawā'iḥ*, somewhat like *Naqd al-nuṣūṣ*, brings together texts written by earlier authors, though Jāmī seems to have been much freer in adapting these than in *Naqd al-nuṣūṣ*. The work demonstrates self-confidence and mastery of the subject matter. He acts as a "speaker" for this school of thought by thoroughly rewriting the original passages, if not by composing his own essays on well-known issues. Moreover, his quatrains, which make up a good proportion of the text, are especially well suited to bringing out the point of the technical discussions in non-technical language.

The general theme of the *Lawā'iḥ* can be summarized with one expression, though Jāmī does not employ it in this specific work: *waḥdat al-wujūd* or "the Oneness of Existence." In fact, Jāmī played a major role in popularizing this term. Whereas it was rarely used before him by followers of Ibn al-'Arabī, Jāmī frequently mentions it in his writings. But even if Oneness of Existence is the book's topic, this does not really take us far in understanding what the book is all about. Contrary to popular (and much scholarly) opinion, *waḥdat al-wujūd* is not a clearly defined doctrine. It is rather a term that was employed as a kind of shorthand to refer to the position of Ibn al-ʿArabī, and it was understood in many different ways by both its supporters and its detractors.[5] Thus, for example, Jāmī's understanding of what the expression implies should in no way be confused with the understanding of Shaykh Aḥmad Sirhindī (d. 1034/1604), who famously criticized it and offered *waḥdat al-shuhūd* ("the oneness of witnessing") as a corrective.[6]

Although Jāmī covers many topics in the work, one can discern two main issues: *tawḥīd* as practice and *tawḥīd* as theory. The practical issue is the devotional imperative of turning one's full attention toward the One. The theoretical issue is discerning between the One and the many, or God and the world. In practical terms, Jāmī is telling his readers that it is necessary to see things correctly in order to be able to remember God as he should be remembered. In theoretical terms, he is differentiating between existence (*wujūd*) per se, or the reality of God, and the existence that is ascribed to the cosmos.

Most of the book is dedicated to explaining how cosmic existence arises from the one and undifferentiated Real Being. In order for the existent things to appear as the universe, there must be some prefiguration of the things within the Real, and there must be a movement whereby the things are transferred from their state of prefiguration to their state of external existence. Hence Jāmī is trying to explain how the Real gives rise to that which is less than fully real (i.e., the cosmos and everything within it).

Jāmī spends most of the first twelve Gleams addressing the practical imperatives of right understanding. He reminds seekers on the path of the importance of one-pointed concentration through "remembrance" or "invocation" of God's name (*dhikr*). Only in this section, in two instances, is there any sign of specifically Naqshbandī teachings. The first instance is one mention of the word *yādkard*, a relatively unusual Persian expression meaning "doing remembrance"; this is the first of the eight or eleven specifically Naqshbandī practices set down by the early shaykhs.[7] Second is the mention of the word *nisbat* ("relation") in five different Gleams (6, 7, 8, 11, 12) in a technical Naqshbandī meaning. However, Jāmī does not highlight the Naqshbandī significance of the two terms, and those not familiar with Naqshbandī practices could easily miss their provenance, as did earlier translators of the text into English and French (and certainly Liu Chih shows no sign of recognizing the specifically Naqshbandī significance).

The Oneness of Existence

From Gleam 13 to the end, Jāmī expounds his basic understanding of the Oneness of Existence. As he says in the conclusion, his purpose in writing the book was calling "attention to the essential encompassment [of all of reality] by the Presence of the Real . . . and the pervasion of all levels of existence by His light." A brief review of some of the technical terminology and philosophical issues that he is investigating may help readers grasp the points of his arguments.

The central concept of course is being or existence. Here Jāmī uses two words interchangeably, Arabic *wujūd* (translated throughout as "existence") and Persian *hastī* (translated as "being"). Like most authors, he treats these two words as synonyms. As he explains in Gleam 14, the term *wujūd* (or *hastī*) has two basic meanings in the intellectual tradition. In the first meaning, the word refers to the fact that something is there, in which case it designates a concept or a mental assertion. In a second sense, it refers to the ultimate reality that undergirds all of reality, what the Peripatetic philosophers call the "Necessary in Existence." It is in the latter sense that the term is meant in this school of thought when it is said that "God is Existence" or "God is Being."

The remaining theoretical sections discuss various ways in which the relationship between the true Being of the Real and the existence of the world and things can be conceptualized. The basic point throughout is that the only true and absolute *wujūd* is God, and whenever *wujūd* is ascribed to something else, the ascription is problematic. It is true from one point of view, but false from another point of view. Thus created things may be said to exist, but when we compare their *wujūd* with God's *wujūd*, we have to recognize that they do not exist in and for themselves.

This whole theoretical discussion of *waḥdat al-wujūd* is an exercise in *tawḥīd*. In other words, discussion of the Oneness of Existence asserts the Shahadah—"There is no god but God"—employing philosophical rather than specifically religious language. If, on the one hand, the Shahadah means that only God is true reality, on the other hand it means that everything other than God is not true reality, even though, in a certain sense, the "others" (*aghyār*) may be said to exist. Hence the others are real in one respect and unreal in another. Ibn al-ʿArabī sums up this discussion with the expression "He/not He" (*huwa lā huwa*), which is to say that all things are identical with God inasmuch as they exist, but different from God inasmuch as they are specific things.[8]

It is not without significance that Jāmī devotes the final Gleam to an explicit discussion of creaturely ambiguity, given that the whole issue of *waḥdat al-wujūd* revolves around it. He points out that Ibn al-ʿArabī takes two different positions concerning human acts—that they are God's acts, and that they are the creatures' acts.[9] If they were not God's acts, then creation would be independent of its Creator. If they were not the creatures' acts, then the prophetic injunctions to do good works would be meaningless. Jāmī explains the apparent contradiction between divine and human activity in terms of two levels of God's "self-disclosure" (*tajallī*).

The divine self-disclosure or self-showing is a constant theme in the text. The term is central to the teachings of Ibn al-ʿArabī's school of thought.[10] It derives from the Koranic account of how Moses asked to see God. When God disclosed himself to a mountain, the mountain shattered to dust, and Moses swooned. So also, coming to an understanding of God's cosmic self-disclosure allows people to see that the mountain of apparent reality has been shattered in the face of the divine Reality. The world itself is nothing but the locus in which God discloses his reality and attributes, and seeing things as they are allows observers to grasp that the independent existence of things is an illusion.

The world is God's self-disclosure because all things derive their existence and characteristics from God's conscious act to show himself, or from Being's effusion of reality. In terms of the famous hadith that is cited toward the beginning of most Sufi theoretical texts from about the seventh/thirteenth century onward, God was a "Hidden Treasure" and desired to be known, so he created the universe so that he might come to be known. The universe and everything within it are God's disclosures of what is hidden in the treasure-chest of his own reality. This reality is nothing but absolute, unconditioned, and undifferentiated Being, and it contains in itself the root of everything that can possibly come to be.

In short, Jāmī addresses three basic theoretical issues. One is Being per se, the second is Being's self-disclosure, and the third is the nature of the things that appear through self-disclosure. Being is the utterly undifferentiated original reality that brings forth all secondary reality, self-disclosure is the bringing forth, and the things are what has been brought forth. Like much of the theoretical writing of Ibn al-ʿArabī's school, *Lawāʾiḥ* traces self-disclosure from the point where it is absolutely hidden to the point where it appears to the senses and human experience. The text speaks of the movement from the absolute oneness of God to the infinite multiplicity of the universe, a movement that has stages and can be conceptualized.

Any review of the primary literature will show that there was no set scheme that had to be followed in delineating these stages of the emergence of the universe from undifferentiation. The process of investigating and explicating the nature of things was looked upon as an exercise in self-realization and verification (*taḥaqquq, taḥqīq*). Disciples often contradicted the formulations of their masters, not because of the one-upmanship that characterizes much of modern philosophy, but because any number of paths can be followed to express the invisible domains. Ibn al-ʿArabī's writings are full of theoretical formulations that differ or disagree with other formulations found elsewhere in his works. For him, the contradictions gush up from the quest of the sage to explain the truth and legitimacy of every standpoint. The verifying sage, who alone is the "perfect human being" (*insān kāmil*), must stand at the "standpoint of no standpoint," or the "station of no station" (*maqām lā maqām*). Only he sees that the Real Being is the dimensionless point in which all contradictions coalesce and all opposites coincide (*jam' al-aḍdād*).

Jāmī provides a relatively detailed explanation of the levels of self-disclosure in Gleam 26. He describes six levels, moving from the domain of absolute undifferentiation to the stage of full differentiation that is the world. This scheme is one version of the well-known doctrine of the Five Divine Presences. Strictly speaking, the first of the six levels, that of "Nonentification" (*lā ta'ayyun*), lies outside the scheme. Nonentification is the Essence understood as an absolute unity in which no "entity" (*'ayn*) or thing can be differentiated from any other.[11]

Several of the Gleams explicate various points of view on the question of the relation between God and the created things. God discloses himself, and the things come to be, distinct and different from God. Yet, the things derive their being and reality, their qualities and characteristics from God. Looking carefully, we see that there is nothing that cannot be traced back to the One Source. So, how exactly is the world to be differentiated from God? There are always distinctions to be drawn in terms of attributes, but, from the point of view of the omnipresence of existence, creation cannot be distinguished from God's presence. The things, again, are He/not He.

If we conceive of God in terms of his self-consciousness, we can speak of God's knowledge of himself. It is here that Ibn al-'Arabī's famous discussion of the "fixed entities" (*a'yān thābita*) enters the picture. In knowing itself, the Real Existence knows everything, which is to say that God knows every concomitant of himself. In other words, he knows all the "things" (*ashyā'*) that exist in any mode whatsoever for all eternity. As objects of the divine knowledge, the entities are called "fixed entities" (and sometimes "fixed things") because they are known to God and fixed in his knowledge forever.

In themselves, without regard to the Real Being that supports and sustains them, the things or entities are "nonexistent" (*ma'dūm*), because they have no existence of their own. When God "creates" a thing, he bestows existence upon it. "Our only word to a thing, when We desire it, is to say to it 'Be!', so it comes to be" (Koran 16:40). At the point of creation, the fixed entity comes into being, all the while remaining fixed in God's knowledge. It now has an existence that appears to belong to it, so we can speak of this rock, this tree, this person, this idea, this book. We now have "existent entities" (*a'yān mawjūda*). However, the "existence" of the entities does not belong to them. As Ibn al-'Arabī says in a well-known passage from the *Fuṣūṣ al-ḥikam*, "The entities, which have nonexistence and are fixed in Him, have never smelt a whiff of existence. So they remain in their state, despite the number of forms in the existent things"[12] (compare Gleam 27). The mystery then remains: What exactly are the things that we observe in the universe and in ourselves? What are we? How are we related to God? There are no straightforward answers. The questions have to be investigated and "verified" by each individual, which brings us back to the exhortations of the first twelve Gleams.

The nonexistent, fixed entities are called by several other names, such as "realities" and "quiddities." Jāmī often refers to them by the word "task" (*sha'n*), a term that Ibn al-ʿArabī derived from the Koranic verse, "Each day He is upon some task" (55:29). These "tasks" of God are the things or realities or entities considered as specific activities of the "Reality of Realities"—God inasmuch as he embraces all realities and entities without exception (Gleam 25). In the broadest sense "tasks" designate everything in God that gives rise to the multiple things of the universe. In Ibn al-ʿArabī's discussions, they are usually associated with the idea of the renewal of creation at each instant (Gleam 26), because of the Koranic verse's mention of "each day." Ibn al-ʿArabī maintains that the "day" of the Divine He-ness (or Essence) is the present instant, which is suffused by the He-ness fully and constantly for all eternity. Hence, at each instant, God is busy with the tasks that are the entities or the creatures, and at each instant the tasks change, so the creatures change.[13] After Ibn al-ʿArabī, however, the association of the tasks with creation's renewal is pushed into the background and the term comes to be employed, as in *Lawā'iḥ*, as another synonym for the fixed entities or the divine attributes and relations.

Although God in himself is unknown to us, we know that he knows all things and that, on the basis of this knowledge, he creates the universe. Hence we can conceptualize his knowledge of himself, that is, the manner in which he looks upon himself and knows all things as requisites of his own infinite and absolute Being. When we look at God as knowing himself, we can call him the "First Entification" (Gleams 17, 24). At this level of reality, all the entities become "entified"—which is to say that they assume form as entities. Although the term "entification" (*taʿayyun*) is seldom used by Ibn al-ʿArabī, it becomes an important technical term with Qūnawī and his followers. Other translations that have been proposed for it, such as "epiphany," "characteristic," and "phenomenon" (all Whinfield), "individuation" (Richard), and "determination" (Izutsu), lose sight of the fact that the word is derived from the term *ʿayn* or "entity." Its basic meaning is to become an entity or to have the situation of being an entity, and an "entity" is simply a thing (what the philosophers call a "quiddity" or "whatness," *māhiyya*). Thus the "fixed entities" come to be discernible at the level known as the "First Entification." In the plural, the term "entification" designates all the situations in which things can be discerned as entities, and hence everything other than the Essence.

The First Entification is also named the "First Self-Disclosure" (Gleams 16, 36), because here we conceive of God as disclosing himself to himself in himself, the first step in a process that eventually leads to the appearance of the universe. Only at the second level of self-disclosure can there be discussion of the things entering into creation.

In Gleam 17, Jāmī explains that the First Entification embraces all the divine names and attributes, which are called the "divine realities." It also embraces the fixed entities of all things, which are the "engendered realities." The term "engendered" (*kawnī*) means that they pertain to the domain of "generation and corruption," which is the whole domain that God addresses when he says to the things "Be!" (*kun*), and they come to be. In contrast, the "divine realities"—such as knowledge, power, mercy, and compasson—are eternal and never "come to be" in themselves. Rather, they are the designations for Being's perfections, and as such they determine the qualities and characteristics that come to be within the engendered realities. Pure and unsullied knowledge, power, mercy, and compassion remain the exclusive attributes of the Real Being as such.

In clarifying the nature of created reality, Jāmī has frequent recourse to the divine names Manifest (*ẓāhir*) and Nonmanifest (*bāṭin*). More specifically, he likes to talk of the "Manifest of Existence" as contrasted with the "Nonmanifest of Existence," a pairing that goes back to the writings of Saʿīd al-Dīn Farghānī, especially the introductions to both the Persian and Arabic versions of his commentary on Ibn al-Fāriḍ's *Poem of the Way*. The Manifest of Existence is the cosmos, and the Nonmanifest of Existence is God; the former is the engendered realities, the latter the divine realities. On closer analysis, however, Existence is one, so both the Manifest and the Nonmanifest are the same Existence. The one Being alone manifests itself in the universe, but it can be seen and understood only as clothed and garmented in the traces of the names and attributes. The fixed entities come to appear as existent entities, but in fact, the only thing that appears and becomes manifest is the Apparent, the Manifest, and that is the One Entity of Being.

Liu Chih's Appropriation of *Lawā'iḥ*

There is little in Liu Chih's *Displaying the Concealment of the Real Realm* that would overtly betray its Islamic origin. Like Wang Tai-yü, Liu Chih avoids mentioning Arabic or Persian words, the only exceptions being *Allāh* and *ādam* (Adam), once each. *Displaying the Concealment* appears as a Neo-Confucian treatise that stresses the transcendence and uniqueness of the Principle on the one hand, and the manner in which the Principle brings about the ten thousand things through various levels of differentiation on the other. Jāmī's recurrent theme of the Oneness of Being appears as a variation on the frequent Neo-Confucian discussion of the unity of principle (*li*) and vital-energy (*ch'i*), or substance (*t'i*) and function (*yung*).

Liu Chih's translation is far from literal, and on several occasions he abbreviates the discussion or adds commentary to the text. This is most obvious with the poetry, which he almost always drops. In the original Persian, the quatrains that are found in every Gleam alleviate the denseness of the philosophical discussion. If the reader has not quite understood what Jāmī is getting at in the prose sections, at least the poetry delights the ear and suggests the point in simpler language. In the translation, however, Liu Chih is interested only in philosophical and metaphysical issues, and with two or three exceptions, he makes no attempt to translate the poems. Hence the Chinese text keeps the high level of discourse throughout, and readers have no opportunity to refresh themselves with poetical diversions.

As Liu Chih explains in a short comment at the end of Gleam 12, he sees *Lawāʾiḥ* as divided into two parts. The first twelve Gleams explain the necessity of *kung* or "endeavor," the next twenty-four Gleams explicate the nature of *i*, a word that means both "righteousness" and "meaning." By endeavor and righteousness/meaning Liu Chih has in mind what would be called in Islamic terms "practice" (*ʿamal*) and "knowledge" or "theory" (*ʿilm, naẓar*). We have already met the term "endeavor" in the title of Liu Chih's book, *Interpretation of the Five Endeavors*, where it is employed to designate Islam's Five Pillars, that is, the five basic practices. However, *Displaying the Concealment* uses the term in the sense of practice in general, just as Wang Tai-yü does in the *Great Learning* when he says, "The endeavor of witnessing the One is indeed the chief task" (p. 88). As Liu Chih remarks at the end of Gleam 12, endeavor is to seek and to cultivate the Tao.

I or "righteousness/meaning" stands after *jen* (humanity) in the lists of the four or five key Confucian virtues. In Mencius, for whom the sense of "righteousness" is strong, the word designates the path that must be followed if people are to achieve true humanity. He writes,

> *Jen* is the human heart and *i* the human path. How sad it is when a man gives up the right path instead of following it and allows his heart to be lost without knowing how to seek it. When his chickens and dogs are lost, he knows that he has to seek for them, but not when his heart is lost. The Tao of learning is nothing but seeking for the lost heart. (VIA.11)

Righteousness/meaning is associated with the spirit of metal among the Five Agents, and it manifests the principle of what is right, correct, just, and appropriate. Its semantic range corresponds roughly with that of Arabic *ḥaqq*, which means truth, rightness, reality, appropriateness, obligation, responsibility. On the level of understanding, the quality of righteousness/meaning becomes manifest in discernment, decision, judgment, and seeing the reality of things. According to Chu Hsi, "*I* in the heart is like a sharp knife. When a thing comes in contact with it, the thing will split into two pieces."[14] Ch'eng Hao says, "*I* means what is proper, the standard for weighing what is of greater or smaller importance."[15] *I*'s connotation of meaning and putting things in their proper places seems to be the reason that Liu Chih makes it the theme of the second part of *Lawā'iḥ*, which discusses the theory of the Oneness of Being. Both Chinese introductions to the text consider the pairing of endeavor and righteousness/meaning as central to its message, but both stress the connotation of "righteousness" rather than "meaning."

Liu Chih's constant mention of the term "Real" is perhaps the major indication of the book's Islamic provenance. He speaks repeatedly of the "Real Being" (*chen-yu*), an expression that is not employed in the Chinese classics. Of course, "being and nonbeing" are often discussed in Taoism, Buddhism, and Neo-Confucianism, but there is no stress on a Real Being that stands beyond the opposition between the two (although both the Taoist "Non-Ultimate" and the Buddhist "Emptiness" can be understood in this sense). We have already met this Real Being that stands beyond being and nonbeing in the *Great Learning*, where Wang Tai-yü insists that "The Real Being does not fall into being and nonbeing" (p. 90). Thus the expression was familiar to Muslims at least from Wang's writings.

Although Jāmī uses the Persian equivalents for Real Being—*wujūd-i ḥaqq* (three times) and *hastī-yi ḥaqq* (three times)—Liu Chih gives the expression much more prominence by using it fifty-seven times. The importance Liu Chih gives to the term is obvious, for example, in Gleam 14, where Jāmī distinguishes in philosophical language between the Being that is attributed to God and that which is attributed to created things. For his part, Liu Chih ignores the literal sense of Jāmī's discussion and expresses the distinction in much simpler language, employing the terms "Real Being" and "illusory being" (*huan-yu*), both of which have come up before, though not in juxtaposition.

"Real Being," then, designates the One Principle, or the Divine Essence. When Liu Chih talks simply of "being," he usually means the illusory being that is attributed to creatures, and it is in this sense that he contrasts being with nonbeing. On two occasions, nonbeing in this sense comes up in connection with the idea of the nonexistence of the fixed entities. Thus, in Gleam 4, Jāmī mentions the realities of things as nonexistent in the divine knowledge, and Liu Chih explains this as the "nonbeing" of the principles, which is not to say that they are totally nonexistent, but that they have no existence per se in the universe. Then the "forms" of the things—that is, their modes of appearance in the universe—are "illusory being." In Gleam 27, Jāmī refers to the root nonexistence of the fixed entities—the fact that the entities never smell a whiff of existence—and Liu Chih employs the expression "Non-Ultimate" for the only time in the text. He seems to be implying that the "Great Ultimate" (a term that he does not mention) is God viewed as Creator of the universe, whereas the "Non-Ultimate" comprises the principles of the ten thousand things as prefigured in God. This would be close to Chu Hsi's explanation of the Non-Ultimate as the state of reality before the appearance of forms and the Great Ultimate as its state after the appearance of forms (see p. 37).

A passage from Gleam 17 suggests that Liu Chih is paying close attention to the complementarity of designations implied by "Great Ultimate" and "Non-Ultimate," perhaps following Wang Tai-yü, who, as we have seen, placed these two at the level of the Numerical One, below the Real One. Jāmī points out that the First Entification is the level where we can conceive of God as encompassing all qualities and characteristics, "whether the receptivity for disengagement from all attributes and respects, or the receptivity for being qualified by all." In other words, God embraces both the attributes that declare him incomparable (*tanzīh*) with all things and those that assert his similarity with creation (*tashbīh*). God is an undifferentiated Being that receives everything we negate from him and everything we ascribe to him, which is to say that in respect of the First Entification, God can be spoken of not only in positive theological terms, but also in the language of negative theology. Liu Chih expresses Jāmī's basic point by saying that this level embraces all the rulings of "being and nonbeing," which can be understood to mean that it embraces both the Great Ultimate and the Non-Ultimate.

Throughout *Displaying the Concealment*, Liu Chih shows little interest in maintaining one-to-one correspondences between the Persian and the Chinese. His concern is rather to make a specific discussion comprehensible in Chinese terms, even if he has to ignore the terminological nuances and throw consistency to the wind. Thus, for example, he discusses the central concept of self-disclosure in several ways, adjusting his terminology according to the context. When Jāmī talks about the "First Self-Disclosure," Liu Chih quite rightly treats the term as synonymous with the "First Entification," and he translates both as "First Movement." Movement, as we have seen, is the yang complement of "quietude." In other contexts, Liu Chih translates self-disclosure as issuance, appearance, manifestation, and manifesting transformation. The fact that he recognizes the centrality of the idea of self-disclosure in *Lawāʾiḥ* can be judged already by the title he has given to the text, which, indeed, can be taken as a definition of the very concept of self-disclosure —*Displaying the Concealment of the Real Realm.*

Liu Chih's most obvious adaptation of *Lawā'iḥ* to the needs of Chinese thinking is in Gleam 18, where he adds a long paragraph that rephrases the discussion in Neo-Confucian terms. In the Persian text, Jāmī presents a standard Islamic version of an Aristotelian/Neoplatonic method of tracing individual things back to the One Real. In this philosophical scheme, which has been called the "tree of Porphyry" in the West, every individual thing is seen to be a member of a species, every species a member of a genus, and every genus a member of a higher genus. The higher genera are gradually reduced in number until they are all subsumed under the "genus of the genera." Among the philosophers, the last stage is usually said to be substance (*jawhar*), but for the Sufis, the final term is Being.

For example, a horse is an "animal." When we consider animals along with plants, then we have "growing things." Growing things along with inanimate things are "bodies." Bodies along with spirits are "substances." Substances along with accidents are "possible existents." Possible existents along with the Necessary Existence are "Existence." Undifferentiated Existence is the One Essence that lies behind all reality.

Although the Greco-Islamic terms in this discussion are totally foreign to the Chinese tradition, the point of the discussion is to reduce the perceived manyness of the world to the One Principle that lurks behind all things, and few theoretical issues are closer to the heart of the Neo-Confucians.[16] Liu Chih knew very well that Jāmī was not trying to teach people the details of Greek philosophical learning. Rather, he was making use of well-known philosophical expressions to teach readers how to see the world correctly. Hence Liu Chih adds at the beginning of Gleam 18 an alternative, Neo-Confucian version of the reduction of things to the One. When he finishes it, he runs through Jāmī's argument, dropping the specifically Greco-Islamic terms and simplifying the discussion so that it corresponds exactly with the Neo-Confucian world view that he has just outlined.

In Liu Chih's rewriting of Gleam 18, Real Being is "substance." Substance, as we have seen repeatedly, is the underlying reality that makes itself manifest as "function." According to Liu Chih, the Real Being's function is knowledge and power, which is to say that the Real Being knows all things and is powerful over all things, and it exercises its power in accordance with its knowledge. So, having knowledge and power, the Real Being acts. Once there is activity, the "principle" (*li*) of the activity can be differentiated from the "vital-energy" (*ch'i*) of the activity. Vital-energy, which is the harmonious interworking of yang and yin, gives rise to the ten thousand things, which are called here the "forms and images." They are forms and images because, as previous passages of *Displaying the Concealment* have explained, the only thing that is truly real is the Real Being itself, and everything else is its manifestation, or the appearance and guise to which it gives rise. So, once there are forms and images, specific activities can be described, whether vegetal attributes like growth and nourishment or animal characteristics like life and spirit. Looking at the ten thousand things from this point of view, we have a full differentiation into different classes and types, which may then be discussed in terms of their names and guises. But all this is simply the outward appearance, and its reality goes back to the One Principle.

Liu Chih's most interesting adaptation of the text is probably what he has done in Gleam 27, where he cleverly avoids a problem caused by Jāmī's mention of two proper names—Ashʿarī, the founder of the Ash'arite school of theology, and Ḥusbāniyya, a name given in Islamic texts to the Sophists. Liu Chih had two obvious alternatives as to how to deal with these names. He could have explained the references, or he could have dropped the names (just as he dropped the most technical part of this chapter, toward the end). Instead, he took inspiration from the root meaning of the terms and interpreted them as symbols for two types of mentality. The name Ashʿarī derives from the same root as *shiʿr*, "poetry," and the word *ḥusbāniyya* comes from the same root as *ḥisāb*, "arithmetic." Liu Chih simply calls the two the "poet" and the "arithmetician," and thereby adds a certain logic to their differing perspectives. Given the general skill with which he translates the text and his wide reading in Arabic and Persian sources, it is difficult to believe that this modification could have been anything but intentional.

The Translations

Lawāʾiḥ was first translated into English in 1906 by E. H. Whinfield and Mīrzā Muḥammad Ḳazvīnī, and this work has been reprinted several times. Although it is one of the best of the early translations of Sufi texts, it is more a paraphrase than a translation, and Whinfield's goal, as is shown clearly by his introduction, was to fit the text into the now discredited idea that Sufism can be explained by the influence of Neoplatonism. He made little attempt to situate the text in its own historical and intellectual context, and indeed that task would have been almost impossible at the time, since Ibn al-ʿArabī and his school of thought were practically unknown in the West. Given the voluminous scholarship on Ibn al-ʿArabī that has appeared since 1906, *Lawāʾiḥ* has long been in need of a new translation.

Yann Richard's French translation, done in 1982 along with a critical edition of the Persian text, is much more accurate and reflects some of the new scholarship, but his introduction and annotations are not quite enough to provide a real sense of what the text is trying to do and how it relates to the general concerns of the Islamic intellectual tradition. And like Whinfield, Richard is not aware of the technical meaning of a good deal of the terminology of Ibn al-ʿArabī's school, and he often employs philosophical vocabulary of questionable relevance.[17] Given the inadequacies of the two earlier translations, we thought it would be appropriate to provide a relatively full introduction and detailed annotations, even if the net result is to pay more attention to Jāmī's original than to Liu Chih's translation. Perhaps, some years from now, it will be possible to offer a much more complete introduction to the intellectual milieu of Chinese Islam so that Liu Chih's context and goals may be better understood.

The Persian original is translated from the text established by Richard, the Chinese version from an edition published in 1925, which includes two introductions by Chinese ulama.[18] Note that Liu Chih's numbering of *Lawā'iḥ* departs slightly from that provided in Richard's edition, since he inserts a heading between Gleam 21 and 22 and drops the heading for Gleam 32. The numbering of the Gleams commonly varies in the manuscripts, and indeed, the numbering in Whinfield's edition allows for only thirty. Liu Chih seems to have had a good manuscript, though his translation is free enough so that we cannot be completely sure. Most of the major discrepancies are clearly dictated by the needs to adapt the Persian text to Chinese thinking.

Finally, it should be noted that there has been some discussion about Liu Chih's authorship of the book. On the title page and in Gleam 12, the translator's name is given as Liu I-ts'an. Leslie agrees with Chin Chit'ang that this is a mistake pertaining to the 1925 edition of the work.[19] One can also not exclude the possibility that I-ts'an is a pen-name. The style of the translation is very similar to Liu Chih's other writing, especially *The Philosophy of Arabia*, in the text of which he already refers to *Lawā'iḥ* by the first half of the Chinese title as given in the translation, "Displaying the Concealment." It is hard to believe that there could have been someone else called Liu I-ts'an, writing with such mastery, who was then otherwise forgotten.

In what follows, Chittick's English translation of the original Persian text is placed on the left-hand pages, and my translation of Liu Chih's Chinese version is placed on the right-hand pages. *Lawā'iḥ* begins with an introduction that Liu Chih did not translate (and ends with a postscript that he also did not translate). Facing Jāmī's introduction are two introductions to the Chinese text, one written by P'eng Hui-o in 1751 and the other by Wei Kang Ch'ui-ch'ih in 1775. Nothing is known about these two authors. In the Chinese text, the first is printed at the beginning of the book, and the second at the end.

6

Gleams

Introduction

"I do not number Thy laudations—how indeed! Every laudation returns to Thee. The precinct of Thy holiness is too majestic for my laudation. Thou art as Thou hast lauded Thyself."[1]

O God, I do not bring Your thanksgiving to my tongue, nor do I count out Your praises. Everything in the pages of the engendered things is of the same kind as laudation and praise, and all return to the precinct of Your magnificence and greatness. What comes from our hands and tongues worthy of Your thanksgiving and praise? You are as You have said Yourself—the pearl of Your laudation is what You Yourself have pierced.

> There in the perfection of Your magnificence,
> the world is a dewdrop from Your ocean of gifts.
> However much we praise and laud You,
> only Your praise and laudation are worthy of You.

In the place where he who voiced "I am the most eloquent"[2] threw down the pennant of eloquence and recognized himself as incapable of pronouncing Your laudation—how can just any stuttering talker let loose his tongue, how can just any confused surmiser adorn his speech? Or rather, making manifest here the admission of incapacity and inadequacy

7

Displaying the Concealment of the Real Realm

Introduction

by

P'eng Hui-o

Displaying the Concealment of the Real Realm is a book written by a great worthy of Arabia, Ch'a-mi. In talk of the "realm," there is no realm that is not real; in talk of the "real," there is nothing real that is not concealed; and in examining "concealment," there is nothing concealed that is not displayed. In sum, there is only the Real, so it can conceal, and there is only concealment, so it can display. Moreover, there is only the true substance in the Real Realm, which can penetrate the concealment of the Real and display the concealment of the concealment.

I enjoyed this book. Altogether it has thirty-six chapters. The first twelve chapters talk about the endeavor to cultivate the Tao and embody the Tao. The next twenty-four chapters clarify the hidden and revealed righteousness of the Real Principle. *Displaying the Concealment of the Real Realm* talks about this in detail.

Why does he talk first about endeavor and then about righteousness? Is it because we go from sincerity to clarity? Is it because we follow function to substance? Neither is correct. Endeavor and righteousness are complementary. They are one and at the same time two, two and at the same time one. In talk of endeavor, righteousness is there, and in talk of righteousness, endeavor is lodged within—neither comes slowly or quickly, before or after.

People use endeavor, but they do not know how endeavor should be used. Thus he talks about endeavor first. People seek after righteousness, but they are mistaken in recognizing it and they take the wrong righteousness as righteousness. Thus he talks about righteousness next. If you lose it, you lose everything, and if you gain it, you gain every-

is itself inadequacy, and seeking to share in this meaning with that leader of the religion and this world is far from beautiful courtesy.

> Who am I? Numbered as who? What person,
> that I might wish to vie with his dogs?
> I know that I won't reach his caravan—
> enough to hear from afar the sound of its bells.

O God, bless Muhammad, who set up the Banner of Praise and owns the Praiseworthy Station,[3] and his household and companions, those who made every effort to attain the goal, and give them plentiful peace!

thing. Therefore, good talk about endeavor includes talk of righteousness.

At root the human heart has a real realm. If various conditions veil and disturb it, this is like a clear mirror covered with dust.[1] Finally, the surface is filled and stopped up, so the root substance is lost.

If you encounter coarse and shallow principles of the Tao and are still perplexed about this, how will you ever be able to see luminously the Utmost Principle? So, you should first follow the ground of your heart so as to use endeavor. The main thesis of this book is to request people to discriminate what is the "human heart," which arises later, from the "Tao heart," which is the root nature; how to rid oneself of the human heart and return to the Tao heart; and how to govern the human heart with the Tao heart.[2]

Within the heart there exists a real realm. It may be sought with the heart, and it may be reached with the heart. This is the meaning of what was said—"In talk of endeavor, righteousness is there."[3] This is seeking the Tao and cultivating the Tao. If the hidden and revealed righteousness of the Real Principle is not clear, then, even if we are not enslaved by divergent paths, the real appearance of the Tao-substance cannot be glimpsed—not one part in ten thousand. So, those who designate themselves as "seekers of the Tao" and "cultivators of the Tao" carry only false names.

Thus the book talks about the hidden and revealed righteousness of the Real Principle, and from beginning to end it is arranged in good order. Its moments and divisions penetrate the changes, while its emptinesses and fullnesses indicate the return, which is the subtleness of the final stage. While separating and talking item by item, either it follows outward explanation to reach the inward, or it follows the inward explanation to reach the outward. Either it follows the concealed explanation to reach the manifestation, or it follows the manifest explanation to reach the concealment. Sometimes it uses illusion to make the real distinct, and sometimes it uses desire to discriminate the principle. Sometimes it uses borrowed illustrations and sometimes contrary deductions, sometimes it uses additional evidence, or it uses indicating points. From every direction explanation comes, and drop by drop it returns to the fountainhead. Bit by bit it indicates the Real Realm, desiring that people depend on the function of endeavor, for all the loose thoughts and considerations will not by themselves plunge into the ground of the Pure and Real. This is the meaning of what was said, "In talk of righteousness, endeavor is lodged within."

To sum up: To employ endeavor is to employ the heart, and to clarify righteousness is to clarify the heart. Therefore, the Classic [*Lawāʾiḥ*, chapter one] says, "Why do you not have one heart and one bearing," that is,

Whispered Prayer

"My God, my God, deliver us from occupation with follies, and show us the realities of things as they are!"[4] Lift the covering of heedlessness from our insight's eye and show us each thing as it is! Disclose not to us nonbeing in being's form, and place no curtain of nonbeing on being's beauty! Make these imaginal forms into the mirror of Your beauty's self-disclosures, not the cause of veiling and distance! Turn these imaginary imprints into the capital of our knowing and seeing, not the instrument of our ignorance and blindness! Our deprivation and rejection come from ourselves—turn us not over to ourselves! Bestow upon us freedom from ourselves, and confer upon us familiarity with Yourself!

O Lord, give me a pure heart, an aware spirit!
    Give me sighs at night and tears at dawn!
In Your self's path, first take my self away from self,
    then show me the way, selfless of self, to Yourself!

O Lord, make all creatures turn against me!
    Put me to the side of all the worldlings!
Turn my heart's face from every direction,
    give my love one direction and one face!

O Lord, free me from deprivation—why not?
    Give me a road to the lane of gnosis—why not?
Your munificence has turned many a disbeliever into
        a Muslim.
    Turn one more disbeliever into a Muslim—why not?

O Lord, free me from need for both worlds,
    lift my head high with poverty's harness![5]
Make me a confidant in the path of the secret,
    turn me aside from every path not to You!

direction. It also says that when you talk about the two ranks, "You will reject the things and run to the Lord."

Time: Ch'ien-lung [era], the sixteenth year, the year *hsin-wei* [1751], the second month of spring, P'ing-ling, Chiang-tso. Written by P'eng Hui-o at the government office of West Hill.

Small Introduction

by

Wei Kang Ch'ui-ch'ih

It was said in ancient times that each person has abilities and inabilities. Others cannot force me to do what I cannot do, and I cannot force others to do what they cannot do. None of us can force others to do what they cannot do, which means that all of us have what we cannot do. Even those who are surely able can only reach the ultimate by means of "not forgetting and not helping."[4] This means that those who are surely able understand the lack of ability.

Concerning the book *Displaying the Concealment of the Real Realm*, Master Ching-ch'u[5] is surely able, and I am surely unable. However, the master did not take me as unable, and he asked me again and again to write the introduction. This is why I do not dare to take the master as unable, and I have often sought advice from him to get his consent. When two help each other, in fact they are needed by each other, and when they meet, both of them will be perfected.

In general, how could the teaching of our Confucianism refuse the practice of the utmost ultimate of "the Central and Ordinary"[6] as transmitted from the ancients? But at present, even if people put on the Confucian hat and wear the Confucian robe, when we trace their deeds and affairs, we see that they pursue only their own profit. When a son pursues his own profit, he does not treat his father as a father, and when a younger brother pursues his own profit, he does not treat his elder brother as an elder brother. If such acts are put forward, then surely what is taught from the gate of the Sage will simply be rejected. Such people are sinners following Yang and Mo,[7] because their faith in the Tao is not genuine and their cultivation of the Tao is not focused. So, no one has the ability to do anything.

Preface

To continue: This is a treatise named *The Gleams* on the explanation of the gnostic sciences and the meanings. It has gleamed forth from the tablets of the secret hearts and spirits of the lords of gnosis and the masters of tasting and finding in appropriate expressions and lustrous allusions.[6] It is hoped that none will see in the midst him who has embarked on this explication or sit on the carpet of avoidance and the mat of protest, since the author has no share save the post of translator, and no portion but the trade of speaker.

I am nothing, and much less than nothing—
    no work comes from nothing and less than nothing.
Whatever secret of Reality I speak,
    no share have I but the speaking.

In the world of poverty, signlessness is best,
    in the story of love, tonguelessness is best.
From him who has not tasted the secrets,
    speaking by way of translation is best.

Like the clear in intellect, I've pierced a few pearls
    to translate the sayings of the high in rank.
Might it be that from know-nothing me, the trusty
    will convey this gift to Hamadan's king?[7]

How wonderful is this book! First it talks about endeavor, then about righteousness. In talking about endeavor, it says that the heart should be one; in talking about righteousness, it says that the reality should be sought. This can truly give rise to the Tao of "cultivating [the body], regulating [the family], governing [the country], bringing peace [to everything under heaven]"[8] and the principle of the Three Bonds and the Five Constants. Without endeavor, no righteousness will be created, and without righteousness, no endeavor will be seen.

In practicing righteousness by means of endeavor, the later scholars look only at their ability and inability. Indeed, if one does what one can, even if one has inabilities, there is nothing wrong. If one does not do what one can, even if one has no inabilities, of what use is this?

Time: Ch'ien-lung [era], the year *i-wei* [1775], the fourth month, its middle third, in the city of Ch'in-ch'eng; by Wei Kang Ch'ui-ch'ih, who added this introduction to the text at the lodging place of T'o-sui, the Sheng-chai house.

THE FIRST GLEAM

"God has not assigned to any man two hearts in his breast" [Koran 33:4]. The Howless Presence, who has given you the blessing of being, has placed within you only one heart, that you may be one-faced and one-hearted in love, turning away from other than Him and turning toward Him—not that you should make one heart into a hundred pieces, each piece wandering after a goal.

O you who've turned to the qibla of faithfulness,
  why make the shell into the kernel's veil?
It's not good for your heart to run after this and that—
  with one heart, one friend is enough for you.

THE SECOND GLEAM

"Dispersion" is that you scatter the heart by means of attachment to numerous things. "Gathering" is that you turn away from everything by witnessing the One. A group supposed that gatheredness lies in gathering the causes, and they stayed in endless dispersion. A band knew for certain that gathering the causes is among the causes of dispersion, and they emptied their hands of all.[8]

O you whose heart has a thousand troubles from all!
  Your heart will have trouble finding ease from all.
Since the heart gains nothing but dispersion from each,
  give your heart to the One and cut yourself off
    from them all!

As long as you dwell in dispersion and doubt,
  the Folk of Gathering see you as the worst of men.
No, by God, no—you're not a man, you're a monkey,
  but out of ignorance, you don't see your own
    monkeyness.

CHAPTER 1

One Heart

The Classic says, "The Real Lord did not give humans two hearts in their bellies." The meaning is that the Imageless Imperial Majesty has bestowed upon you your image, and He entrusted not but one heart to your image. Why do you not have one heart and one bearing, reject the things, and run to the Lord? Do not make one heart into a hundred divisions, each division following a selfish intention, thereby making your heart into a scrapbook.

CHAPTER 2

Collectedness and Division

"Division" means to bring about number through occupation with the diverse things and the consequences of affairs. "Collectedness" means to return from the image to the One with clear seeing. Some people have doubted this meaning and have said that collectedness means to collect all the conditions. They did not know that by collecting all the conditions, their hearts were finally drifting into division. Only the wise men discerned with certainty that collecting all the conditions certainly leads into division. They washed their hands of the conditions and cast them aside.

O traveler, speak not on every topic!
    Run only the road of reaching the Lord of lords.
The cause of dispersion is the world's causes—
    don't try to gather the heart by gathering causes!

O heart, how long searching for perfection in school?
    How long perfecting the rules of philosophy and
        geometry?
Any thought other than God's remembrance is evil
        suggestion.
    Have shame before God! How long this evil suggestion?

THE THIRD GLEAM

The Real—glory be to Him and high indeed is He!—is present everywhere, gazing in each state at the manifest and nonmanifest of all. What a loss—that you have lifted your eyes from His countenance and look at others! You have left the path of contentment with Him and pursue another road.

She came at dawn—that heart-taker of fevered lovers.
    She said, "O heavy load on my thoughts!
"Shame on you! I look in your direction,
    but you've turned your eyes toward the others!"

We've run in love's path all our life,
    we've tried hard for union all our life.
A glimpse of Your image is better for the gaze
    than the beauty of all the beauties all our life.

CHAPTER 3

Seeing the Tao

The Real Lord is timeless and placeless, but He always looks at the inward and outward of the ten thousand beings. Alas, you people do not see what He sees, but instead you see other things. You do not walk the Tao of the Real Lord, but instead you walk different paths.

THE FOURTH GLEAM

Everything other than the Real—exalted and high is He!—is exposed to disappearance and annihilation. Its reality is a nonexistent object of knowledge, its form an illusory existent.[9] Yesterday it had no being and no appearance, and today it has an appearance without being. It is obvious what will open up from it tomorrow.

Why do you give the reins of acquiescence into the hands of wishes and hopes? Why do you lean back on these varnishings that undergo annihilation? Pull your heart out from everything and bind it to God! Cut off from everything and join with God! It is He who has always been and always will be. No thorn of any newly arrived thing scratches the face of His subsistence.

Every heart-tugging form that shows its face to you
  will soon be stolen from your eyes by the spheres.
Go, give your heart to someone who, in the stages of existence,
  has always been with you and always will be.

Gone—that I should turn my face to the qibla of the fair,
  inscribing the words of their heartache on the tablet of
    my heart.
I aim for the eternal beauty—
  I've had my fill of all loveliness not eternal.

Anything that does not let you turn to subsistence
  will at last make you the target of annihilation's arrow.
If you will be parting from a thing when you die,
  better to part from it now while you're still alive.

O great man, let it be property or offspring,
  it is clear how long it will subsist.
Happy is he whose heart is tied to that Heart-taker
  to whom are joined, heart and soul, the Folk of Heart.

CHAPTER 4

Alteration and Perishment

Everything other than the Lord will certainly alter and perish. Its principle belongs to hidden nonbeing, while its image is illusory being. Yesterday at origin, it was nonbeing and had not been seen, and today it is seen, yet it remains nonbeing from the very beginning. Thus you must awaken to what will be tomorrow.

Not knowing, you have surrendered the bridle of submissiveness to the hand of indolence and hope. You lean the back of trust on the edge of the illusory and perishable. Why not escape and cut your body and heart off from all the conditions? With one heart, care for and be united with the Real Lord! Only the Real Lord is eternally constant and will not perish. No thorn of anything newborn can scratch the face of everlastingness.

THE FIFTH GLEAM

The absolutely beautiful is the Presence of the Possessor of Majesty and Bounteous Giving. Every beauty and perfection manifest in all the levels is the shining ray of His beauty and perfection, and by it have the owners of the levels gained the features of beauty and the attributes of perfection. Whenever you know someone to be a knower, that is the trace of His knowerness. Wherever you see someone to be a seer, that is the fruit of His seerness. In short, all are His attributes, descended from the pinnacle of universality and unboundedness, and disclosed in the depths of particularity and binding.[10]

Thus, you should take the path from the part to the whole and turn your face from binding to unboundedness. You should not consider the part as distinct from the whole, lest the bound hold you back from the unbounded.

I went to look at the roses, but that candle of Ṭirāz
    saw me in the rosebeds and sweetly said,
"I'm the root, the meadow's roses are My branch—
    why be held back from the root by the branches?"

What will you do with that elegant stature and lovely cheek?
    What will do with those chains of curling locks?
From every side, the unbounded beauty is shining—
    O unaware, what will you do with bounded loveliness?

THE SIXTH GLEAM

Although the child of Adam, because of corporeality, has extreme density, in terms of spirituality he has the utmost subtletly. He takes on the property of everything toward which he turns, and he receives the color of everything to which he attends. This is why the philosophers have said, "When the rational soul discloses itself in forms that coincide with the realities and when it realizes their true properties, it becomes as if it were all of existence."[11]

CHAPTER 5

Completion and Beauty

The Perfectly Penetrating Beauty is the imperial majesty, the utmost honor, and the utmost nobility. All the completion and beauty that are seen in the ten thousand levels are results of the flow of the Complete Beauty's surplus light. What the ten thousand levels gain are the shadows and echoes of the Complete Beauty. So, the knowledge and discernment of all things are the traces of Its knowing and discerning, the seeing and hearing of all things are the fruit of Its seeing and hearing. In sum, all are the pervading and going of the great function of the Honorable Majesty, having come down from the peak of penetration and wholeness to be seen in the outskirts of division and obstruction.[9]

CHAPTER 6

Search and Examination

The body of human beings is turbid, but their nature is the most spiritual. Because of form, they receive shapes, and when they encounter things, they become tinged by them. A wise man said, "When human nature can embody the Real Principle and be seen, the images qua images cannot obstruct. When the Real and the image become united and they perfect the form, this is almost the same body as heaven and earth."[10]

Moreover, the generality of creatures, because of their intense conjunction with this corporeal form and their perfect preoccupation with this material figure, have become such that they do not know themselves apart from it and cannot make the distinction. [Rūmī writes] in the *Mathnawī*,

> You are this very thought, brother,
> the rest of you is bones and fiber.
> If your thought is a rose, you're a rosegarden,
> but if it's a thorn, you're firewood.[12]

So, you must strive to conceal yourself from your own gaze. You must turn toward that Essence and occupy yourself with that Reality whose beauty's loci of disclosure are the degrees of the existents and whose perfection's mirrors are the levels of the engendered things.

You must persevere in this relation[13] such that it thoroughly mixes with your soul and such that your own being disappears from your gaze. If you turn toward self, you will have turned toward Him, and when you express self, you will have expressed Him. The bounded becomes the Unbounded, and "I am the Real" turns into "He is the Real."[14]

> If a rose passes into your heart, you're a rose,
> if a restless nightingale, you're a nightingale.
> You're a part, and the Real is the whole. If for a time
> you take up thought of the whole, you'll be the whole.

> From the mixture of soul and body, you are my goal.
> In dying and living, you are my goal.
> Long may you live, for I am leaving the midst!
> If I say "I" about me, you are my goal.

> When will it be, when?—torn the dress of being,
> blazing the beauty of the unbounded Face,[15]
> consumed the heart by the assaults of His light,
> drowned the soul by the attacks of yearning!

The multitude are deeply lost and deluded in form's disposition. Drawn into illusion and shadow, they are no longer aware and they do not want to depart from form.

The man who carefully guards [the Tao] forgets himself and forgets the things. He examines the substance and searches for the Real; he clarifies that the levels of the ten thousand beings are all locations in which the Graceful Beauty flows perpetually, and that the ranks of all things are the places in which the Complete Power manifests and exposes itself.

He obtains in this place the real vein of the utmost Tao, and he employs his power in this place through mysterious endeavor and subtle application. His heart is transformed such that enjoying self is enjoying things, preserving self is preserving the Lord, and portraying self is portraying the Lord. The obstructed is the penetrating.

THE SEVENTH GLEAM

You must exercise this eminent relation such that in every moment and in every state you will never be empty of this relation—whether in coming or going, eating or sleeping, hearing or speaking. In short, in all movement and rest you must be present with the moment, lest it pass in vain; or rather, you must be aware of the breath, lest it come out in heedlessness.

From year to year though You don't show Your face,
there's no worry my love for You will vanish.
In every place, with every person, in every state, I have
hope in my heart and Your image in my eye.[16]

THE EIGHTH GLEAM

Just as it is necessary to extend the mentioned relation to comprise all the moments and all the times, so also the most important goal is to increase its quality by denuding oneself of the garments of the engendered things and ridding oneself of observing the forms of possible existence. This can only be done through intense effort and complete exertion to negate thoughts and illusions. The more thoughts are negated and evil suggestions hidden, the stronger that relation will be.

You must strive so that dispersed thoughts strike their tents outside the breast's courtyard and the light of the Real Being's manifestation—glory be to Him!—casts its rays on your nonmanifest realm. It will take you away from you and free you from the jostling of the others. No consciousness of yourself will remain, nor any consciousness of the self's lack of consciousness. Rather, nothing will subsist but God, the One, the Unitary.

O Lord, help—so that I may escape from my own animality,
so that I may cut myself off from the bad and escape
from my own evil!
Take my self away from myself in Your own Being
so that I may escape my selfhood and selflessness.

CHAPTER 7

Storing and Piling Up

Storing and piling up this Tao must be such that you not be without it even for a moment, whether in sleeping or eating, in talking or silence. In all movement and non-movement, you must preserve your heart, so that nothing commands you to vanity. You must be self-awake, so that you do not end up in confusion and ignorance.

CHAPTER 8

Conquering Self

You already know the Tao's vastness and far-reachingness, which embraces and puts together all the world's turnings and meetings. So, you must examine the substance and forget the form. By expanding the scale [of examination], you must search for the clues.[11] This cannot easily be attained without adding caution, employing strength, conquering self,[12] and leaving selfishness. The more selfishness is conquered, the clearer the Tao becomes. The more you move away from guesswork, the stronger will be the Tao.

If you are watchful, confused considerations will run away, the light of the Real Being will start displaying, and the ten thousand things will all be provided within self.[13] There will be no disturbance by the external things. There will be no self-awareness, nor will there be awareness of non-awareness of self.[14] There will be nothing acted upon—only the Unique One, the Real Lord.

When someone's custom is annihilation and his rule poverty,
he has no unveiling, no certainty, no gnosis, no religion.
He has left the midst, God alone remains, God—
This is the meaning of "When poverty is complete,
he is God."[17]

THE NINTH GLEAM

"Annihilation" is that the Real Being's manifestation overmasters the nonmanifest realm such that no consciousness of other than He remains. "Annihilation of the annihilation" is that no consciousness of this unconsciousness remains.[18]

It should be clear that "annihilation of annihilation" is included in annihilation. If the companion of annihilation is conscious of his own annihilation, he is not a companion of annihilation, for both the attribute of annihilation and the one described by it pertain to other than the Real. So, being conscious of it negates annihilation.

When you want your self to subsist like this,
how can you subtract a barleycorn from
your being's crop?
If you are conscious of the tip of a hair
and speak of annihilation's road, you've left the road.

CHAPTER 9

Conquering the Conquering

"Conquering" means that the Real Being's manifestation overcomes the heart, and there is no awareness of external things. "Conquering the conquering" means that there is no awareness of the non-awareness.

The second kind of conquering is stored in the first. If someone who has been conquered is aware of the conquering, he has not yet been conquered. In this case what is called "conquering" and "conqueringness" still belongs to human affairs. Awareness of human affairs is not conquering.

THE TENTH GLEAM

"Asserting unity" [*tawḥīd*] is to make the heart one. In other words, it is to deliver and disengage it from attachment to what is other than the Real, both from the side of seeking and desire, and from the direction of knowledge and gnosis. In other words, seeking and desire are to be cut off from all objects of seeking and desire, and all objects of knowledge and intellect are to be eliminated from its insight's gaze. It turns its attentiveness away from every face, and no consciousness or awareness of other than the Real remains.

O man of the journey, "asserting unity" in the Sufi's terms
 is to deliver the heart from attending to others.
This intimation of the birds' final stations
 have I voiced for you, if you understand the
 "language of the birds" [27:16].[19]

THE ELEVENTH GLEAM

As long as Adam's child is caught in the trap of caprice and fancy, his constancy in this relation will be difficult. But when the traces of the attractions of Gentleness become manifest within him and preoccupation with the objects of sensation and intellect goes far from his nonmanifest realm, taking pleasure in this relation will dominate over the corporeal pleasures and spiritual comforts. The toil of struggle will disappear from the midst, and the pleasure of witnessing will cling to his soul. His mind will turn away from the jostling of the others, and the tongue of his state will begin to hum this tune:

O nightingale of the soul, I'm drunk from remembering you,
 O footfall of heartache, I'm low from remembering you.
All the world's pleasures are trampled under foot
 by the taste that comes to hand from remembering you.

CHAPTER 10

Returning to the One

"Returning to the One" is for the heart to be in the One. It is cutting off and breaking away from attachment to external things, so that the self's seeking, loving, knowledge, and discernment are cut off and broken away from all that is sought after, all that is loved, all that is known, and all that is discerned. There will be only awareness of the Lord, and awareness of the Lord is non-awareness.

CHAPTER 11

Uplifting the Awareness

Human beings constantly fall into the net of selfish desires, so clarity of perseverance in the Tao becomes difficult. If the ebb and flow of the Utmost Mercy's uplifting the awareness comes to be seen in them and if the affairs and tasks of the hidden and the manifest are purified in their heart, then only does the taste of the Tao begin to overcome the taste of the bodily mandate. Laborious toil is eased, and the subtle realm becomes manifest. Selfish intention is removed, and a song of joy arises.

THE TWELFTH GLEAM

When the truthful seeker finds the precursor of attraction's relation—that is, taking pleasure from remembering the Real in himself[20]—then he must appoint his complete aspiration to nurturing and strengthening this relation and he must hold himself back from everything that negates it. He should know that, for example, if he were to spend everlasting life on this relation, he would have done nothing and would not have performed what it rightly demands.

Love strummed a tune on my heart's lute
turning me into love from head to foot.
In truth, for ages I will never emerge
from paying what's due for a moment of love.

THE THIRTEENTH GLEAM

The Reality of the Real—glory be to Him!—is nothing but Being, and His Being has no decline or lowness. It is hallowed beyond the brand of change and alteration, and rid of the blemish of plurality and multiplicity. Without the sign of any sign, It does not fit into knowledge or plain-viewing. All the how-manys and hows appear from It, but It has no how-many or how. Everything is perceived through It, but It is outside the compass of perception. The head's eye is dazzled in witnessing Its beauty, and the secret-heart's sight is darkened without observing Its perfection.

O You to whose love I gave my spirit,
You are above and below, not above nor below.
Everything's essence is apart from existence and
endures through existence,
but Your Essence is plain Existence and utter Being.

That heart-desired Friend is so colorless, O heart!
Don't be content all at once with color, O heart!
The root of all color is that colorlessness—
"Who colors better than God" [2:138], O heart?

CHAPTER 12

Real Guarding

Once the truly sincere seeker obtains the guidance that is the uplifting of his awareness, he must focus his heart and guard it closely so that it settles down peacefully and does not transgress any boundary. He must know that this Tao is the most difficult thing to obtain, and so also, it is difficult to advance toward the ultimacy of what ought to be.

I-ts'an says: *Displaying the Concealment* has a total of thirty-six chapters. The preceding twelve chapters explain the endeavor of seeking the Tao and cultivating the Tao. The next twenty-four chapters begin to clarify the hidden and manifest righteousness [meaning] of the Real Principle.

CHAPTER 13

Real Being

The Real Being is only the One, and It has neither place nor sequence. It is not tainted by the name of change and alteration, nor does It have anything to do with the meaning of multiplicity. It is the Lord of the ten thousand transformations, but at root It undergoes no transformation. It is the subtleness of the ten thousand traces, but at root It has no trace. No learning can carry It, no eye can see It. It manifests all colors and guises,[15] but Itself has no color and guise. It is aware of the ten thousand things, but Itself is beyond the ten thousand things. If you want to observe Its beauty, the light of your eyes will first be dazzled. If you want to divulge Its subtleness, your throat and tongue will first become dumb. If you want to think about Its concealment, your heart's wisdom will first be perplexed.

THE FOURTEENTH GLEAM

The word "existence" is sometimes used to mean realization and obtainment,[21] which are verbal meanings and respective concepts. In this respect, it is among the "secondary intelligibles," over and against which there is nothing in the external world. Rather, "existence" occurs to the quiddities in intellection. Thus have the verifying philosophers and theologians verified.

Sometimes the word "existence" is said, but what is meant is a Reality that has being through Its own Essence, while the rest of the existents have being through It. In reality, there is no existent other than It in the external world. The other existents occur to It and endure through It. Thus has given witness the tasting of the great and perfect gnostics and the lofty folk of certainty.

The application of this word to the Presence of the Real—glory be to Him and high indeed is He!—is in the second meaning, not the first.

The folk of the bindings judge by reason that being
occurs only to the entities and realities.
The lords of witnessing see in unveiling that entities
all occur, and existence is the locus of their occurrence.

CHAPTER 14

Being

Being has two meanings—illusory being and Real Being. "Illusory being" is the being of altering penetration. Although it is being in name, in reality it is nonbeing. It does not go beyond human rational understanding and talk of the manifesting images.

"Real Being" is the being of the utmost Reality, and It Itself is the Root Substance and the Reality upon which all beings depend. Beside this Being, there is no being. The ten thousand beings are produced by reliance on this Being, and they stand by depending upon It.

When the word "being" is used for the name of the Lord, it has only this meaning—not the first.

THE FIFTEENTH GLEAM

"Attributes" are other than the "Essence" in regard to what rational faculties understand, but they are identical with the Essence in regard to realization and obtainment.[22]

For example, the Essence is the "Knower" in respect of the attribute of knowledge, the "Powerful" in respect of power, the "Desiring" in respect of desire. There is no doubt that, just as these are different from one another in terms of concept, they are also different from the Essence. However, in terms of realization and being, they are the same as the Essence, in the sense that there is no plurality of existences. Rather, there is one existence, while the names and attributes are its relations and respects.

O You whose Essence is pure of any stain in every task,
concerning You neither "how" can be asked nor "where."
In intellection, all attributes are other than Your Essence,
but in realization, all are the same.

CHAPTER 15

Substance and Function

Substance and function are not the same, but they cannot be separated. They are not the same if we talk about meaning, but they cannot be separated if we talk about their reality.

For example, "knowledge" must be the Substance's knowledge, and "power" must be the Substance's power. Humanity and severity, love and hate, are all like this. In meaning they are distinct, but in reality they belong to one Substance. Moreover, in the beginning, before manifestation, there was only the One, and all the names and designations are only the similative marks of the Substance.

THE SIXTEENTH GLEAM

The Essence as such is denuded of all names and attributes and rid of every relation and attribution. It is qualified by these affairs in respect of Its attentiveness toward the world of manifestation in the First Self-Disclosure, which is that It discloses Itself by Itself to Itself. Then the relations of knowledge, light, existence, and witnessing are realized.

The relation of knowledge entails knowerness and knownness. Light requires manifestness and making manifest. Existence and witnessing issue forth in finding-existence and being-found-in-existence, witnesserness and witnessedness.

In the same way, manifestation, which is a requirement of light, is preceded by nonmanifestation, and nonmanifestation has an essential priority and firstness in relation to manifestation. Thus the names First and Last, Manifest and Nonmanifest are designated.

So also, in the Second Self-Disclosure, and the Third—as far as God wills—the relations and attributions are multiplied. The more the multiplication of the relations and names, the more His manifestation, or rather, His hiddenness. "So glory be to Him who veiled Himself through the loci of His light's manifestation and became manifest by letting down His curtains!"[23]

His hiddenness is in respect of the unmixedness and unboundedness of the Essence, and His manifestation in respect of the loci of manifestation and the entifications.

I said to my rose-cheeked lovely, "O you with bud-like mouth,
    why keep hiding your face like flirting girls?"
She laughed and said, "Unlike the beauties of your world,
    in the curtain I'm seen, but without it I'm hidden."

Your cheek can't be seen without mask,
    your eyes can't be seen without veil.
As long as the sun's fully shining,
    its fountain will never be seen.

When the sun strikes its banner of light on the sphere,
    it dazzles the eyes from afar with its rays.
When it shines from behind a curtain of clouds,
    the gazer can see it without falling short.

CHAPTER 16

Names and Similatives

The Root Substance cannot be named or given similatives. It can only be named and given similatives inasmuch as It faces toward the outward world. In the "First Movement," when It saw by Itself within Itself, there came into being the marks of knowing, seeing, bestowing, and conferring.

In talk of "knowing," there must be a knower and something known. In talk of "seeing," there must be one who sees and something seen. In talk of "bestowing and conferring," there must be a bestower and conferrer, something bestowed and conferred, and a receiver of the bestowal and conferral. Thus, similative marks arise and the names become different.

Manifestation is posterior to hiddenness, so hiddenness is the Root Beginning. If there is the Great Beginning, then there are the names "hidden" and "manifest," "beginning" and "end."

The Second Movement, the Third Movement, and so on, are ceaselessly produced, and the names and marks become inexhaustible. The more secret the hiddenness, the more evident the manifestation; the more splendid the manifestation, the more concealed the hiddenness.[16] Hence it is said, "How mysterious is the Real Lord—by manifesting light He hides Himself, and by letting down curtains He displays Himself!"

The hiddenness speaks of His pervasion and penetration, the manifestation speaks of His issuance and appearance.

THE SEVENTEENTH GLEAM

The First Entification is an unmixed oneness and a sheer receptivity that comprises all receptivities, whether the receptivity for disengagement from all attributes and respects, or the receptivity for being qualified by all.

In respect of disengagement from all respects—even from the receptivity for this disengagement—it is the level of Unity, and to it belong nonmanifestation, firstness, and beginninglessness. In respect of its qualification by all attributes and respects, it is the level of One-and-allness,[24] and to it belong manifestation, lastness,[25] and endlessness.

Some of the respects of the level of One-and-allness are such that the Essence is qualified by them in respect of the level of gathering,[26] whether their precondition be the realization and existence of some of the engendered realities, as with creatorness, providerness, and so on; or not, as with life, knowledge, desire, and so on. These are the "names and attributes" of the Divinity and Lordship. The form of the Essence's knownness while It is clothed in these names and attributes is "the divine realities." The fact that the Manifest of Existence becomes clothed in them does not necessitate the plurality of existence.

Other [respects] are such that the Essence is clothed by them in respect of the engendered levels, like the differentiae, the specificities, and the entifications,[27] which are the features that distinguish the external entities from each other. The forms of the Essence's knownness as clothed in these respects are "the engendered realities."[28] When the Manifest of Existence becomes clothed with their properties and traces, this necessitates the plurality of existence.

Some of these engendered realities—when Existence pervades them through the unity of the gathering of Its tasks and when their traces and properties become manifest through It—have the preparedness to manifest all the divine attributes, with the exception of essential necessity,[29] according to the diversity of the levels of manifestation and in terms of strength and weakness, dominatingness and being dominated over. Such, for example, are the perfect human individuals[30] among the prophets and friends of God. Others have the preparedness to manifest some [attributes] without others, according to the mentioned diversity, and such are the other existents.

CHAPTER 17

The Origin of Transformation

The First Movement is the upright one and the subtle conveyance that embraces and puts together all the ruling[17] conveyances of being and nonbeing.

If we talk only about substance, that is the level of the Only-One. If we talk about substance together with function, that is the level of the First-One. The level of the Only-One is the inward, the origin, and the beginning. The level of the First-One is the outward, the derivative, and the end.

As for the similative marks of the level of the First-One, if we talk about them as the Total Whole, then, facing the things are names of transforming, producing, bestowing, and granting; and not facing the things are names of knowledge, life, power, and act. These are the names of the Real Being's substance and function. The Root Nature clothed in all these names is the known images, which are the principles that are possessed totally by the Real Being. At this time there are as yet no numbers.

If we talk about [these similative marks] as divisions and separations, they are called the "dividing chapters," the "individual truths," the "manifestations," and the "revealings," all of which are the mutually divided images of the external things. The Root Nature clothed in all these similatives is the known images that are the principles possessed by each thing's being. Now there are numbers for the first time.

All the principles that are possessed by each thing's being are obtained when the Real Being pervades and goes into the midst of the things, after which It is capable of manifesting and revealing all the ruling traces. Those who obtain these completely are the sages and worthies. Those who obtain these partially are all the ignorant people and the ten thousand things.

Through the unity of the gathering of Its divine and engendered tasks, the Presence of the Essence pervades and discloses Itself beginninglessly and endlessly in all these realities, which are the differentiations of the level of the One-and-allness—whether in the world of spirits, the world of images, or the world of sensation and the witnessed; whether in this world or the last world.[31]

The goal of all this is the realization and manifestation of the "Name-derived Perfection," which is the perfection of disclosure and seeing disclosure. "The perfection of disclosure" means His manifestation in terms of these respects. "The perfection of seeing disclosure" means His witnessing Himself in terms of these same respects.[32] These are a manifestation and a witnessing that are plainly viewed and in entity, like the manifestation and witnessing of the undifferentiated within the differentiated.

In contrast, the "Essential Perfection" is the Essence's manifestation to Its own Self within Its own Self for the sake of Its own Self without respect to other and otherness. It is a manifestation that is knowledged and absent, like the manifestation of the differentiated within the undifferentiated.

"Unbounded wealth" is required by the Essential Perfection. The meaning of unbounded wealth is that the tasks, states, and respects of the Essence as well as their properties and requirements—all of which appear in the levels of the divine and engendered realities—are witnessed by and fixed for the Essence in a universal, undifferentiated mode within Its own nonmanifestation by the inclusion of all within Its oneness, along with all their forms and properties as they have become manifest and will become manifest, fixed, and witnessed in the levels.[33] In this regard, the Essence is wealthy beyond all the existent things, just as God has said: "Surely God is wealthy beyond the worlds" [29:6].

The skirt of Love's wealth is pure, pure,
    of the stain of need for a handful of dust.
Disclosers and gazers are all Itself—
    if we not be in the midst, what harm will be done?

Every task and attribute of the Real Being
    is known and realized in Himself.
In the midst of the bounded things in need of themselves,
    His wealth is unbounded by seeing them.

The Necessary is wealthy beyond the existence of good and evil,
    the One is wealthy beyond the levels of the numbers.
Since He sees them all within Himself eternally,
    He is wealthy beyond seeing them outside of Himself.

The Only-One's Root Nature, together with lordness, thingness, and all the subtle functions of the beginning and the end, always displays Itself in and pervades throughout the ten thousand principles that are possessed by the level of the First-One—whether it be in the world of nature or the world of images, the world of color or the world of the colorless, this world or the next world.

Thus, all are nothing but the reality and fulfillment of the completeness of the Real Being's names. This is the level of "the manifesting transformation," and it is the transformation of the Total Whole within dividing separativeness.

As for the completeness of the Real Being's Root Nature, in it there is no division between the things and the "I"; Self is for Self, manifesting Self in Self. This is the level of "the silent transformation," and it is the transformation of dividing separativeness within the Total Whole.

This is the root power and immeasurable wealth of the real completeness. All the root affairs and encounters of the world, all the similative marks, and all the manifesting transformations of the necessary, ruling patterns of all the levels of lordness and thingness—all are as a unified image put together in the One. Likewise, the ruling images that are revealed and seen have already been seen in totality within the Root Nature. This is a wealth beyond the ten thousand beings. The Classic says, "Only the Real Lord is wealthy beyond the ten thousand worlds."

THE EIGHTEENTH GLEAM

When you eliminate the individuations and entifications of the individuals of all species included under animal, the individuals of each species are gathered under the "species." When you eliminate the distinguishing features of those species—that is, the differentiae and the specificities—all are gathered under the reality of "animal." When you eliminate the distinguishing features of animal and everything included along with it under growing body, all are gathered in "growing body."

When you eliminate the distinguishing features of the growing body and everything included along with it under body, then all are gathered in the reality of "body." When you eliminate the distinguishing features of body and everything included along with it—I mean intellects and souls—under substance, all are gathered under the reality of "substance." When you eliminate that through which substance and accident become distinguished, all are gathered under the reality of "possible thing."

CHAPTER 18

The Total Order

When there is Real Being, there is real knowledge. When there is real knowledge, there is real power. Knowledge and power are the function of the Substance, and they put forth acting and making. After the putting forth of acting and making, principle and vital-energy become divided. After the division of principle and vital-energy, the forms and images are revealed. After the forms and images are revealed, growth and nourishment take form. After growth and nourishment take form, spirit and life are produced. Then the kinds of things become discriminated one from another and the classes of things are divided according to the name. The names and guises depend upon each other, but these are not true things. There is only the Real Being, which by Itself manifests all Its root affairs first on the level of knowledge, which is the total container of the Principle. Then, on the level of power, the images are revealed dividedly and become the external things. The external things all depend on the names and guises of the Real Being. Spirit and life depend on growth and nourishment, growth and nourishment depend on form's disposition, form's disposition depends on vital-energy, vital-energy depends on the Principle, and the Principle is the subtle container of the Real Being's knowledge and power.

If you remove the names and guises that divide and distinguish all spirit and life, all are nothing but growing and nourishing bodies.

In the same way, if you remove the names and guises that divide and distinguish all growing and nourishing bodies, all are nothing but one disposition of vital-energy. If you remove the names and guises that divide and distinguish all the dispositions of vital-energy, all are nothing but one principle.

When you eliminate that through which the Necessary and the possible become distinguished, both are gathered under the reality of the Unbounded Existent. This is the same as the Reality of Existence. It exists through Its own Essence, not through an existence added to Its own Essence. "Necessity" is the attribute of Its manifest, and "possibility" is the attribute of Its nonmanifest. [By possibility] I mean the "fixed entities" that are obtained when He discloses Himself to Himself clothed in His own tasks. These distinguishing features—whether the differentiae and specificities or the entifications and individuations—are all "divine tasks" that are included and contained in the Oneness of the Essence. First, at the level of knowledge, these features come forth in the form of the fixed entities, and second, at the level of the eye,[34] they take on the form of the external entities by being clothed in the [fixed entities'] properties and traces through the Manifest of Existence, which is the locus of disclosure and the mirror for the Nonmanifest of Existence.

Hence there is nothing in the external domain except One Reality which, by means of becoming clothed in the tasks and the attributes, appears multiple and plural to those who are imprisoned in the confines of the levels and bound by their properties and traces.

For my lesson I took all of engendered existence
    and reviewed it page after page.
In truth, I saw nothing there and read nothing
    but the Real's Essence and the Real's essential tasks.

How long this talk of bodies, dimensions, directions?
    Until when this discussion of minerals, animals, plants?
Only one Essence is realized—not "essences."
    This illusory manyness comes from the tasks and the
        attributes.

In the same way, if you remove the names and guises that divide and distinguish all the principles of the things, all are nothing but the knowledge and power of the one Real Being. Again, if you remove the names and guises that divide and distinguish all knowledge and power, all are nothing but the one root nature of the Real, Perfect Penetration.

This is the Only-One, the Real Being, but the manifest names and guises are not the same. Those who see narrowly do not reach what is the Root, and thus they think that the Lord is outside the things. The fact is that the Lord delimits Himself through the ten thousand things.

THE NINETEENTH GLEAM

What is meant by the "inclusion of the manyness of the tasks in the oneness of the Essence" is not the inclusion of the part in the whole, nor the inclusion of the contained in the container. Rather, what is meant is the inclusion of the descriptions and the requirements in the described thing and the requirer, like the inclusion of one-halfness, one-thirdness, one-fourthness, one-fifthness, ad infinitum, in the essence of the numerical one. After all, these relations are included within it and have no manifestation whatsoever so long as it does not become part of two, three, four, and five through repetition of manifestation in the levels.[35]

From this it is known that the Real's encompassment of all existents is like the requirer's encompassment of the requirements, not like the whole's encompassment of the part, nor the container's of the contained. High indeed is God beyond what is not appropriate for the precinct of His holiness!

> The task's inclusion in the Real's Essence is well-known.
> The task is like a description, and the Real's Essence is described.
> Learn this rule, for where God is
> there is neither part nor whole, container nor contained.

CHAPTER 19

The Subtle Container

The manyness of the affairs contained in the One Substance is not like a part contained in a whole, nor like water contained in a container. Rather, it is the substance's containment of the function and the requirer's containment of the required. For example, one is one-half of two, one-third of three, one-fourth of four, and so on, to one part of one hundred thousand billion. All these are contained in the root nature of "one," and "one" has beforehand the power to be the principle of one part of all numbers. However, as long as the various numbers are not added, its power will never become manifest. This is also like the power of giving light, keeping warm, and cooking food that are contained in fire. The fire possesses from beforehand all these powers, but as long as it does not encounter various things, these do not become manifest.

Because of this we know that the Real Substance embraces the ten thousand beings just as the requirer embraces the required—not as the whole embraces the parts, nor as a container preserves water.

THE TWENTIETH GLEAM

The manifestation and hiddenness of the tasks and respects is because they do or do not become clothed in the Manifest of Existence, but this does not necessitate the alteration of the Reality of Existence and Its true attributes. Rather, the relations and attributions are built on change, but this does not entail change in the Essence. If Amr should stand up on Zayd's right hand and sit down at his left hand, Zayd's relation with him becomes different, but his essence and true attributes are still established.

In the same way, the Reality of Existence does not increase in perfection by becoming clothed in eminent affairs, nor does It accept deficiency by becoming manifest in base loci of manifestation. Although sunlight shines on the pure and the filthy, no alteration finds the way to the simplicity of its luminosity—it gains no fragrance from musk, no color from roses, no shame from thorns, and no blame from stones.[36]

> When the sun adorns the world with its radiance,
> well does it shine on pure and on filthy.
> No filth leaves a stain on its light,
> and nothing pure increases its purity.

CHAPTER 20

Change and Alteration

All the similative marks of the Root Affair undergo change and alteration according to the hiding and revealing of the external images, but this change and alteration of the similative marks cannot change and alter the substance and function of the Reality-Principle. The similative marks' change and alteration occurs in nonbeing and has nothing to do with the Root Substance. If A is sitting on the right side of B, then stands up and sits on the left side of B, the similative marks of A and B change and alter, but the substance and function of the root nature of A and B remain as they were.

When the Real Being clothes Itself with noble things, It does not increase in benefit, and when It is revealed in mean things, It does not increase in loss. Sunlight shines everywhere, but it is not touched by the smell of musk, nor does it receive the color of flowers, nor is it destroyed by a sword.

THE TWENTY-FIRST GLEAM

The Unbounded is never without the bounded, and the bounded does not take form without the Unbounded. However, the bounded has need for the Unbounded, and the Unbounded is independent of the bounded. Hence requiring is from both sides, but need is from one side. This is like the movement of a hand and the movement of a key in the hand.

O You in whose holy sanctum none has any place,
    the world appears from You, but You do not appear.
We and You will never be separate,
    but we need You, and You don't need us.

Moreover, the Unbounded requires any of the bounded things by way of substitution. It does not require a specific bounded thing. But since the Unbounded has no substitute, the qibla of every bounded thing's need is He, none other.

Nearness to You can't be found through causes and occasions,
    it can't be found without the beginningless bounty.
Whoever it may be, a substitute can be taken.
    You have no substitute, so Your substitute can't be found.

O You whose elevated Essence is neither substance nor accident,
    whose bounty and generosity are not motivated by
        purpose.
No matter who may not be there, You can replace him,
    but if someone does not have You, none can replace You.

CHAPTER 21

Penetration and Obstruction (1)

Penetration does not reveal Itself without obstruction, and obstruction does not assume form without penetration. However, obstruction necessarily seeks penetration, whereas penetration does not seek obstruction. Thus, the demand is from both sides, but the seeking is from one side, like the meaning of a hand's movement and a fan's movement.

Moreover, penetration demands obstruction by way of alteration and change; it does not demand a specific obstruction. At root, penetration does not alter or change, so the ten thousand obstructed things seek penetration specifically, nothing else.

The Unbounded's lack of need for the bounded is in respect of the Essence. Otherwise, it is impossible for there to be the manifestation of the names of Divinity and the realization of the relations of Lordship without the bounded.

O You whose beauty has incited my yearning and seeking,
Your soughtness is a branch of my seeking!
If not for the mirror of my loverness,
the beauty of Your Belovedness would not have appeared.

No, rather the lover is the Real and the beloved He, the seeker is the Real and the sought He. He is the Sought and the Beloved in the station of Unity's gathering, and the seeker and the lover in the level of differentiation and manyness.

O You toward whom no one journeys but You,
neither mosque nor monastery is empty of You!
I saw all the seekers and everything sought—
all are You, with no one else in the midst.

CHAPTER 22

Penetration and Obstruction (2)

If we talk about substance, penetration does not seek obstruction. However, if we talk about function, it certainly demands obstruction. Without obstruction, the names of the Real Substance and the affairs of the Real Function cannot be presented and disclosed. Obstruction is penetration, that is, the manifestation of penetration.

Therefore, it is said that the obstructer is the Real and the obstructed is also the Real; the seeker is the Real, and the sought is also the Real. The sought and the obstructed are at the level of the Total One, but the seeker and the obstructer are in the site of separation and division.

THE TWENTY-SECOND GLEAM

The "reality" of each thing is the entification of Existence within the Presence of Knowledge in respect of the task of which the thing is the locus of manifestation; or, it is Existence Itself, entified by that task in that Presence.

The "existent things" consist of the entifications of Existence in respect of the coloration of the Manifest of Existence by the traces and properties of the things' realities; or, [they are] Existence Itself entified by these very respects such that the realities remain always hidden in the Nonmanifest of Existence, while their properties and traces are apparent in the Manifest of Existence. After all, the vanishment of the knowledged forms from the Nonmanifest of Existence is absurd, or else ignorance would be required—high indeed is God beyond that![37]

> We are the modes and respects of Existence
> and occur for the Essence of Existence outside
> and inside knowledge.
> We are curtained by the veil of nonbeing's darkness,
> our reflections manifest in the mirror of Existence.

So, in terms of reality and existence, each thing is either entified Existence; or it is the entification that has occurred for Existence, and the entification is the entified thing's attribute. Although in respect of the concept, "attribute" is other than "object to which it is attributed," in respect of existence, they are the same. A disparity in terms of concept and a unification in terms of existence necessitate the soundness of the predication.[38]

> Neighbor, companion, fellow voyager—all are He.
> In beggar's rags, in king's satin—all are He.
> In the banquet of dispersion and the private hall of gathering,
> all are He, by God—by God, all are He![39]

CHAPTER 23

The Principle of the Images

The "principle" of all things is the Real Being's knowledge and the movement of a similative of Its root affair; or, it is the root of the Real Being by Itself in the midst of knowledge, moving as a similative of the real, root affair.

The "form" of everything is the outward of the Real Being and the ruling images of all the principles, which become manifest; or, it is the root of the Real Being, which itself is manifest clothed with those ruling images. What we call "principle" is the subtle within knowledge, and what we call "form" is the revealed through power. Knowledge and power are the functions of the Real Being. If the function is discussed as real and as reality, it is the substance.

Hence, all that is called a "thing" can be said to be dependent upon the Real Being, or it can be said to be the movement of the Real Being. We can also say that it is the root of the Real Being. The meanings of the reality are different, but they belong to the one reality. This is why the Origin is at once divided and unified.

THE TWENTY-THIRD GLEAM

Although the reality of Existence is asserted and predicated for all mental and external existents, it has disparate levels, some above others. In each level it has specific names, attributes, relations, and respects that are not in the other levels, such as the level of Divinity and Lordship, or the level of servanthood and creatureliness.

So, for example, ascribing the names of the Divine Level—such as Allah, All-Merciful, and so on—to the engendered level is the same as unbelief and nothing but heresy. In the same way, ascribing to the Divine Level names that are specific to the engendered level is extreme misguidance and utmost abandonment.

O you who suppose you're a realized master,
a man truthful in sincerity and certainty!
Each level of existence has a property—
if you don't preserve the levels, you're a heretic.

CHAPTER 24

The Allotment of the Names

Although the Real Being can be explained in the ten thousand kinds of secret and manifest things, the levels and orders are not the same, and their classes and degrees should not be disturbed. This is because each level has a specific and unique name and designation. The similative marks are different in the distinct levels, like the level of Lord-rulerness and the level of thingness.

If the names unique to the level of Lordness—like An-la and the designation of the universal compassion— are mentioned in the level of the ten thousand things, this is the utmost degree of perverse rebellion. If the names unique to the level of thingness are mentioned in the level of Lordness, this is the ultimate perplexity and confusion.

THE TWENTY-FOURTH GLEAM

The True Existent is not more than one. It is the same as Real Existence and Unbounded Being. However, It has many levels.[40]

First is the level of nonentification, nonconfinement, and unboundedness by any binding or respect. In this regard, It is incomparable with the attribution of descriptions and attributes and hallowed beyond the denotation of words and phrases. Tradition has no tongue to express Its majesty, and intellect has no possibility of alluding to Its inmost perfection. The lords of unveiling are veiled from perceiving Its reality, and the masters of knowledge are agitated at the impossibility of knowing It. The extreme limit of Its sign is signlessness, and the utmost end of Its gnosis is bewilderment.

O You in whom explication and plain viewing are nothing,
 the fancy of all certainties and suppositions nothing!
No sign whatsoever can be given of Your Essence—
 there where You are, all signs are nothing.

The gnostic's soul may well be aware,
 but how does he enter Your holy sanctum?
The hands of unveiling's folk and witnessing's lords
 fall short of the skirt of perceiving You.

That Love which is our inseparable part—
 far be it from It to be perceived by intellect!
Happy the moment when certainty dawns from Its light,
 freeing us from darkness and all of our doubt!

The second level is His entification by an entification that comprehends all the active, necessary, divine entifications and all the passive, possible, engendered entifications. This level is named the "First Entification" because it is the first of the entifications of Existence's Reality. Above it is the level of Nonentification, nothing else.

The third level is the unity of the gathering of all the active, trace-inducing entifications. This is the level of Divinity.

CHAPTER 25

The Real Level

The Real Being is only one, not many. It is the True Being and the Perfectly Penetrating Being. It has many levels.

The first level is the level of Non-Movement, which is the subtle penetration without any obstruction. It has nothing to do with similative marks, nor does It reveal Itself in sound and hearing. The man of ears and eyes has no place to use his hearing and clarity, and the man of wisdom and wakefulness has no place to turn his spiritual insight. It is the Great Function with total completeness. Wanting to search out Its concealment, the man of clarity becomes perplexed, and wanting to penetrate Its meaning, the man of speech becomes dumb. It has no trace to be followed and no principle of meaning to be examined.

The second level is Its movement. This movement embraces all the necessary movements of Lordness and all the powerful movements of thingness. This level is called the "First Movement," because the true principle of the Real Being is the beginning of the ten thousand movements. Above it is the level of Non-Movement, nothing else.

The third level is the true Only-One, embracing and putting together all the movements of the root act's bestowal of traces. This is the level of Lordness.

The fourth level is the differentiation of the level of Divinity. This is the level of the names and their Presences.

The respect of these two levels is in regard to the Manifest of Existence, whose specific description is Necessity.[41]

The fifth level is the unity of the gathering of all the passive entifications, whose task is accepting traces and being passive. This is the engendered, possible level.

The sixth level is the engendered level's differentiation, which is the level of the cosmos.

The occurrence of these two levels is in respect of the Manifest of Knowledge, one of whose requirements is possibility. It is His disclosure of Himself to Himself in the forms of the realities and entities of the possible things.

So, in reality, Existence is not more than one. It pervades all these levels and all the realities ordered within them. Within these levels and realities, It is the same as these levels and realities. So also, within It, these levels and realities were the same as It, since "God was, and nothing was with Him."[42]

> Being manifests Itself in everything,
> and if you want to keep track of Its state in each,
> Go, look at the bubbles on top of the wine, how
> the wine is they in them, and they are wine in the wine.

> On the tablet of nonexistence, the gleams of Eternity's light
> gleamed forth, but of the confidants of this secret,
> none is like Adam.
> Don't count the Real as apart from the world, for
> the world is in the Real, and in the world the Real
> is none but the world.

The fourth level is the level of the dividing separativeness of the level of Lordness. This is the level of the manifestation of the names and designations of all the root act's movements.

These two levels act as "the outward of the Real Being." What we call "the necessary rulings of the Real Principle" are specific to this station of the division.

The fifth level is the Only-One that embraces and puts together all the movements of the powerful acts. This is the principle of all beings, following the level of Lordness, and it sees by itself for itself. This is the level of the powerful act and thingness.

The sixth level is the level of the dividing separativeness of the level of thingness, that is, the world.

What is manifested by these two levels is called "the external surface"; the pivot of ceaseless production is the necessary way. In this level the Real Being becomes clothed in the images of all the principles and forms of the ten thousand things, and It manifests and transforms in self-doing.

In sum, Its reality does not coexist with the manyness of the things. There is only One Real, which pervades and goes into the levels and orders of the inward and outward of the ten thousand beings. When existing in the principles of all the images, this One Real is the same as the principles of all the images. So also, when the principles of all the images exist in the Real Being, they are the same as the Real Being. "At origin the Real Lord does not share with anything."

It is also said, "If you want to discriminate the Real from the things, you should look at water and waves."

You should not say that the Real and the world were separate before the time of A-tan. Apart from the world, it is not possible to talk about the Real.

> When the world is in the Real,
> it is this very Real,
> and when the Real is in the world,
> It is not other than the world.

THE TWENTY-FIFTH GLEAM

The "Reality of Realities," which is the Divine Essence—high indeed is Its task!—is the reality of all things. Within the limit of Its own Essence, It is a One to which number has no path. However, in respect of the multiple self-disclosures and plural entifications in the levels, now It is the substantial, subordinating realities, and now the accidental, subordinate realities.

So, One Essence is shown as multiple substances and accidents by means of the plural attributes. In regard to the Reality, It is a one that is not plural or multiple in any way.

> O you who have not scratched out the letters of this and that,
> fancying twoness is proof of His distance and anger.
> Without remiss and error, know that in all engendered things,
> there is One Entity alone—only One Essence.

In regard to disengagement from and unboundedness by the mentioned entifications and bindings, this One Entity is the Real. In regard to the plurality and multiplicity that appear because of Its being clothed in the entifications, It is the creatures and the cosmos. So, the cosmos is the manifest of the Real, and the Real is the nonmanifest of the cosmos.[43] Before manifestation, the cosmos was the same as the Real, and after manifestation, the Real is the same as the cosmos. It is one Reality, and manifestation and nonmanifestation, firstness and lastness, are its relations and respects. "He is the First and the Last and the Manifest and the Nonmanifest" [57:3].

> The lovers' bandit in the shape of the fair is the Real.
> No—plainly viewed on all horizons is the Real.
> That which is the world in regard to binding,
> in unboundedness, by God, that itself is the Real.

> When the Real becomes plain through the differentiations of the tasks,
> the world comes to be witnessed, full of gain and loss.
> If the world and the worldlings go back to undifferentiation,
> then the Real will come into the midst.

CHAPTER 26

The Reality of the Things

The "principle" of the ten thousand beings is the Real Being's Root Nature. This means that when the reality-principle of the ten thousand beings is in the site of the Root Nature, in reality it is One Substance concerning which "two" and "nonbeing" must not be said. However, in discussing various levels and orders, there is a manyness of issuances and appearances. At one moment there is the principle of perfect concealment and hiddenness, at another moment the principle of continuous manifestation and revelation.

There is One Substance, yet all the images of concealment and secretness and of manifestation and revelation are seen as many. In its reality and origin, it is never many, for there is nothing but One Substance.

In discussion of perfect penetration and self-existence, this One Substance has no relation whatsoever to any of the manifesting obstructions, for It is the Real. In discussion of the manifesting obstructions, It becomes many, for It is the things. The world is the outward of the Real, and the Real is the inward of the world. Before manifestation, the world was that very Real, and after manifestation the Real is the world. A sage said, "Great indeed is the Real Lord—when He is hidden, His name is 'Real,' and when He is manifest, His name is 'things.'" In reality, He is one principle. Outward and inward, beginning and end, are all His similative marks. A wise man said, "The ten thousand images are not constant. Endlessly being born and at rest, sometimes they are the revolving and changing of the ruling images, sometimes the coming and going of the Real Being. All are with the Substance, but all pass away, and none that perish rise again."

THE TWENTY-SIXTH GLEAM

In the Bezel of Shu'ayb [chapter twelve of the *Fuṣūṣ al-ḥikam*] the Shaykh [Ibn al-'Arabī] says that the cosmos consists of accidents gathered together in the One Entity, which is the reality of Being. It undergoes change and renewal at every breath and every instant. At every instant a world goes to nonexistence and its likeness comes into existence, but most of the world's folk are heedless of this meaning, just as God has said: "No indeed, but they are uncertain of a new creation" [50:15].

Among the lords of theory, no one became informed of this meaning except the Ash'arites in regard to those parts of the cosmos that are the accidents, for they said, "The accident does not subsist for two moments;" and the Husbanids, who are known as the "Sophists," concerning all the parts of cosmos, whether substances or accidents. But each group was mistaken in a certain mode.[44]

As for the Ash'arites, [they were mistaken] because they affirmed plural substances apart from the reality of Existence and held that the changing, renewing accidents endured through them. They did not know that the cosmos in all its parts is nothing but accidents undergoing renewal and change at every breath and gathered together in the One Entity. At each instant, they disappear from this Entity, and their likenesses are clothed by It. Hence, the one who gazes falls into error by means of the succession of the likenesses. He fancies that the affair is one and continuous. Thus the Ash'arites say that the likenesses succeed one another in the accident's locus, without any instant being empty of an individual accident similar to the first individual. So the gazer supposes that it is one continuous affair.

An ocean, not decreasing, not increasing,
    waves going, waves coming—
Since the world is made up of waves,
    it never lasts for two moments, or rather, two instants.

The world—if you can take a lesson—
    is an appearance that flows in overtaking stages.
Within all the stages of the flowing appearance
    is a mystery—the pervading Reality of Realities.

As for the error of the Sophists, it is that, despite their saying that constant alteration fills the whole cosmos, they did not become alert to the fact that the One Reality is clothed in the forms and accidents of the

CHAPTER 27

The World

A former worthy said that the world is a collectedness that collects all the manifesting images and gathers and assembles them in the root nature of the Real One. Moreover, the alteration, change, and ceaseless production of the world accords with the pervading and the going, the ebb and the flow, of vital-energy. In a moment it perishes and in a moment it arises; one world perishes and another world is produced, but the multitude do not grasp this meaning.

The poet was caught up with images and lost the principle, and the arithmetician disregarded the principle and became involved with emptiness.[18]

The poet sought after the principle outside the Real Principle. He said, "The principles are in numbers. The images of alteration, change, and ceaseless production depend upon these principles and are established through them." He did not know that all is of One Root, and that the world and the ten thousand things are only the complexity of the names and images. In accordance with vital-energy's number, they change and become new, but originally they are gathered together in One Root. However, this One Root's hiding and revealing are not perpetual. At one moment it becomes manifest in this image, at another moment it appears in that image. The onlooker sees that the ruling images revolve and flow and that what is seen later and what was seen before are similar in form and pattern. So, he finally comes to suppose that this is one perpetual affair.

cosmos and comes to appear as entified and plural existents. It has no manifestation in the engendered levels save through these forms and accidents, just as these have no existence in the external world without It.

> The Sophists, who know nothing of intelligence,
> say that the world is a passing image.
> Yes, the world is all image, but
> within it a Reality discloses Itself eternally.

As for the lords of unveiling and witnessing, they see that the Presence of the Real discloses Itself at each breath with another self-disclosure and that there is no repetition at all in Its self-disclosure. In other words, It does not disclose Itself at two instants through one entification and one task. Rather, at each breath It becomes manifest through another entification, and at each instant It discloses Itself in another task.

> Being, which is not seen plainly in one task for two instants,
> at every instant discloses Itself in another task.
> Search for this point in "Each day [He is] upon some task" [55:29]
> if you need proof from the Speech of the Real.

The secret in this is that the Presence of the Real has contrary names, some of gentleness and some of subjugation.[45] All are perpetually at work, and ineffectuality is not permitted for any of them.[46] Hence, when one of the possible realities is prepared for existence because of the obtainment of the preconditions and the elimination of the impediments, the all-merciful mercy[47] grasps it and effuses existence upon it. Then the Manifest of Existence, by mean of becoming clothed in this reality's traces and properties, entifies Itself in a specific entification and discloses Itself in terms of this entification. After that It is stripped of the entification because of the subjugation of True Unity, which entails the dissolution of the entifications and traces of the formal manyness.[48] At the very instant of stripping, because of what is entailed by the all-merciful mercy, It becomes entified with another specific entification that is similar to the previous entification. At the second instant It is dissolved by Unity's subjugation, and another entification is obtained through the all-merciful mercy. So it continues, as long as God wills. Hence, in no two instants does self-disclosure occur through one entification.

At each instant a world goes to nonexistence and another like it comes to exist. However, those who are veiled, because of the succession of likenesses and the mutual correspondence of the states, fancy that the

Although the arithmetician talked about the alteration and change of the world, it was not clear to him that the Reality is that of the One Real and that, by becoming clothed in the forms and images of the world and the ten thousand beings, It manifests and transforms. Without forms and images, It does not manifest and transform, and all the forms and images are in reality the outward of the Real Being. To say that the forms and images are the outward of the Real Being means that the Real Being is the inward of the forms and images. However, he did not wake up to this and was mistaken, for he said that the world is void and empty because illusory considerations give rise to images.

The poet did not arrive and the arithmetician went too far. Only those who are with the real discernment see luminously that the Imperial Majesty of the One Real appears at every breath, and Its appearance is never repeated. In two moments It does not appear in one affair, and in two affairs It does not appear at one moment. At this moment It appears in this affair, at that moment It appears in that affair. These are not the same and they do not coexist.

In this, there is a concealed meaning. The Real Lord has names of opposition. Some are names of humanity, and some are names of severity.[19] They always exist together and they do not harm [each other's] deeds. When humanity moves, a thing is produced, and when severity moves, a thing perishes. Neither production nor perishing is eternal. Therefore it is said that whatever becomes manifest is in utmost difference, and it never happens that it becomes manifest with one particular movement in several moments.

As soon as one world perishes, a different world that is similar to it is produced accordingly. Those who are covered with a veil see the ten thousand images revolving and pervading and the four seasons changing in transition, and they finally suppose that the being of the world exists as a whole in one moment and that the order of the four seasons always exists according to one pulse.

world's existence stays in one state and, over consecutive times, has one manner.

> Glory be to God! What a marvelous loving God,
> embracing bounty, generosity, mercy, and munificence!
> At every breath He takes a world to nonexistence,
> and in that very moment He brings another like it.

> God it is who gives every sort of gift,
> but each of His names gives a gift apart.
> To the world's reality at every instant
> one name gives annihilation, another subsistence.

The proof that the cosmos is the totality of accidents gathered together in the One Entity, which is the Reality of Existence, is that, as much as the realities of the existents are defined, nothing becomes manifest in their definitions but accidents. For example, it is said, "The human is a rationally-speaking animal." "Animal" is a growing, sensate body, moving by volition. "Body" is a substance receptive to the three dimensions. "Substance" is an existent that is not in a substrate. "Existent" is an essence that has been realized and obtained.

Everything mentioned in these definitions pertains to accidents, except for the indeterminate essence that is regarded in these concepts.

Thus the meaning of "rationally-speaking" is an essence that has rational speech, the meaning of "growing" is an essence that has growth, and so on with the rest. This indeterminate essence is identical with the

They do not know that the world is the root nature of the Real One. The images that are gathered together and assembled within it can never be portrayed along with the principles of the ten thousand things. Even if you want to portray them, you can portray nothing but their images. For example, if we try to portray the human being, we say, "The human being is a living thing with the power of speech." A "living" thing is simply a disposition that has the power of awareness and movement and the power of growth and nourishment. "Disposition" is simply a vital-energy that receives various forms, vessels, congealings, and combinations. "Vital-energy" is simply a principle that becomes manifest from the bestowed mandate of the Real Being.

All are portrayed like this, and they are simply names and images, except for the substance of the undifferentiated nature within all the names and images. Those who reach the final stage cannot portray it with names and images.

Real Existence and True Being that endures by Itself and makes these accidents endure.

The lords of theory say that concepts like this are not differentiae. Rather, they are requirements of differentiae that are given expression as "differentiae" because the differentiae's realities cannot be expressed as distinct from others except through these requirements, or through requirements that would be even more hidden. But this is a prohibited premise and an unacceptable speech. Supposing we grant it, then, when something is essential for substance, it would be accidental in relation to the One Entity. Although it would be within the reality of substance, it would be outside the One Entity while enduring by It.

The claim that there is here a substantial something beyond the One Entity is in the furthest limit of nullity, especially when the lords of the Reality's unveiling—which is lit from the candle-niche of prophecy—bear witness in contradiction, and the opponent is unable to offer any proof. "And God speaks the truth, and He guides on the path" [33:4].

Don't seek to realize the meanings from the expressions,
    don't seek without lifting the bindings and respects.
If you want to find *Healing* from the disease of ignorance,
    don't seek *The Canon* of *Deliverance* from *The Allusions*.[49]

You are content with stopping at *The Stopping Places*—
    aiming for *The Goals* has kept you from the goal.
If you don't remove the veils, you will never find
    the lights of Reality rising from *The Rising Places*.[50]

Strive to lift the veils, not to gather books—
    if you gather books, you'll never lift the veils.
How can love appear from the folds of your books?
    Fold them up, turn to God, and repent!

Thus, when we say "the power of speech," this means a substance that necessarily has the power of speech; "growth and nourishment" means a substance that necessarily has the power of growth and nourishment. When we remove the names and images of the power of speech and of growth and nourishment, this is the substance of undifferentiated nature. This substance of undifferentiated nature is the very substance of the Real Being, the True Being. It stands by Itself and makes all images stand.

THE TWENTY-SEVENTH GLEAM[51]

The greatest veil and the densest mask over the beauty of the true Oneness is the essential bindings and plurality that occur in the Manifest of Existence by means of Its becoming clothed in the properties and traces of the entities fixed in the Presence of Knowledge, which is the Nonmanifest of Existence.

It appears to those who are veiled that the entities have become existent in the external world. In fact, no aroma of external existence has reached their nostrils; they have always been and will always be in their root nonexistence.[52] What is existent and witnessed is the Reality of Existence, but in respect of being clothed in the properties and traces of the entities, not in regard to being disengaged from them, because in this regard, nonmanifestation and hiddenness are Its requirements. Thus, in reality, the Reality of Existence remains in Its true Oneness as It was without beginning and as It will be without end. However, because of being veiled by the form of manyness's properties and traces, It comes forth in the view of the "others" as bound and entified and appears as plural and multiple.

Existence is an ocean, its waves eternal—
    of it the world's folk have seen only waves.
Look at the waves coming from the inside of the ocean
    to the outside, the ocean hidden within.

Gaze on the world, the divine secret hidden—
    like the water of life, hidden in darkness.
Swarms of fish appear from the sea,
    the ocean hidden by the swarming fish.

CHAPTER 28

Images and Similatives

The greatest and thickest veil over the Real One's beautiful face is the Root Nature's displayed obstructions and manifest numbers. By clothing various forms and images, the Root Being displays the traces of forms and colors on Its external surface.

Those who are separated by the veil think that all the forms and images have become external things. They do not know that the external things have not yet taken form and always remain in the Non-Ultimate, and each one of them is fully complete and presently disclosed in the Root Nature. What is gained and seen at present is nothing but the Real Being. The Real Being is only one, and from the beginning to the end, It is as It is. The sight and hearing of the blind and dumb are nothing but blockage, obstruction, and manyness.

> The old ocean gives birth to new waves—
> seeing the waves, you don't see the ocean.
> The ocean is hidden inside the waves,
> but the waves are manifest outside the ocean.

THE TWENTY-EIGHTH GLEAM

Whenever something appears within something else, the manifest is other than the locus of manifestation. In other words, the manifest is one thing, and the locus of manifestation is another. Moreover, what appears from the manifest in the locus of manifestation is the semblance and form, not the essence and reality. This is not so, however, for the Real Existence and Unbounded Being. Wherever It is manifest, It is identical with the loci of manifestation, and in all the loci of manifestation, It is manifest through Its Essence.

They say that the mirror-like heart is wonderful.
See within it the faces of your beloveds—wonderful!
No one wonders at the beloved's face in mirrors.
To be oneself both beloved and mirror—
that is wonderful!

O You whose form has given mirrors all their luster,
without Your form no mirror has ever been seen.
No, no—all the mirrors show Your Self
in Its subtlety, not Your form.

THE TWENTY-NINTH GLEAM

The Reality of Being, along with all the tasks, attributes, relations, and respects that are the realities of all the existents, pervades the reality of each existent. This is why it has been said, "Everything is in everything." The author of the *Gulshan-i rāz* says,

Split the heart of a single drop—
out will come a hundred pure oceans.[53]

Being is the Essence of the Exalted God—
all things are in It, It too within all things.
This is the explanation of the gnostic's saying,
"Everything is included in everything."

CHAPTER 29

Manifestation

Whenever the world manifests the shape of a form for the first time, what becomes manifest is not the site of manifestation. What becomes manifest is one thing, the site of manifestation something else. Moreover, what becomes manifest is a form and a shadow, not the true substance. Water and mirrors are like this. Only the Root of the Real Being's perfect penetration is not like this. What becomes manifest is the same as the site of manifestation. Everything manifest in the sites of manifestation is the Root Substance.

CHAPTER 30

The Principle

One Principle possesses all and contains the ten thousand principles. The ten thousand principles are gathered together and contained by the one Principle. Therefore it has been said, "In each of the ten thousand things, there are the ten thousand principles."[20]

A worthy said, "If you open the heart of one drop, a hundred rivers flow out evenly."

THE THIRTIETH GLEAM

Every power and act that emerges in the manifest from the loci of manifestation is in reality manifest from the Real manifest within those loci of manifestation, not from the loci themselves. In "The Wisdom of the High," the Shaykh says, "The entity has no act. Rather, the act belongs to its Lord within it. So the entity is at peace from the attribution of any act to it."[54]

Hence, power and act are attributed to the servants from the direction of the Real's manifestation in their form, not from the direction of their souls. Read "And God created you and what you do" [37:96], and know that your existence, power, and act come from the Presence of the Howless.

From us are sought only incapacity and nonbeing—
being and its subordinates are all held back.
It is He who appears in our form—
that is why power and act are ascribed to us.

Since your essence is negated, O man of understanding,
keep silence in ascribing acts to yourself.
Listen to a sweet proverb, don't show a sour face—
"First put up the roof, then paint."

How long this praise of self to spite the envier?
How long promoting goods that no one buys?
You are nonexistent, and imagining your being
is perverse. How long this perverse imagining?

CHAPTER 31

Power and Act

All the power and acts that are made manifest from various sites of manifestation are in reality manifest from the Real Being, not from the site of manifestation. Therefore it is said, "People do not have acts. Acts are only from the Lord. Yet people are happy with what returns to themselves."[21]

Hence, whenever we talk about the power and acts that are attributed to human beings, it is correct to say that they are the Real Being becoming manifest in the human image, not that they are becoming manifest through the human substance. The Classic says, "The Real Lord transforms you and what you do."

THE THIRTY-FIRST GLEAM

The attributes, states, and acts that are manifest in the loci of manifestation are, in reality, ascribed to the Real that is manifest in these loci of manifestation. So, if from time to time an evil or a deficiency occurs in some of them, this may be from the direction of the nonexistence of something else, because existence qua existence is sheer good. Whenever an evil is imagined from an affair of existence, this is because some other affair of existence does not exist, not because of that affair of existence qua affair of existence.

Every description pertaining to good and perfection
    is a description of the pure and transcendent Essence.
Every attribute counted as evil and bane
    goes back to the inadequacy of the receptivities.

THE THIRTY-SECOND GLEAM

The philosophers have claimed it to be self-evident that existence is sheer good. To clarify this, they have brought various examples. They say, for example, that hail brings about fruit's corruption and that it is evil in relation to fruit. Its evilness is not in regard to the fact that it is one of the qualities, because, in this regard, it is one of the perfections. Rather, it is in regard to the fact that it has caused the fruit not to arrive at its appropriate perfections.

In the same way, for example, killing is evil. Its evilness is not in regard to the killer's power to kill, or the weapon's cuttingness, or the receptivity of the bodily member to cutting. Rather, it is in regard to life's disappearance, and this is an affair of nonexistence. And so on with other examples.

Wherever existence journeys, O heart,
    know for certain that it is Sheer Good, O heart.
Every evil comes from nonexistence, not from existence,
    so all evil is entailed by the "other," O heart.

CHAPTER 32

Good and Evil

All the natures, the feelings, and the turnings of vital-energy, and all the acting and making that become manifest in all the sites of manifestation, are in reality related to the Real Being, who becomes manifest in all these sites of manifestation. Thus, if an evil or an injury is seen in a site of manifestation, the reason may be the nonbeing of a different affair, because everything that has being is unmixedly limpid and "utmost good."[22] So, if something is regarded as evil, this is because of the nonbeing of another affair, not because this affair has being.

For example, hail harms fruits, and it is evil in relation to fruit. However, what makes it evil is not that the pattern and shape of hail's being is not good, for in discussing the shape and pattern, it is judged to be complete. Rather, that is because it caused the fruit not to reach completeness.

So also, killing is evil. What makes it evil is not the power of the killer, the sharpness of the knife or the sword, or the ease of separating the limbs from the one killed. Rather, it is simply because life has been changed and removed. The change and removal of life is nonbeing.

Therefore, it is said that all being is good, and evil is also good. However, goodness is completeness, and it is from the affair of the Root Nature; evilness is injury, and it belongs to a thing's being receptive toward the endowment of ruin and such things.

THE THIRTY-THIRD GLEAM

In the book *al-Nuṣūṣ*, Shaykh Ṣadr al-Dīn Qūnawī—may God hallow his secret heart!—says,

> Knowledge is subordinate to existence in the sense that, whenever any of the realities has existence, there is knowledge. The disparity of the knowledge is in terms of the disparity of the realities in receiving existence, perfectly or deficiently. Hence, what is receptive to existence more completely and perfectly is receptive to knowledge in the same mode, and what is receptive to existence more deficiently is qualified by knowledge in the same mode.[55]

The springhead of this disparity is that the properties of necessity and possibility dominate and are dominated over. In any reality where the properties of necessity are more dominant, existence and knowledge are more perfect. In any reality where the properties of possibility are more dominant, existence and knowledge are more deficient. Most likely, the judgment that occurs in the words of the Shaykh—that knowledge specifically is subordinate to existence—is by way of providing an example. Otherwise, all the perfections subordinate to existence, such as life, power, desire, and so on, have the same state.

One of them—God hallow their secret hearts!—has said that no individual existent is naked of the attribute of knowledge, but knowledge has two modes. One is called "knowledge" in keeping with common usage, and the other is not called "knowledge" in common usage. However, the lords of the reality hold that both sorts pertain to the category of knowledge, for they witness the fact that the Real's essential knowledge pervades all existents.

Pertaining to the second sort is water, which is not considered a "knower" in common usage. However, we see that it distinguishes between highness and lowness. It turns away from highness and flows to the side of lowness. In the same way, it enters into a porous body and it wets the surface of a solid body and passes by; and so on. Hence, it is because of the specificity of knowledge that water flows according to what is entailed by the receptivity of the receptacle and the lack of opposition to it. However, at this level knowledge has become manifest in the form of nature.

CHAPTER 33

Knowledge and Power

The ten thousand things all have knowledge, and each of them has difference of more or less. The difference of more or less is based on the completeness or incompleteness of receptivity toward the endowment of the Real Being. When something receives the Real Being completely, its knowledge is also complete. When something receives the Real Being slightly and lackingly, its knowledge is little in itself.

What is the beginning condition of that which is complete and incomplete? It is related to the supremacy and subservience that people obtain from the Real Principle and the principle of things. Within all the principles of the things, the more the Real Principle is supreme, the more knowledge is complete. The more the things' nature is supreme, the more knowledge is diminished in itself.

Truly, the Real Being's knowledge goes throughout the ten thousand beings. Therefore, without any doubt, all things large or small, manifest or concealed, have knowledge. However there are two sorts of knowledge. One can be called "knowledge" according to the common people's opinion, and the other cannot be called "knowledge" according to their opinion. Both kinds are called "having knowledge" by those who possess real eyes.

For example, in the common people's opinion, it is not said that water has knowledge. Nonetheless, we see that water has the power of dividing between high and low. It leaves the high and has the power to go down. When it encounters emptiness, it enters into it, and when it encounters fullness, it runs against it. If it is possible for it to go, it goes; if not, it stops. All these come from the power of knowledge.

So also should be judged knowledge's pervading all the other existents—or rather, the pervasion of every single existent by every perfection that is subordinate to existence.

Through the attributes hidden within It
Being pervades all the entities of the world.
In the entity receptive to It, every description
is plainly seen in the measure of the entity's receptivity.

THE THIRTY-FOURTH GLEAM

From the direction of the unmixedness of Its own unboundedness, the reality of Being pervades the essences of all existents such that, within these essences, It is the same as these essences. So also Its perfect attributes, because of their universality and unboundedness, pervade all the attributes of the existents such that, in the midst of the existents' attributes, these perfect attributes are the same as those attributes, just as those attributes were the same as these in the perfect attributes themselves.

For example, in the midst of the world's knowledge of the particulars, the attribute of knowledge is the same as knowledge of the particulars; in the midst of the world's knowledge of the universals, it is the same as knowledge of universals; in the midst of active and passive knowledge, it is the same as active and passive knowledge; and in the midst of knowledge through tasting and finding, it is the same as knowledge through tasting and finding. This reaches the point that, in the midst of the knowledge of those existents that are not held to be knowing in terms of common usage, it is the same as the knowledge that is appropriate to their state. So also should be judged all the other attributes and perfections.

O You whose Essence pervades the entities' essences,
whose descriptions lurk behind their attributes,
Like Your Essence, Your descriptions are unbounded
but not naked of binding in the loci of manifestation.

Not only knowledge, but also all the powerful affairs possessed by the Real Being pervade fully and go throughout the ten thousand beings. All ten thousand things are endowed with the powerful affairs of the Real Being. However, some have supremacy and some are subservient, and the difference of more or less is nothing but the difference of completeness and incompleteness.[23]

CHAPTER 34

The Union of Reality and Thing

The Substance of the Real Being, which pervades and goes into the ten thousand substances, is the Substance of the ten thousand beings, and so also, the Substance of the ten thousand beings, which are put together in the Real Substance, is the Substance of the Real Being. The functions of the Real Being, which are distributed to the ten thousand beings, are the functions of the ten thousand beings, and so also the functions of the ten thousand beings, which are contained in the Real Function, are the functions of the Real Being.

Apart from the Real Substance, nothing is to be thought a substance, and apart from the Real Function, nothing is to be thought a function. Thus it is said that there is nothing, only the Real.

THE THIRTY-FIFTH GLEAM

The reality of Being is the "Essence" of the Presence of the Real—glory be to Him, and high indeed is He! The Essence's tasks, relations, and respects are His "attributes." His making Himself manifest as clothed in these relations and respects is His "act" and "trace-inducing." The manifest entifications that are put in order by this making manifest are His "traces."

To Himself through His essential tasks, He who sits behind the curtain
began displaying within manifestation's loci, which are this world and religion.
O seeker of certainty, see in this subtle point of mine
what are "Essence," "attribute," "act," and "trace."

THE THIRTY-SIXTH GLEAM

In some places in the *Fuṣūṣ*, the Shaykh's words indicate that the existence of the entities of the possible things and of the perfections subordinate to existence are attributed to the Presence of the Real (glory be to Him and high indeed is He!); in other places, that everything attributed to the Presence of the Real is this very effusion of existence, nothing else, and that existence's subordinates are among the things entailed by the entities.

These two statements are reconciled by the fact that the Presence of the Real has two self-disclosures. One is the absent, knowledged self-disclosure, which the Sufis have called "the most holy effusion."[56] It is the Real's manifestation to Himself from eternity without beginning in the Presence of Knowledge within the entities' forms, receptivities, and preparednesses.

CHAPTER 35

The Union of Substance and Function

All is one Real. The True Being is Its "substance," and knowledge and power are Its "function." The manifestation of Its function is Its "act," and the revealing of Its images is Its "trace."

CHAPTER 36

Discriminating Meanings

Some chapters say that the substance and function of the ten thousand things are wholly related to the Real Lord. It is also said that what is related to the Lord is only the substance of things; their functions are related to the self-perfection of the things. Why?

This is because the Real Being has two manifesting transformations, the transformation of the principle, and the transformation of the form. The transformation of the principle is put together in knowledge and contained in the inward. Its act is silent transformation, and, from the beginning, it possesses the substance of the root nature of the ten thousand beings.

The second is the witnessed, existential self-disclosure, which is called the "holy effusion." It consists of the manifestation of the Existence of the Real colored by the properties and traces of the entities. This second self-disclosure is put in order by the first self-disclosure. It is the locus of manifestation for the perfections that came to be included through the first self-disclosure in the receptivities and preparednesses of the entities.

> One munificence of Yours paints a hundred sorts of beggar,
> one munificence gives to each its separate share.
> The first munificence has no beginning, and it puts
> the second munificence into order without end.

Hence, the attribution of existence and its subordinate perfections to the Real—glory be to Him and high indeed is He!—is in respect of the totality of the two self-disclosures. The attribution of existence to the Real along with the attribution of its subordinates to the entities is in respect of the second self-disclosure. After all, nothing is put in order by the second self-disclosure except effusing existence on the entities and making manifest what had come to be included within them by what was entailed by the first self-disclosure.

> Listen to a difficult word and an abstruse mystery
> about the acts and attributes appended to the entities.
> From one direction, all are attributed to us,
> in another mode, all are attributed to the Real.

The transformation of the form is seen in power and is issued into the outward. Its act is creative transformation, which is the function required for perfecting the ten thousand things. The silent transformation is the Unique Act, and the creative transformation combines with the acts of the things. The "substance" is that which possesses the principle of the things before the thing, and the "function" issues forth properly following the substance.

It is said that both substance and function are related to the Lord when there is talk about silent and creative transformations together. It is said that the substance is related to the Lord, but the function to the things, when there is talk specifically about the creative transformation. In sum, all are in reality the Real's acts, and the things are the imprints and traces of the Real's acts.

Postscript

What was intended by these expressions and sought by these allusions was alerting to the essential encompassment by the Presence of the Real—glory be to Him and high indeed is He!—and to the pervasion of all levels of existence by His light. Then the aware travelers and alert seekers will not be neglectful of witnessing the beauty of His Essence while witnessing any essence, nor will they become heedless of examining the perfection of His attributes in the manifestation of any attribute.

What was mentioned was sufficient to accomplish what was intended and adequate to clarify what was sought. Therefore, it was confined to this measure and is cut short with these few quatrains:

Jāmī, enough! How long weaving words?
How long casting spells and telling tales?
Manifesting realities in words is illusion—
O simple man, how long playing with illusions?

In the rags of poverty, covering defects is better,
on the subtle points of love, sharpness of wit is better.
Since words are a mask on the face of the goal,
silence is better than talking and listening.

Until when will you cry and shout like a bell?
For a moment, keep silent from this empty talk.
You will not become a treasure for realities's pearls
as long as you do not become all ear like an oyster.

O you whose nature has taken on the disquiet of words,
if you're of the folk of knowledge, watch your words.
Don't loose your tongue in unveiling the secrets of Being—
that pearl can't be pierced with the diamond of words.

Scratch one line through defects, another through virtue,
then pull back the veil from the Absent Beauty.
That beauty's disclosure is not outside of you,
so pull feet under skirt and head under hood.

O you whose shroud has been rent by heartache for Him,
don't stain your pure consciousness with speech.
Since you can stay dumb about it, if you open
your lips after this—may dirt fill your mouth![57]

Notes

Foreword

1. Lee Cheuk Yin, "Islamic Values in Confucian Terms: Wang Daiyu (a. 1580–1658) and His Zhenjiao Zhenquan (Genuine Annotation of the Orthodox Teachings)," in *Islam and Confucianism: A Civilizational Dialogue*, edited by Osman Bakar and Cheng Gek Nai (Kuala Lumpur: Center for Civilizational Dialogue, University of Malaya, 1997), pp. 75–94.

2. Jacqueline Armijo-Hussein, "Sayyid Adjall Shams Al Din: A Muslim from Central Asia, Serving the Mongols in China and Bringing 'Civilization' to Yunnan" (Harvard Ph.D. Dissertation, 1998).

3. See Raphael Israeli, *Islam in China: A Critical Bibliography* (Westport: Greenwood Press, 1994) and Donald Daniel Leslie, *Islam in Traditional China: A Short History to 1800* (Canberra: Canberra College of Advanced Education, 1986). See also Bai Shouyi, *Zhongguo huijiao xiaoshi* ("A short history of Chinese Islam"), in *Zhongguo yisilanjiao shi cungao* ("The preserved manuscripts on the history of Chinese Islam," Yinchuan: Ningxia renmin chubanshe, 1988).

4. Jin Yijiu, *Yisilanxiao shi* ("History of Islam," Beijing: The Chinese Academy of Social Sciences, 1990), pp. 440–56.

5. See Zhang Xiong's dissertation on Matteo Ricci with emphasis on the shift from "cultural accommodation" to "intellectual colonization" (History of Science, Harvard University, 1995).

6. See Kuwata Rokuro and An Mutao, trans., "Mingmo Qingchu zhi huiru" ("The Muslim Confucians at the end of the Ming and early Qing"), in *Zhongguo yisilanjiao shi cankao ziliao xuanbian* ("Selections of reference materials on the history of Chinese Islam"), edited by Li Xinghua and Feng Jinyuan (Yinchuan: Ningxia renmin chubanshe, 1985), Vol. 1, pp. 584–88.

7. This statement, chapter XXII of the *Doctrine of the Mean*, may not appear as textual evidence of Liu's anthropocosmic vision, but it is obvious that the logic of mutuality between Heaven and man (in the gender neutral sense of humanity) implicit in the statement underlies much of Liu's understanding of Confucian moral metaphysics.

Introduction

1. Fletcher, *Studies on Chinese and Islamic Inner Asia*, p. XI.3.

2. On Chinese Islamic literature, see Leslie, *Islamic Literature in Chinese*; idem, *Islam in Traditional China*; Isaac Mason, "Notes on Chinese Mohammedan Literature."

3. Ford, "Some Chinese Muslims of the Seventeenth and Eighteenth Centuries," p. 147.

4. Ibid., p. 146.

5. Leslie, *Islam in Traditional China*, p. 137.

6. Tazaka Kōdō, *Chugoku ni okeru kaikyō no denrai to sono gutsū*, pp. 1354–57; Tazaka cites the concurring views of Nohara Shiro and Kuwata Rokuro.

7. Zürcher, "Jesuit Accommodation and the Chinese Cultural Imperative," p. 64.

8. I have discussed this in detail in *The Tao of Islam*. For a general survey of the Islamic tradition in terms of this theological bipolarity, see Sachiko Murata and W. C. Chittick, *The Vision of Islam*.

9. Compare the translation of this passage in Wing-tsit Chan, *A Source Book in Chinese Philosophy*, pp. 86–87.

1. *Chinese-Language Islam*

1. For a survey of Islam in China today, see Gladney, *Muslim Chinese: Ethnic Nationalism in the People's Republic.*

2. Leslie, *Islam in Traditional China*, p. 31.

3. According to Leslie (*Islam in Traditional China*, p. 70), different dates were given by the Chinese Muslims themselves. By far the most thorough study of Islam's history in China is the already mentioned work by Tazaka, *Chugoku ni okeru kaikyō no denrai to sono gutsū*. For an overview, see Rossabi, "Islam in China." For a good study of six of the classic Chinese-language works on Islam, see Françoise Aubin, "En islam chinois."

4. For a detailed discussion of the Islamic tradition in terms of these three dimensions, see Murata and Chittick, *The Vision of Islam*.

5. To speak of "the school of Ibn al-ʿArabī" is problematic. The expression should not be taken as delineating a narrow group of authors with fixed viewpoints. Rather, it designates a broad approach to theoretical issues within the context of a great deal of diversity. See Chittick, "The School of Ibn ʿArabī." For a scholarly investigation of many facets of Ibn al-ʿArabī's controversial legacy in the central Islamic lands, see Alexander D. Knysh, *Ibn ʿArabi in the Later Islamic Tradition.*

6. D. Leslie and M. Wassel provide details as to how transliteration was attempted for Arabic into Chinese and Chinese into Arabic in "Arabic and Persian Sources used by Liu Chih." See also Aubin, "En islam chinois," especially pp. 496–98.

7. For a few more examples of Chinese terminology, see Aubin, "Taṣawwuf 6. In Chinese Islam;" idem, "En islam chinois."

8. Leslie, *Islam in Traditional China*, p. 117.

9. See, for example, Wang Tai-yü, *Cheng-chiao chen-ch'üan* (1987), pp. iv–vii, 1, 3–4, 6; anonymous, *Hui-hui yuan-lai*, pp. 15–18; Yu Zhengui and Yang Huaizhong, *Chung-kuo i-ssu-lan wen-hsien chu-i t'i-yao*, pp. 69–73; Jin Yijiu, "Notes of the Quarter," p. 332.

10. Wang, *Cheng-chiao* (1987), p. 4.

11. Cited in Chittick, *The Sufi Path of Love*, p. 138.

12. Wang, *Cheng-chiao* (1987), p. 6.

13. Wang, *Cheng-chiao* (1987), p. 254. However, some scholars have suggested that this expression in fact means "the old days of master Wang," that is, the time before Wang left Nanjing (Tazaka, *Chugoku*, p. 1368).

14. Wang, *Cheng-chiao*, p. 16.

15. Ibid.

16. Ibid., p. 3.

17. A recently erected stele in the Ching-chio mosque in Nanjing, which I visited in the fall of 1997, tells us that both Wang and Liu Chih taught and preached in the mosque.

18. The earliest source of this story seems to be the anonymous *Wang Kung Tai-yü t'an-tao* ("The way of discussion of Master Wang Tai-yü"), which is not known to have been published before 1894; it was reprinted as an appendix to the 1927 edition of *Hui-hui yüan-lai* ("The original coming of the Muslims [to China]"). See Mason, "Notes," number 165.

19. Wang, *Cheng-chiao* (1987), pp. 328–30. This is a short biography of Wang Tai-yü by Chin Chi-t'ang.

20. Wang, *Cheng-chiao* (1987), pp. 9–10.

21. Tazaka employs this text, from Wang's *Real Commentary* (*Cheng-chiao* (1987), p. 16), to support his contention that Wang did not compromise with traditional Chinese teachings (*Chugoku*, p. 1415).

22. Wang, *Cheng-chiao* (1987), preface, p. 3.

23. See especially the chapter, "The Naqshbandiyya in Northwest China," in Fletcher, *Studies on Chinese and Islamic Inner Asia*.

24. Tazaka thinks that Wang is the first to refer to Islam as "the Pure and Real," though the expression had been used by Buddhists, Taoists, Jews, and Nestorians to refer to their own teachings (*Chugoku*, pp. 122–28).

25. See A. D. W. Forbes, "Liu Chih," *Encyclopaedia of Islam*.

26. Nohara Shiro, "Tempō tenrei taku yōkai no hōyaku ni saishite," p. 81.

27. Ford, "Some Chinese Muslims," p. 150.

28. Ibid.

29. The next most frequently cited book in Liu Chih's introduction is *Mawāqif* (nine times), then what he calls *Tafsīr* (four times). Finally, he quotes once from a book he calls *Aḥkām-i kawākib*, apparently a Persian work on astronomy. *Tafsīr* is presumably one of the two commentaries on the Koran that he mentions in his list of sources at the beginning of the work, neither identified with any certainty. Leslie and Wassel ("Arabic and Persian Sources," pp. 91–92) think that *Mawāqif*, whose title Liu Chih translates as "The complete classic of the extended investigation" (*Ko-chih ch'üan-ching*), is probably the Arabic text on Kalam by the eighth/fourteenth century scholar Ījī (d. 756/1355), or possibly the well-known work by the fourth/tenth century Sufi Niffarī. However, given the content of the actual citations, they could not have been drawn from either work, and most likely they derive from a Sufi work on cosmology. The title, in fact, may not be *Mawāqif*; Tazaka reads it as *Mawāhib*, and has no idea what it may be. Liu Chih mentions this same book in his life of the Prophet along with what he calls "The classic of the human mirror" (*Jen-ching ching*; Arabic *mir'āt al-insān*). There he says that both books deal with the learning of "the three ultimates"

(*san-chi*)—heaven, earth, and the human being. Discussions of cosmology in conjunction with human perfection pertain to later Sufi learning, not to the science of Kalam. Suʿād al-Waḥīdī seems to think that *Mawāqif* refers to *al-Mawāqif al-ilāhiyya*, a work by the 11th/17th century Sufi Ibn Qaḍīb al-Bān (see her article, "al-Falsafat al-islāmiyya fi'l-ṣīn," note 71, pp. 101–2), and the contents of this work make this a distinct possibility.

30. The whole text was translated into Japanese, and in 1921 Isaac Mason published an abridged English version as *The Arabian Prophet*. I have examined the translations, and both suffer from the translators' lack of knowledge of Islam, though they do provide a good idea of the contents of the work.

31. Liu Chih is known to have been the author of at least three and probably eight or more other works as well. See Leslie, *Islamic Literature*, pp. 92–93.

32. In his list of sources, he mentions several other Sufi works, including *Kashf al-maḥjūb* of Hujwīrī, *Kashf al-asrār* of Maybudī, and *Tadhkirat al-awliyā*ʾ of ʿAṭṭār. Tazaka gives twelve titles on Sufism, *Chugoku*, pp. 1286–89. For the lists themselves, see Leslie and Wassel, "Arabic and Persian Sources."

33. F. Aubin, "La Chine," p. 264.

34. On Ma, see Lin, "Three Eminent Chinese 'Ulama' of Yunnan," pp. 109–12. On the Arabic text, see Akiro Matsumoto, "Ma Rengen." I thank Professor Matsumoto for kindly sending me a copy of this book.

35. For a description of the Arabic text, see Matsumoto, "Ma Rengen." See also the article of Suʿād al-Waḥīdī, "Al-Falsafat al-islāmiyyat fi'l-ṣīn." I extend my gratitude here to Françoise Aubin, who showed remarkable generosity in the way that she speedily sent me a copy of *Sharḥ-i laṭāʾif* as soon as I wrote to her inquiring about the text.

36. For details, including discussion of a translation said to have been made in the middle of the nineteenth century, see Aubin, "Les traductions du Coran en chinois."

37. Leslie, *Islamic Literature*, pp. 33–34. The book was badly translated into English by E. H. Palmer as *Oriental Mysticism: A Treatise on the Sufistic and Unitarian Theosophy of the Persians*.

38. Tazaka, *Chugoku*, pp. 1425, 1431; Fu T'ung-hsien, *Chung-kuo hui-chiao shih*; Japanese translation as *Chugoku kaikyoshi*, pp. 140, 198. Leslie and Wassel claim that there was also a second translation of *Mirṣād al-ʿibād*, but until the two versions are compared, the evidence will remain unconvincing (Leslie and Wassel, "Arabic and Persian Sources," pp. 89–90). *Mirṣād* has an excellent English translation by H. Algar as *The Path of God's Bondsmen from Origin to Return*.

39. Leslie lists two translations of *Maqṣad-i aqṣā*, a dated one by She Yün-shan and an undated one with a different title by P'o Na-ch'ih (*Islamic Literature*, pp. 32–34). Yu and Yang (*Chung-kuo*, p. 111) say that P'o Na-ch'ih is She's pen-name. In a survey of seventeen mosques carried out in the Inner Mongolian district in 1944, Saguchi found Ch'ang's grammar in eight of the mosques ("Chugoku isuramu no kyōten").

40. The Tenri Library seems to have the only copy of this translation outside China (Leslie, *Islamic Literature*, p. 43). It is in two volumes with a brief introduction by P'o without date; the full Persian title is given in transliteration at the beginning of the second volume. *Lamaʿāt* was translated into English by Chittick and Wilson as *Fakhruddin Iraqi: Divine Flashes*.

41. Leslie, *Islamic Literature*, p. 23; Tazaka, *Chugoku*, pp. 1278–80, 1405–10.

42. Leslie, *Islamic Literature*, p. 49. I checked the Chinese text against *Nihāyat al-mas'ūl fī riwāyat al-rasūl*, a work by ʿAbd al-Salām ibn ʿAlī ibn Ḥusayn Abarqūhī. This is a careful translation of the Arabic *Mawlūd al-nabī*, the book by ʿAfīf's father, Saʿīd al-Dīn Muḥammad ibn Masʿūd al-Kāzirūnī. According to the editor of *Nihāyat al-mas'ūl*, Abarqūhī's translation was made during the lifetime of al-Kāzirūnī, who died in 758/1357. ʿAfīf al-Dīn made his own translation, which has not been published, in 760/1359. The editor says that there is no great difference between the two translations. If this is so, we are on safe ground in employing *Nihāyat al-mas'ūl* to judge the faithfulness of Liu Chih's Chinese version.

43. Tazaka, *Chugoku*, pp. 1365 and 1426, note 6.

44. Ma Fu-chu, *Han-i tao-hsin chiu-ching*, p. 1. See Chang-Kuan Lin, "Three Eminent Chinese ʿUlama' of Yunnan," pp. 103–8.

45. The translator, J. Peter Hobson, does not give the original title, but renders it as "The Three-Character Rhymed Classic on the Kaʿbah." Lin (previous note) does not appear to mention this work in his list of Ma's writings.

46. Ma, *Ta-hua tsung-kuei*, p. 3.

47. Yu and Yang, *Chung-kuo i-ssu-lan*, pp. 89–94.

48. Chan, *Source Book*, p. 14.

49. Ibid., pp. 460, 589–90.

50. Ch'en, *Neo-Confucian Terms Explained*, p. 105.

51. Ibid., p. 112.

52. See *Source Book*, 460–65. For the diagram itself, a different translation, and much commentary, see Kalton, *To Become a Sage*, pp. 37–50.

53. *Source Book*, pp. 464–65. Cf. Ch'en, *Neo-Confucian Terms Explained*, pp. 115–20, 188–89.

54. *Source Book*, p. 519.

55. Ibid., p. 641. In this passage and several others that are cited from *Source Book* and *Neo-Confucian Terms Explained*, I have modified the text slightly for the sake of preserving consistency in translating Chinese terms.

56. *Neo-Confucian Terms*, p. 190 (see also p. 39).

57. On the significance of the heart in the Koran and Islamic thought, see my *Tao of Islam*, Chapter 10.

58. *Source Book*, p. 614.

59. Ibid., p. 638.

60. Ibid., p. 789.

61. Ibid., p. 594.

62. For a good discussion of these two terms in the Neo-Confucian context, see the first two chapters of Ch'en, *Neo-Confucian Terms*, pp. 37–56.

63. *Source Book*, p. 23.

64. Wilhelm, *I Ching*, p. 371; cf. Lynn, *The Classic of Changes*, p. 129.

65. *Source Book*, p. 597.

66. Ibid., p. 613.

67. Ibid., p. 621.

68. Ibid., p. 667.

2. *The Works of Wang Tai-yü*

1. This edition, dated 1827, is found in the Tenri Library.

2. The edition employed is Wang, *Cheng-chiao* (1987).

3. Ibn al-ʿArabī makes the same basic argument when he distinguishes between the God (*ilāh*) and the "godded-over" (*maʾlūh*), or between the Lord (*rabb*) and the vassal (*marbūb*). See Chittick, *The Sufi Path of Knowledge*, chapter 4.

4. The reference is probably to Koran 67:2: "[Blessed is He . . .] who created death and life to try you, which of you is most beautiful in works."

5. This seems to be a different translation of Koran 67:2.

6. The reference is to the accounts in the hadith literature that tell how the angels were sent to the earth to gather clay for Adam's body, on condition that they return it to the earth at the body's death. See Murata and Chittick, *Vision*, pp. 92–93.

7. "Clean and Aware" (*ching-chio*) is the name of the mosque in Nanjing where Wang was teaching.

8. "Causes and conditions" translates *yin-yüan*, an expression used by Buddhists to designate the whole configuration of causes and effects commonly known as "interdependent arising."

9. The reference is of course to the Zen practice of ritual beating when a disciple is lax in his meditation.

10. I have provided a number of passages in *Tao of Islam* which deal with this same issue. Most sophisticated is probably that by Muʾayyid al-Dīn Jandī (d. ca. 1300) in his commentary on Ibn al-ʿArabī's *Fuṣūṣ al-ḥikam* (*Tao*, pp. 94, 196–99).

11. See Chan, *Source Book*, p. 463; *To Become a Sage*, p. 38.

12. *Source Book*, p. 597.

13. See Birdwhistell, *Transition to Neo-Confucianism*, pp. 66 ff.

14. *Source Book*, p. 790. It is worth noting that the expression was much debated, as can be judged from the fact that Ch'en devotes to it by far the longest section of *Neo-Confucian Terms Explained* (pp. 142–68).

15. *Source Book*, pp. 790, 643.

16. Ibid., p. 644.

17. Wang may have in mind the Koranic verse, "Surely the religion [*al-dīn*] with God is the submission [*al-islām*]" (3:19).

18. This is the famous hadith, "The search for knowledge is incumbent upon every Muslim, male and female."

19. These two sentences are reminiscent of two prophetic sayings: "I seek refuge in God from a knowledge without use" and "Knowledge without action is a tree without fruit." The necessary connection between knowledge and practice is thoroughly discussed in both Islamic and Confucian texts. For Chu Hsi's views, see *Source Book*, pp. 609–10.

20. *Source Book*, pp. 340, 317–18, 525.

21. Wang certainly has in mind the saying constantly cited in Sufi texts, "He who knows himself knows his Lord."

22. Cited in Ch'en's chapter on the two terms, *Neo-Confucian Terms Explained*, p. 86.

23. Perhaps Wang has in mind verses like this: "We have charged the human

being that he act beautifully toward his parents" (46:15; cf. 2:83, 6:151, 17:22–24, 29:8).

24. This hadith is found in Bukhārī, Muslim, and other standard sources. Rāzī cites it twice in *Mirṣād al-ʿibād* (Algar, *Path*, pp. 415, 474).

25. This is probably a reference to the hadith cited earlier (p. 38). The analogy of the human being to a country ruled by a king is a popular one in Islamic texts, employed by, among others, Ghazālī toward the beginning of his *Kīmiyā-yi saʿādat*.

26. The standard Persian translation of this saying (which follows the Arabic text rather closely), is given by ʿAṭṭār in *Tadhkirat al-awliyāʾ* (p. 97): "Bāyazīd was asked about renunciation [*zuhd*]. He replied, 'Renunciation has no worth. I was a renouncer for three days—on the first day in this world, on the second day in the next world, and on the third day in everything other than God.'"

27. This is most likely an allusion to the purported hadith, commonly cited in Sufi texts, "Die before you die!"

28. One of the several versions of this hadith reads, "Reflect upon God's blessings, but do not reflect upon God." Another has, "Reflect upon everything, but do not reflect upon God's Essence." Suyūṭī, *al-Jāmiʿ al-ṣaghīr*, vol. 3, pp. 262–63.

29. The Koranic verse Wang has in mind seems to be 49:13, which can be translated, "Surely the noblest among you in God's sight is the most godwary." Godwariness (*taqwā*) derives from a root that means to take care and to fear. It implies carefully taking into account one's own ultimate destiny by fearing the consequences of disobeying God. It is often considered the most important and comprehensive of the virtues, which helps explain why it is sometimes translated as "piety." Sufi authors frequently discuss its ramifications in terms similar to those Wang offers here. For a summary of the word's Koranic significance, see Murata and Chittick, *Vision of Islam*, pp. 282–85.

30. The worthy who visited Rābiʿa was Ḥasan of Basra. For ʿAṭṭār's version of this story, which in no way suggests Wang's conclusion, see ʿAṭṭār, *Muslim Saints and Mystics*, pp. 44–45 (read "fat soup" for "a little onion pulp").

31. Wang probably has in mind the common description of wine as *umm al-khabāʾith*, "the mother of loathsome things," which can be traced back to a saying by ʿUthmān, the fourth caliph (cited in Nasāʾī, Ashriba 44).

32. This chapter is a good commentary on the Koranic verse that reads, "The life of this world is naught but a game [*laʿb*] and a diversion [*lahw*]" (6:32, 29:64, 47:36, 57:20).

33. The saying has the tone of a hadith, but I could not find the Arabic. A hadith of the same sort tells us, "This world is the home of those who have no home and the property of those who have no property. Those who gather for it have no intelligence." Cited by Suyūṭī in *al-Jāmiʿ al-ṣaghīr* 3:545.

34. This is a hadith that is cited among others in Rāzī's *Mirṣād al-ʿibād* (Algar, *Path*, pp. 93).

35. The discussion in this paragraph has a decidedly Taoist flavor. Cf. *Source Book*, p. 326.

36. The transliteration of Arabic *ḥawwā* as Chinese *hao-wa* illustrates one of the literary tools of the Chinese Muslims that deserves serious study. Usually, the meaning of the characters making up transliterated words has no relation with the meaning of the original Arabic or Persian words. However, sometimes

the meaning suggests something of the significance of the original. *Hao-wa* is a good example. Everyone knows that the mother is highly honored in Confucianism. But it also needs to be remembered that in Islamic thinking, Eve is the honored mother of the human race and the wife of the first prophet; the Koran makes no suggestion that Eve was any more forgetful than Adam. The word *hao-wa* is made up of two characters, both of which contain the radical for woman. *Hao*'s second radical is "child," so at first glance it reads "woman/child." The dictionaries give the meaning of *hao* as good, excellent, beautiful, intimate; to like, to love. As for *wa*, it is the proper name of the sister of Fu Hsi, the legendary emperor who arranged the eight trigrams of the *I Ching*. Wa herself is portrayed as a supernatural being who possessed all sorts of powers to transform the ten thousand things. Thus the Chinese reader, seeing the transliteration *hao-wa*, will naturally associate Eve with the primeval and supernatural beauty of womanhood.

37. As noted earlier, Buddhists use the expression "causes and conditions" for "interdependent arising."

38. Perhaps Wang has in mind the verse, "They know an outward something of this world's life, but of the next world they are heedless" (30:7).

39. *Source Book*, p. 790.

40. Ibid., p. 8.

41. The Koranic reference was cited earlier (note 32).

42. This is a reference to the covenant of Alast (Koran 7:172) made between God and the children of Adam before they entered this world. Again Wang uses the Taoist expression "before heaven," commonly paired with "after heaven."

43. The term "flowers in the sky," which can be translated literally as "empty flowers," is often employed in Buddhist texts. The world as perceived by the unenlightened is compared to flowers that are seen in the sky because of distorted vision. See, for example, the short essay by Dōgen, translated in Cleary, *Shōbōgenzō*, pp. 66–75. Wang mentions the expression again in the *Great Learning*, but there he is rather critical of the Buddhist interpretation

44. This famous saying is usually attributed to the Prophet, though it is not found in the standard hadith sources, and some authorities consider it to belong to ʿAlī.

3. *Wang Tai-yü's* Great Learning

1. *Source Book*, p. 84.

2. Ibid., p. 85.

3. Ibid., p. 84–86; cf. the translation by Legge in *Confucius*, pp. 354–59.

4. *Source Book*, p. 474.

5. Compare Jāmī's differentiation of the divine levels in Gleam 24.

6. The distinction between these two sorts of unity, *aḥadiyya* and *wāḥidiyya*, is frequently discussed by followers of Ibn al-ʿArabī. See, for example, Gleam 17.

7. Tu, "Embodying the Universe," p. 178.

8. Ibid., p. 180; cf. *Source Book*, p. 523. Ch'en writes, "The sage . . . is com-

pletely merged with the Principle of Heaven in one body without any alteration." *Neo-Confucian Terms Explained*, p. 193.

9. *Source Book*, p. 685.

10. Ibid., p. 675.

11. On the second, see Chittick, *Sufi Path of Knowledge*, Chapter 20; for the third, see idem, *Sufi Path of Love*, pp. 173–75. The first is discussed in both books.

12. The 1987 edition does not have this notation, but this is no proof that it was not found in the 1931 edition, upon the basis of which the 1987 edition was prepared.

13. Mason, "Note on Chinese Mohammedan Literature," p. 185.

14. Tazaka, *Chugoku*, pp. 1392–95.

15. Wang, *Cheng-chiao* (1987), p. 326.

16. The *Interpretation* is a book of sixty-three short chapters, in twenty-nine folios, on the Five Pillars of Islam (see Leslie, *Islamic Literature*, p. 48, no. 35). Seven chapters discuss the general foundation of the Five Pillars, twenty-five the principles of the Five Pillars, and thirty-one the meaning of the Five Pillars. I could not find in it any expressions similar to those of the *Great Learning*.

17. Leslie records editions that appeared in 1794, 1832, 1876, 1852, 1875, 1918, 1921, and 1931 (*Islamic Literature*, p 24). I could obtain only one of these, that of 1921 (both from Harvard Yenching Library and from Tōyō Bunko). However, I also obtained two other editions—the most recent, 1987 edition, and an undated edition from Tenri University Library. The Tenri catalogue lists the latter together with an edition of Wang's *True Answers of the Very Real* dated 1827. The binding of the two books is similar, but the *Great Learning* itself is not dated, and the librarian in charge had no idea why, in 1944, these two books had been catalogued together. The three editions that I could obtain can be described as follows: (1) The undated edition from Tenri University. The cover tells us that the book was written by the Old Man of the Pure and Real and that the engraved blocks belong to the Pure and Real Hall (Ch'ing-chen T'ang). The book includes the undated introduction by Ch'ing-chen Pi-jen ("the Rustic of the Pure and Real") and a table of contents. (2) The 1921 edition. The cover inscription reads: "the elder of the real Hui of Chin-ling [Nanjing], Master Wang Tai-yü eminently wrote *A Summary of the Important Points for Enlightening the Young*." It also says that the engraving blocks are held by The Pure and Real Book Store (Ch'ing-chen Shu-pao-she) on Ox Street in Beijing. The book has the introduction by the Rustic of the Pure and Real and a second introduction by Yang Tsan-hsün, dated 1852. This edition also has "A discarded pearl," which is the preface to a completely different book, *Ch'ing-chen chih-nan* by Ma Chu (a book written in 1683). But the author of this introduction is not known, nor is it included in the 1869 and 1988 editions of Ma's book. (3). The 1987 edition in the collected works of Wang. This is presented as based upon the 1931 edition, but the characters have been modernized. The 1931 edition was published by the Chung-hua book shop. In addition to the introduction by the Rustic of the Pure and Real, it has a preface by Chin Shih-ho of Nanjing, who says that he is a descendent of Chin T'ien-chu, the author of *Ch'ing-chen shih-i*, written in 1738. There is a Japanese translation of the *Great Learning* by Kadono Tatsudo, but he follows Tazaka and therefore leaves out the "General Discussion."

18. The introduction to his poetry reads as follows: "Know that those who have received the ultimate Tao of the Pure and Real are human beings. Intention and thought are the human's root. To know the real and false of the sages and worthies is to serve honorably and without mistake. Examining the heterodoxy and truth of the teachings is to run in the right direction without delusion. However, if there is no wisdom and insight, there is no discrimination, even though this is the first duty in cultivating the Tao. In leisure time I casually composed eight poems. I began with wisdom and insight, and the sequence that follows discusses the man of clear wisdom." The topics are as follows: knowledge and wisdom, the human level, intention and thought, the sages, the worthies, the teachings of *shih* (Buddhism), the mysterious gate (Taoism), and creating images.

4. The Great Learning of the Pure and Real

1. This sentence may be inspired by a line from Wang's poem at the end of *The Great Learning*.

2. In other words, compare Islam to Confucianism. The Confucians often discuss their own path in terms of its wideness and broadness. As Ch'en remarks, "This is why the teachings of the Buddha, Lao Tzu, Chuang Tzu, and Lieh Tzu (c. 450–c. 375 BC) are heretical and perverse and are the robbers of our Way. The concrete learning of the Confucian School, however, is as level as the broad and smooth highway." *Neo-Confucian Terms Explained*, p. 109.

3. The expression "one thread" (*i-kuan*) is drawn from the *Analects*, where Confucius says that one thread runs through all his teachings (4.15, 15.2). Wang employs the expression in the *Great Learning* itself. Ch'en begins his chapter on the term by writing, "*I* ["one"] is simply principle, which is undifferentiated in its totality, the one great foundation. *Kuan* is this one principle spreading out in its operation and penetrating the ten thousand things. The heart of the sage, undifferentiated in its totality, is simply one principle, which is the great foundation." *Neo-Confucian Terms Explained*, p. 94.

4. Again, this is typical Confucian language to describe the true Tao that should be pursued.

5. There is no question that in this passage Wang has his eye on the Confucian *Great Learning* (as quoted in the introduction). However, he may have been familiar with this hadith, found in Rāzī's *Mirṣād al-ʿibād* (Algar, *Path*, p. 179): "By Him in whose hand is my soul! The faith of none of you will be upright [*mustaqīm*] until his heart is upright, his heart will not be upright until his tongue is upright, and his tongue will not be upright until his deeds are upright."

6. This passage expands on the Koranic verse of the Trust that was accepted only by human beings: "We offered the Trust to the heavens and the earth and the mountains, but they refused to carry it and were afraid of it. And the human being carried it" (33:72).

7. Color (*se*) and subtlety (*miao*) can be taken as equivalents to the Arabic pairs manifest (*ẓāhir*) and nonmanifest (*bāṭin*), or form (*ṣūra*) and meaning (*maʿnā*), or body (*jism*) and spirit (*rūḥ*). Color is what can be seen of the human being, and subtlety is what cannot be seen but appears through its traces.

8. Probably a reference to Koran 3:18, "God witnesses that there is no god but He."

9. Perhaps Wang has in mind the famous hadith of the Hidden Treasure: "I was a hidden treasure but was not known, so I created the creatures that I might be known."

10. On the Islamic side, Wang may have in view the verse, "Were there gods other than God in earth and heaven, these two would surely be corrupted" (21:22).

11. Compare the numerous verses of the Koran that refer to these and similar natural phenomena as "signs" of God; also the verses that declare God's creation and custom to be unchanging, such as 30:30 and 33:23.

12. The well-known prophetic saying is "God created Adam in His form." However, Wang seems to have in view another version that I have seen only in Rāzī's *Mirṣād al-ʿibād*, where it is cited three times: "Surely God created Adam, then He disclosed Himself [*tajallā*] in him" (Algar, *Path*, pp. 144, 310, 322).

13. This is the translation of a formula that is recited during the daily prayer: "I bear witness that there is no god but God alone, without associate, and I bear witness that Muhammad is His servant and His messenger." That Wang should place these words in Adam's mouth accords with the Islamic belief that Islam represents the religion of the *fiṭra*, or the innate disposition of human beings, and that Adam was the first Muslim.

14. According to an often quoted hadith, Muhammad said, "I was a prophet when Adam was between water and clay." This is often interpreted to mean that he was Adam's father in spirit, though his child in body. Hence it makes sense for Muhammad to have stirred Adam to repentance.

15. The reference is to the first sentence of the treatise.

16. The idea is well known. Perhaps its most famous expression is found in an Arabic poem by the fifth/eleventh century Sufi ʿAbdallāh Anṣārī: "None has affirmed the Unity of the One, since all who affirm it deny it. . . . His own assertion of His unity is His assertion of unity—those who depict it have gone astray." See Murata, *Tao*, p. 49.

17. This may be a translation of Koran 42:11, which is typically cited in theological discussions of this sort: "Nothing is as His likeness."

18. This passage has a bit of a Taoist flavor. Lao Tzu writes, "Tao invariably takes no action, and yet there is nothing left undone" (37). At the same time, this specific approach to negative theology has many precedents in Islamic works. Already in the sermons of ʿAlī, the Prophet's cousin and son-in-law and the fourth caliph, we find statements like this:

> He is a Being, not as the result of temporal origination, an Existent not from nonexistence. He is with everything, not through association; and He is other than anything, not through separation. He is active, not in the sense of possessing movement and instruments. . . . He originated creation and gave to it its beginning without employing deliberation, profiting from experience, occasioning movement, or being disrupted by the cares of the soul. (Adapted from W. Chittick, *A Shiʿite Anthology*, p. 30.)

19. This seems to be a reference to the hadith often quoted by the Sufis, "God was, and nothing was with Him."

20. *Tao Te Ching* 1.
21. *Tao Te Ching* 1.
22. Perhaps Wang has in mind Koran 68:1: "*Nūn*. By the Pen and what they are inscribing." Although *nūn* (i.e., the letter n) is usually taken as one of the disconnected letters found at the beginning of many surahs, some of the earliest commentators interpreted it to mean, or at least to allude to, "inkwell," which the word *nūn* would mean if it were written out. Thus the verse can be read as an oath referring to the cosmic Inkwell, along with the divine Pen or pens that are dipped into the Inkwell, and whatever the pens are writing (e.g., the destinies of the creatures, or the existence and reality of the creatures). Ibn al-ʿArabī devotes part of Chapter 60 of his *Futūḥāt al-makkiyya* to expanding on this imagery. He explains how Inkwell, Pen, and Preserved Tablet can be understood as references to the cosmic hierarchy. The One manifests its knowledge first in undifferentiated form (the Inkwell), then through the differentiating act (the Pen), and then through the actual differentiations, which are the creatures written out on the Tablet before they enter into external existence.
23. In other words, the perfect human possesses the basic attributes of heaven and earth, since, as we were told in the Synopsis, "heaven must cover and earth must carry." The discussion is reminiscent of the "all-comprehensiveness" (*jāmiʿiyya*) that is ascribed in Sufi texts to the perfect human being.
24. Creative (*ch'ien*) and Receptive (*k'un*) are the first two hexagrams of the *I Ching*. There is also a reference to the *Analects*, where Confucius says in defense of a student, "Yu has ascended the hall, but he has not yet entered the room" (11:14).
25. Perhaps a translation with explanation of the saying, "He who knows himself knows his Lord." Or perhaps this saying has been conflated with the hadith, "He who sees me has seen the Real."
26. Koranic parallels for this passage can be found in many verses that speak of God's signs. For a Neo-Confucian parallel, compare Ch'en's description of the Tao of heaven in *Neo-Confucian Terms Explained*, pp. 97–98.
27. Wang probably has in mind the famous hadith of *nawāfil*, the relevant part of which tells us that when God loves his servant, he is then the sight with which the servant sees, the ear with which he hears, the hand with which he takes, and the foot with which he walks. See Murata, *Tao*, p. 253.
28. "Inward and outward" here recalls Chu Hsi's commentary on the *Great Learning*: "Then the inward and the outward, the refined and the coarse, of all things will be reached, and the complete substance and great function of our heart will be clear" (cf. Chan, *Source Book*, p. 89).
29. This may be a translation of a well-known saying of Junayd: "When the newly arrived thing is juxtaposed with the Eternal, no trace of it remains."
30. Probably Wang has in mind this hadith: "I recognized my Lord through my Lord, and were it not for my Lord's bounty, I would not have recognized my Lord." Though not attested in the standard sources, it is cited in Rāzī's *Mirṣād al-ʿibād* (Algar, *Path*, pp. 78, 246). In his Chinese version of *Mirṣād*, Wu Tzu-hsien offers a much looser translation.
31. Wang probably has Koran 67:2 in mind, which he quotes later in the text.
32. This may be a translation of Koran 37:96, a text often cited in discussions of the nature of human activity: "God created you and what you do."

33. Rūmī uses the same argument in the *Mathnawī*. "If [the painter] cannot make ugly pictures, he is imperfect: That is why God creates both unbeliever and sincere servant" (II 2542; cited in Chittick, *The Sufi Path of Love*, p. 55).

34. There is an allusion here to the Confucian *Great Learning*: "Things have roots and branches, affairs have beginnings and ends. Knowing what is before and what is after—then one is close to the Tao" (cf. Chan, *Source Book*, p. 86). The word *central* (*chung*) calls to mind the *Doctrine of the Mean* (*chung-yung*).

35. This can be taken as a reference both to the Islamic idea of *fiṭra*, the innate disposition of all people to profess *tawḥīd*, and to Mencius's declaration of the essential goodness of human nature (e.g., 6A.6), a teaching that became normative for the Confucian tradition. Compare Ch'en: "This is the goodness bestowed on us by the Lord on High, and this is the normal nature the people keep. Because all people share it and thus their minds are unobstructed, intelligent, and not beclouded, it is called the clear virtue (*ming-te*)" (*Neo-Confucian Terms Explained*, p. 177). On *fiṭra*, see Murata and Chittick, *Vision*, pp. 137–39.

36. As Wing-tsit Chan points out, "The analogy of the ocean and many waves for the relationship between substance and function is a favorite Buddhist one" (*Source Book*, p. 769). It is also a favorite Islamic one. Compare Jāmī's quatrain in Gleam 27 and its translation by Liu Chih.

37. Wang cites the first two lines of this poem as part of the poem "life and death" in his collection of twelve poems.

38. This may be a reference to the hadith of the Hidden Treasure.

39. Clearly a translation of the saying, "He who knows himself knows his Lord."

40. These two clauses are almost identical with a sentence already cited from Wang's *True Answers* (p. 45).

41. A translation of Koran 51:56: "I created jinn and mankind only that they should worship Me." Already the Prophet's companion Ibn ʿAbbās interpreted "worship" to mean "know."

42. This may be a reference to Koran 25:43: "Have you seen him who takes his own caprice to be his god?"

43. Compare Mencius: "Even if you had the keen eyes of Li Lou and the skill of Kung-shu Tzu, you could not draw rectangles and circles without square and compass. . . . The compass and square are the ultimate of circle and rectangle. The sage is the ultimate of the human bonds" (4A.1–2).

44. The word is *yeh*, the standard Chinese term for this Buddhist concept.

45. This is the third version of Koran 67:2 that we have seen in Wang's writings.

46. The material in brackets is added to make sense of this proverbial expression. Someone dreamed that he was a great king, but then he woke up to the millet that was in fact his everyday fare.

47. In chapter ten of the *Real Commentary*, Wang quotes this same passage from *Hsing-li ta-ch'üan*.

48. These are the words of the Buddha when he emerged from the womb.

49. The famous T'ang dynasty physician Ch'en Ts'ang-ch'i wrote in *Pen-ts'ao shih-i* that human flesh can cure wasting diseases, and from that time on filial piety would sometimes drive people to feed their own flesh to their parents (Kuwabara Jitsuzō, *Chugoku no kōdō*, pp. 121–24).

50. Compare Chu Hsi's remarks on Buddhism and Taoism: "The mere fact that they discard the Three Bonds . . . and the Five Constants . . . is already a

crime of the greatest magnitude. Nothing more need to be said about the rest" (*Source Book*, p. 646). Ch'en writes, "The Taoists want purity and vacuity and loathe to do things, and the Buddhists reject human affairs. They all look upon principle as something above things and mysterious, and regard human affairs as on the lower level and coarse and therefore want to avoid them" (*Neo-Confucian Terms Explained*, p. 107).

51. Wang may be criticizing Taoists here, but he is making use of Chuang Tzu's own imagery to do so. In 14:5 Chuang Tzu writes, "Scattering chaff blinds the eye such that heaven, earth, and the four directions change their sites." Wang uses the same imagery several times in the *Real Commentary*.

5. Liu Chih's Translation of Lawāʾiḥ

1. See for example Knysh, *Ibn ʿArabi in the Later Islamic Tradition*. See also Chittick, "Notes on Ibn al-ʿArabī's Influence in India."

2. For a translation of the précis, plus a good portion of Jāmī's commentary, see Chittick, "Ibn ʿArabi's Own Summary of the *Fuṣūṣ*."

3. See the translation by Nicholas Heer, *The Precious Pearl*.

4. For two examples of Jāmī's poetry, see Murata, *Tao*, pp. 35–37, 62.

5. For a brief history of the expression and its varying definitions, see Chittick, "Rūmī and *waḥdat al-wujūd*."

6. See Chittick, "*Waḥdat al-shuhūd* and *waḥdat al-wudjūd*," *Encyclopaedia of Islam*.

7. For a list of the eleven practices, see Richard's French translation of the *Lawāʾiḥ*, pp. 12–14.

8. On the expression, see Chittick, *Sufi Path of Knowledge*, pp. 113–15.

9. These two positions are reducible to the contrary stances of the Ash'arite and Mu'tazilite theologians. On Ibn al-ʿArabī's middle position between the two, see "Acts of God and Acts of Man" in Chittick, *Sufi Path of Knowledge*, pp. 205–11.

10. See Chittick, *Self-Disclosure of God*, especially chapters three and four.

11. The scheme Jāmī provides here is different from other, better known schemes. He himself provides three other versions in *Naqd al-nuṣūṣ*, pp. 29–32. For a brief review of some of the standard formulations beginning with Ṣadr al-Dīn Qūnawī, who seems to have coined the expression "Five Divine Presences," see Chittick, "The Five Divine Presences: From al-Qūnawī to al-Qayṣarī." For an explication of the scheme in terms rather close to those that Jāmī employs, see the introduction to Chittick and Wilson, *Fakhruddin ʿIraqi: Divine Flashes*.

12. *Fuṣūṣ al-ḥikam*, p. 76.

13. On the "tasks" in Ibn al-ʿArabī's teachings, see Chittick, *Sufi Path of Knowledge*, pp. 98ff.

14. Quoted in Ch'en, *Neo-Confucian Terms Explained*, p. 71.

15. Chan, *Source Book*, p. 537.

16. See, for example, Chu Hsi's explanations of principle and the Great Ultimate in *Source Book*, pp. 634–41.

17. We have checked our translation against Richard's and are fully aware of the many passages where our interpretation does not agree with his. In choosing English equivalents for technical terms, we have followed those employed in Chittick's studies of Ibn al-ʿArabī, with a few exceptions.

18. A microfilm of the Chinese edition was kindly supplied by the Tōyō Bunko library in Tokyo. I have not found references to any other edition in the catalogues. A copy of the same edition is found in the New York Public Library.

19. *Islamic Literature in Chinese*, p. 41.

6. Gleams

1. This is a hadith that is found in most of the authoritative collections.

2. Al-Ghazālī cites this as a hadith (*Iḥyāʾ ʿulūm al-dīn* 2.10.4). A similar hadith tells us, "I am the most articulate of the Arabs" (*ana aʿrab al-ʿarab*), which is explained as meaning the "most eloquent" (*afṣaḥ*). See Suyūṭī, *al-Jāmiʿ al-ṣaghīr* 3:38.

3. The "banner of praise" and the "praiseworthy station" are both mentioned in the hadith literature as belonging to Muhammad on the day of resurrection (cf. Chittick, *Sufi Path of Knowledge*, pp. 239–40).

4. There is an allusion in this Arabic prayer to a hadith often cited in Sufi texts, "O God, show us things as they are."

5. Poverty (*faqr*) is a common designation for Sufism. For a good collection of classical Sufi sayings about it, see Nurbakhsh, *Spiritual Poverty in Sufism*, pp. 1–38.

6. Gnosis (*ʿirfān*), tasting (*dhawq*), and finding (*wijdān*) are all standard designations for the suprarational knowledge that is most commonly called "unveiling" (*kashf*). See Chittick, *Sufi Path of Knowledge*, pp. 148–49, 168–70.

7. There is word-play here, since *hamadān* can also be understood to mean "know-everything." It is not completely clear who this figure is, but, despite the fact that the probable date of the composition of the work is 870, Whinfield and Richard both think it was Shāh Manūchihr, whom Jāmī met on the way to Mecca in 877 (Whinfield, *Lawāʾiḥ*, p. 4; Richard, *Jaillissements*, pp. 27–28).

8. The discussion of gathering (*jamʿ*) and dispersion (*tafriqa*, also *farq*) goes back to the early Sufi manuals (for a good collection of Sufi texts illustrating how the terms are contrasted, see Nurbakhsh, *Sufism*, pp. 41–64). "Causes" translates *asbāb* (plural of *sabab*), which suggests secondary, apparent causes rather than primary, real causes. In Sufi terminology, all the things in the universe are "causes" in this sense. To immerse oneself in the causes in a search for ultimate truth is to remain in dispersion and separation. In the Sufi view, this is the handicap of all the rational sciences. The Sufi path is rather to empty oneself of all causes, to "polish the heart" by cleansing it of the rust of things, and to find God's light in the heart.

9. As already noted the "realities" of things are the same as the "fixed entities" (*aʿyān thābita*). They are "nonexistent" because they have no existence of their own.

10. "Unboundedness" and "binding" translate *iṭlāq* and *taqyīd*. This is a standard pair of Arabic terms used to contrast the Real Existence of God with the existence of things (on this pairing in Ibn al-ʿArabī, see Chittick, *Sufi Path of Knowledge*, index under "delimitation"; and idem, *Self-Disclosure*, index under "unbounded"). In a philosophical context, *muṭlaq* is usually translated as "absolute," but this is often inadequate in Sufi texts, especially if we translate *muqayyad* as "relative" (as does Whinfield in this passage; Richard uses *absolu* and *determination*, and, for the adjectival form, *inconditionné* and *conditionné*). "Unboundedness" and "binding" give a better sense of the concrete meaning implied by the terms. For his part, Liu Chih translates the two terms rather consistently throughout the text as "penetrating" and "obstructed" (see especially Gleam 21). The Chinese pairing suggests the concrete meaning of the Arabic words, but this is lost when we have recourse to abstract terms like "absolute" and "relative."

It was noted earlier that penetration and obstruction are commonly contrasted in Neo-Confucian thought. We saw that Chu Hsi explains the difference between human beings and animals in terms of their possession of a principle that penetrates the obstructions of impurity (p. 41). Discussions of the two terms often apply them to the issue of achieving perfection by actualizing the heart's oneness with Principle or by realizing the fullness of *jen*. Thus Chu Hsi was asked, "How can the heart by means of Tao penetrate all things without limit?" He replied, "The heart is not like a side door which can be enlarged by force. We must eliminate the obstructions of selfish desires, and then it will be pure and clear and able to know all" (Chan, *Source Book*, p. 630). In Islamic terms, this penetration of all things is a characteristic of the Real Being, which is unbounded and infinite, whereas each specific thing represents a binding and blocking of its infinite light. As Rūmī put it, "If you pour the ocean into a jug, how much will it hold? One day's store" (*Mathnawī* I 20).

11. For "philosophers" Jāmī uses the term *ḥukamāʾ*, plural of *ḥakīm*, meaning "wise" or "sage," but he means the term in the sense of *falāsifa*, the "philosophers," as is commonly the case in both Persian and Arabic. This is manifestly clear in his usage of the same word in the full title of his *Precious Pearl*. Avicenna offers an example of the teaching Jāmī has in mind:

> The soul continues on like this until she fully achieves in herself the guise of all of existence. She turns into an intelligible world, parallel with all the existent cosmos. She witnesses what is absolute comeliness, absolute good, and real, absolute beauty while she is unified with it, imprinted with its likeness and guise, strung upon its thread, and coming to be of its substance. (Ibn Sīnā, *al-Shifāʾ*, pp. 425–26. Cf. Ibn Sīnā, *al-Najāt*, p. 293.)

12. *Mathnawī* II 277–78.

13. As already explained, "relation" (*nisbat*) in this passage and in Gleams 7, 8, 11, and 12 is a Naqshbandī technical term. It refers to a subtle connection that is established between the disciple and the master through picturing the image of the master's face and concentrating on the name of God. Jāmī provides a detailed explanation of the term in *Sharḥ-i rubāʿiyyāt* (edited by Afshār, pp. 88–89). He begins with two quatrains, both of which play on the name of the founder

of the order, Naqshband, which means literally "picture-binder" and can be taken as a reference to this specific practice. I quote the quatrains and the beginning of his explanation:

> When you see a king on the throne of poverty,/ one aware with certainty of the mysteries of reality,/ If you picture his form on the tablet of the heart,/ You will find a road from that picture to the Picture-binder.
>
> Those in pain know the mystery of love's heartache,/ but the pleasant-living and the self-satisfied do not know./ One can go from the picture to the pictureless—/The picture-binders know this wondrous picture.
>
> In attentiveness [*tawajjuh*] and nurturing the nonmanifest relation [*parwarish-i nisbat-i bāṭin*], the path [*ṭarīqa*] of the Master [Bahā᾽ al-Dīn Naqshband] and his vicegerents is as follows: Whenever they want to occupy themselves with the relation, first they bring into imagination the form of the individual from whom they have received it, until the warmth and their accustomed quality appears. Then, while clinging to that quality along with that form and image, which is the mirror of the unbounded Spirit, they turn the attentiveness toward the heart, which is the all-gathering reality [*ḥaqīqat-i jāmiʿa*] of the human being and of which the totality of the engendered universe, both high and low, is the differentiation. Although the heart is incomparable with dwelling in bodies, there is a relation between it and this pine-cone shaped lump of flesh. Hence, one must turn the attentiveness toward the pine-cone shaped flesh. One must assign to it eyes, reflection, imagination, and all faculties and be present with it, and one must sit at the heart's door. We have no doubt that in this state, the quality of selflessness [*bī-khwudī*] and absence [*ghaybat*] will show its face. One must assume that this quality is a road and follow it. Whenever a thought comes that is turned toward the reality of one's heart, one must negate it. One must not occupy oneself with that particular thing, and one must flee into undifferentiation to the Universal so that it may be negated. The time of the quality and the selflessness must be extended and not interrupted. (pp. 88–89)

For a discussion of this practice in the Naqshbandī order, see Chodkiewicz, "Quelques aspects des techniques spirituelles dans la *ṭarīqa* naqshbandiyya."

14. "I am the Real" is of course Ḥallāj's famous declaration.

15. The "unbounded Face" (*wajh-i muṭlaq*) is the face of God seen in all things but not limited and defined by any of them. It is referred to in the Koranic verse, "Wherever you turn, there is the face of God" (2:115). For Ibn al-ʿArabī on this face, see Chittick, *Self-Disclosure*, chapters 3 and 4.

16. This quatrain is reminiscent of another quatrain that Jāmī explains both in his *Sharḥ-i rubāʿiyyāt* and in a short, independent treatise, which goes by several names, on the Naqshbandī method. In both cases, Jāmī is explaining the nature of the already mentioned relation. The quatrain reads, "Bring to hand the thread of good fortune, brother,/ and pass not this precious life in loss: / Constantly, everywhere, with everyone, in every work, / keep the eye of the heart on the Companion in secret!" Jāmī's explanation of this quatrain (pp. 91–92) seems to be an earlier version of the Seventh Gleam:

One must exercise this relation such that one is never empty of this relation. If one is heedless of it for a moment, one must return to the work in the manner that was said. One must be present constantly. In the house and the bazaar, in buying and selling, in eating and drinking, and in all states one must keep the corner of the heart's eye on one's own all-gathering reality. One must place it before one's eyes and keep it present. One must not become heedless of it through particular forms. Rather, one must know that all things endure through it, and one must try to witness it in all existents, whether they are considered beautiful or not beautiful, until one sees oneself in all. One must know that all things are the mirror of one's own perfect beauty. Or rather, one must see that all are parts of oneself. . . . One must know that this all-gathering reality is the locus of manifestation for the totality of God's Essence and attributes, not that God dwells within it—high is God beyond that! Rather this is like the manifestation of a form in a mirror.

17. As noted, "poverty" is a common designation for the Sufi path. For the text on poverty from which Jāmī may have taken this specific saying, see Chittick and Wilson, *Fakhruddin ʿIraqi: Divine Flashes*, pp. 111–13.

18. Jāmī has in view here standard Sufi discussions of annihilation. For a good collection of these, see Nurbakhsh, *Sufism*, pp. 85–115. However, "annihilation of annihilation" is not a common expression, so he may be looking at specific Naqshbandī teachings. In *Nafaḥāt al-uns* (p. 395) he quotes a saying from ʿAlāʾ al-Dīn ʿAṭṭār (d. 802/1400), a major disciple of Bahāʾ al-Dīn Naqshband: "When the Kingdom and the Sovereignty [i.e., both worlds] come to be hidden from the seeker and are forgotten, this is 'annihilation.' When the being of the wayfarer comes to be hidden from the wayfarer himself, this is 'annihilation of annihilation.'"

19. The Sufis take "the language of the birds" as a Koranic allusion to the mysteries of the path to God. It is of course the title of Farīd al-Dīn ʿAṭṭār's famous poem, whose title is usually mistranslated in English. See ʿAṭṭār, *The Conference of the Birds*.

20. Whinfield's translation here is more or less correct but it loses the technical nature of the discussion, whereas Richard misses the point entirely, as shown by his punctuation. The text should read *yādkard-i ḥaqq*, not *yād kard, ḥaqq*. *Yādkard* is a relatively unusual word, since, as already pointed out, it is a technical term pertaining specifically to Naqshbandī teachings. Jāmī says that it is a technical term (*iṣṭilāḥ*) in his *Sharḥ-i rubāʿiyyāt* (p. 99). He defines it as "remembrance [*dhikr*] of the Real by the tongue or the heart." He has taken most of his discussion of the term from Bahāʾ al-Dīn Naqshband's *Qudsiyya*, p. 36.

21. The word translated as "obtainment" is *ḥuṣūl*, whose basic meaning is to come to hand, as gold from a mine or harvest from a planting. Dictionaries give English equivalents such as setting in, occurrence, happening, attainment, achievement. Whinfield and Ḳazvīnī render the whole phrase rather loosely as "the state of being or existing," and Richard translates *ḥuṣūl* into French as *acquisition*.

22. The Ash'arites resolved the theological issue here in the Kullabite formula, "They [the attributes] are neither He nor other than He," a statement that Ibn al-ʿArabī sometimes rejects. He often formulates the issue in terms of what he

calls the "two denotations" of the Essence. See Chittick, *Sufi Path of Knowledge*, pp. 36–37; Chodkiewicz et al., *Les Illuminations de La Mecque/The Mecca Revelations*, p. 114 (*Futūḥāt* IV 197.22).

23. This Arabic prayer is probably Jāmī's own composition. The pattern goes back to a famous prayer uttered by Abū Bakr, the first caliph: "Glory be to Him who assigned the creatures no path to His knowledge save the incapacity to know Him!"

24. "One-and-allness" translates *wāḥidiyya*, a term that began to be contrasted with "Unity" (*aḥadiyya*) with the writings of Qūnawī and Farghānī. As explained on p. 75, these two terms are derived from two Koranic names of God, *aḥad* and *wāḥid*, both of which mean "one." According to many commentators, God is *aḥad* inasmuch as he is uniquely one, incomparable, and transcendent, and he is *wāḥid* inasmuch as his one reality gives rise to all things. Hence "unity" can be said to designate a transcendent oneness that is contrasted with the manyness of the things, whereas "One-and-allness" can designate the immanent oneness that is implied by the plurality of divine names and attributes, a oneness that entails all multiplicity. Whinfield translates the two terms as "unity" and "singleness." Richard, following Henry Corbin, translates them as *unitude divine* and *unité seconde*. Liu Chih's translation of the two as "Only-One" (*chih-i*) and "First-One" (*ti-i*) nicely catches their contrasting meanings.

25. "Lastness" (*ākhiriyya*), which is derived from the divine name Last (*ākhir*), means also "latterness." The word *ākhir* is both a comparative and a superlative adjective, so if one thing comes after another—in this case *wāḥid* after *aḥad*—the second is the "latter" and hence deserves this attribute.

26. "Gathering" (*jamʿ*) is God's attribute inasmuch as all attributes and possibilities are prefigured within Him. The term is derived from the word *jāmiʿ*, which is both a Koranic divine name ("All-gathering" or "All-comprehensive") and a basic description of the name Allah, which is called the "all-gathering name" (*al-ism al-jāmiʿ*), because all the other divine names come under its compass. In Ibn al-ʿArabī's vocabulary, the attribute of gathering is closely associated with the perfect human being, who is the "all-gathering engendered thing" (*al-kawn al-jāmiʿ*), mentioned at the beginning of the first chapter of the *Fuṣūṣ* (see also Chittick, *Self-Disclosure*, pp. 171, 178–81). In Gleam 2, gathering was discussed in much the same manner as it is discussed in the classic Sufi manuals, where it designates the collectedness and concentration achieved by one-pointed focus on the One. The present context reminds us that for Ibn al-ʿArabī's school of thought, the theoretical elaboration of the classic concepts of gathering and dispersion demands attention to the true nature of human beings as "all-gathering engendered things," created in the image of the One who embraces all of reality.

27. The first two terms, differentia (*faṣl*) and specificity (*khāṣṣa*), are philosophical designations for the characteristics that set things apart from each other, whereas "entification" (*taʿayyun*) came to be used among Ibn al-ʿArabī's followers to designate all things inasmuch as they are distinct entities having specific characteristics.

28. As this passage illustrates, "divine" (*ilāhī*) and "engendered" (*kawnī*) are contrasting terms. The first designates what pertains specifically to God considered as the Divinity (*ulūhiyya*), the second to everything that derives from the

engendering act of God, which is his saying to a thing "Be!" (*kun*). "Realities" are the things as known to God, or, the things as present within the Reality of Realities (Gleam 25). The engendered realities may be considered in their non-existence, in which case they are identical with the fixed entities, or they may be considered as existent in the world, in which case they may be called the "existent entities" and, as in the next paragraph, the "external entities." On the entities, see Chittick, *Sufi Path of Knowledge*, pp. 83–88. Richard translates the term *ʿayn* ("entity") as "individual essence," which is misleading and loses sight of the context of the discussion. On why "essence" is inappropriate for *ʿayn*, see Chittick, *Self-Disclosure*, p. 389n9.

29. Essential necessity (*wujūb-i dhātī*) is the fact that the Being of the Essence is necessary, which is to say that the Essence cannot not be. Every other divine attribute can become manifest generally in creation and specifically in perfect human beings. Created things always remain "possible things" (*mumkin*), which is to say that their existence can never belong to them by essence, only by borrowing from the Necessary in Being. They can have necessity, but only "through the other" (*bi'l-ghayr*), not through their own essences.

30. "Individuals" translates *afrād*, which seems to have no specifically Sufi meaning here. It is used in the same sense at the beginning of the next Gleam, when Jāmī mentions the "individuals of the species." In Ibn al-ʿArabī's vocabulary, it can better be translated as "solitaries" and designates those perfect human beings who are outside the scope of the Pole (*quṭb*). See Chittick, *Self-Disclosure*, p. 142 (and index for other references).

31. These are two standard divisions of the worlds. Vertically, there are three worlds: the world of bodies, of images, and of spirits. Horizontally, there are two: the world in which we now dwell and the world of the resurrection and beyond. See Murata and Chittick, *Vision*, p. 224.

32. This pairing of terms—"disclosure" (*jalāʾ*) and "seeing disclosure" (*istijlāʾ*)—seems to have been made current by Qūnawī. For an explanation of some of what it implies, see the discussion of "distinct-manifestation" and "distinct-vision" in Chittick and Wilson, *Fakhruddin ʿIraqi: Divine Flashes*, pp. 21 ff. For some of Farghānī's explications, see *Muntaha'l-madārik*, vol. 1, pp. 45–46, 72. Liu Chih seems to consider this discussion too technical, since he drops the passage.

33. Jāmī has taken this complex sentence almost verbatim from Farghānī, *Mashāriq al-darārī*, p. 17. The basic meaning of the Koranic term *ghinā* is wealth and riches, though it can also be translated as "independence" or "lack of need." Here Liu Chih chooses to look at the primary sense of the word, and we follow his lead. Ibn al-ʿArabī frequently discusses this divine attribute to assert the transcendence of the divine Essence (see Chittick, *Sufi Path of Knowledge* and *Self-Disclosure*, indexes under "independence"), and Farghānī's passage summarizes the basic point: The Essence is utterly transcendent because it has no need of anything whatsoever outside itself, given that everything is already present within it by virtue of its infinite knowledge. After the phrase, "by the inclusion of all within Its oneness," Farghānī's original sentence has, "like the inclusion of all the numbers and their levels in *one* [*wāḥid*], and *unit* [*aḥad*]." Compare the even more complex Arabic version of this sentence in Farghānī, *Muntaha'l-madārik*, vol. 1, pp. 13–14.

34. "Eye" here translates *ʿayn*, which elsewhere in this passage is translated as "entity." In this specific context, however, it is contrasted with *ʿilm* or "knowledge," which means the stage of the fixed entities in their nonmanifestation. Hence *ʿayn* refers to the stage in which the entities fixed in knowledge become manifest to the eye as existent entities. Whinfield has caught the implication of the term by translating it freely as "sensible world."

35. This passage is probably derived from a much more complicated version of the discussion found in Farghānī, *Muntaha'l-madārik*, vol. 1, p. 7.

36. Jāmī is answering here one of the attacks made by opponents of Ibn al-ʿArabī's school such as Ibn Taymiyya and ʿAlāʾ al-Dawla Simnānī. As Knysh tells us in his review of Ibn Taymiyya's polemic, "According to the Hanbali scholar, Ibn ʿArabi makes no distinction between the existence of God and that of 'jinn, devils, unbelievers, sinners, dogs, swine.'" *Ibn ʿArabi in the Later Islamic Tradition*, p. 100.

37. The "knowledged forms" (*ṣuwar-i ʿilmiyya*) are God's "objects of knowledge" (*maʿlūmāt*) and, as the Koran tells us, "Not a leaf falls, but He knows it" (6:59). It would be absurd to suggest that God does not know the leaf, or else he would be touched by ignorance. And since God is outside of time, he knows all things for all eternity. Ibn al-ʿArabī calls this divine omniscience God's "conclusive argument" against the creatures. See Chittick, *Sufi Path of Knowledge*, pp. 297–301.

38. "Predication" (*ḥaml*) is to ascribe a "predicate" (*maḥmūl*), that is, an attribute or characteristic, to a "subject" (*mawḍūʿ*), that is, whatever is described by the attribute. The point is the same that was made more briefly in Gleam 15—that the attributes are identical with the Essence in respect of existence and different in terms of denotation.

39. On the expression "All are He" (*hama ūst*) and its connection to the debate in later Sufism over the term *waḥdat al-wujūd* ("the oneness of existence"), see Chittick, "*Waḥdat al-shuhūd* and *waḥdat al-wudjūd*," *Encyclopaedia of Islam*.

40. A good portion of this description of the six levels seems to be taken from Jandī, *Sharḥ Fuṣūṣ al-ḥikam*, p. 613.

41. The Manifest of Existence (*ẓāhir-i wujūd*) is often contrasted with the Nonmanifest of Existence (*bāṭin-i wujūd*), as we saw in Gleams 18 and 22. Here, however, it is contrasted with the Manifest of Knowledge (*ẓāhir-i ʿilm*), which will be mentioned shortly. The contrast is discussed in detail by Farghānī (and the sentences relevant to these two terms in the present passage are not found in Jandī's version). Farghānī explains that at the level of Divinity—the level that Ibn al-ʿArabī sometimes calls the "One/Many"—there is both the oneness of the Real Existence and the manyness of the divine knowledge. In other words, God is truly one through his Being, but he embraces the principles of all multiplicity through his knowledge of all realities. This true oneness is called the "Manifest of Existence," and the manyness is called the "Manifest of Knowledge." The Manifest of Existence is the form of Unity (*aḥadiyya*) and has the attribute of necessity; it has a real oneness and a relative manyness. The Manifest of Knowledge is the form of One-and-allness (*wāḥidiyya*) and has the attribute of possibility. In other words, the objects of God's knowledge are the "possible things" (*mumkināt*), to which God may give external existence. The Manifest of

Knowledge has a real manyness and a relative oneness (*Mashāriq al-darārī*, p. 22; cf. *Muntaha'l- madārik*, vol. 1, p. 15). As for the "Nonmanifest of Existence" and the "Nonmanifest of Knowledge," these two pertain to the Essence and its tasks.

42. A saying of the Prophet, made famous in this version by Ibn al-ʿArabī. See Chittick, *Sufi Path of Knowledge*, p. 393n13.

43. Compare Ibn al-ʿArabī, "So the nonmanifest of the Real is the manifest of creation, and the nonmanifest of creation is the manifest of the Real" (Chittick, *Self-Disclosure*, p. 370). For many other passages in which Ibn al-ʿArabī describes God and the world in terms of manifest and nonmanifest, see ibid., pp. 205–23.

44. For an analysis of this argument in the *Fuṣūṣ*, see Izutsu, *Sufism and Taoism*, pp. 212–15. For passages from the *Futūḥāt* covering the same ground, see Chittick, *Sufi Path of Knowledge*, pp. 97 ff.; idem, *Self-Disclosure*, pp. 19, 248–49.

45. Ibn al-ʿArabī frequently discuss the two categories of contrary (*mutaqābil*) names, some associated with mercy, majesty, and gentleness (*luṭf*), some with wrath, beauty, and subjugation (*qahr*). See indexes, under "contrariety," of Chittick, *Sufi Path of Knowledge*, and idem, *Self-Disclosure*.

46. "Ineffectuality" renders *taʿṭīl*, which is a technical term in Kalam for the heretical position of declaring that God is not actively at work in the cosmos. The *muʿaṭṭila*, or "those who believe in ineffectuality," are commonly criticized in theological texts.

47. The "all-merciful mercy" (*raḥmat-i raḥmāniyya*) is contrasted with the "compassionate mercy" (*raḥmat-i raḥīmiyya*). The first pertains to the Breath of the All-merciful that gives existence to the cosmos, and the second to mercy that gives rise to paradise, as contrasted with the wrath that gives rise to hell.

48. The term *subjugation* is derived from the divine name *qahhār*, the "All-subjugating," which is paired with the divine name one (*wāḥid*) in all six of its Koranic occurrences. The verse most often cited to show its relevance to the present discussion—that is, the fact that it negates all "otherness"—refers to the Last Day, that is, the day when true relationships become clear to everyone. "The day they sally forth, and naught of theirs is hidden from God. 'Whose is the kingdom's today?' 'God's, the One, the All-subjugating'" (40:16).

49. These are the four most famous books of Avicenna, the greatest of the Muslim philosophers: *al-Shifāʾ*, *al-Qānūn*, *al-Najāt*, and *al-Ishārāt wa'l-tanbīhāt*.

50. These are the names of books by three famous scholars: *al-Mawāqif* in Kalam by ʿAḍud al-Dīn Ījī (d. 756/1355), *al-Maqāṣid* in Kalam by Saʿd al-Dīn Taftāzānī (d. 793/1390), and *al-Maṭāliʿ* in logic by Sirāj al-Dīn Urmawī (d. 682/1283).

51. This Gleam is probably inspired by the last *naṣṣ* of Qūnawī's *Nuṣūṣ*, p. 88.

52. This sentence refers to a passage from the fourth chapter of the *Fuṣūṣ al-ḥikam* that was quoted earlier (p. 119).

53. Maḥmūd Shabistarī, *Gulshan-i rāz*, in Lāhījī, *Mafātīḥ al-iʿjāz*, verse no. 145 (with slight textual discrepancies).

54. *Fuṣūṣ al-ḥikam*, p. 91.

55. Jāmī's Persian translation of the Arabic passage is accurate, but not exact. The text is found toward the beginning of *al-Nuṣūṣ*, p. 13.

56. The source of this expression is towards the beginning of the first chapter of the *Fuṣūṣ al-ḥikam*, where Ibn al-ʿArabī writes, "Among the characteristics

of the divine ruling is that He never proportions a locus that does not receive a divine spirit, which He has called 'blowing into it.' . . . The receptacle derives only from His most holy effusion" (p. 49). Jāmī says "Sufis" not because he does not know that Ibn al-ʿArabī coined the expression, but because the complementary expression, "holy effusion," is not found in his writings (see Ḥakīm, *al-Muʿjam al-ṣūfī*, pp. 888–92). Its source may be the writings of Ṣadr al-Dīn Qūnawī, specifically toward the beginning of his *Mirʾāt al-ʿārifīn* ("The mirror of the gnostics"), where he writes, "Glory be to Him who entified the entities through the most ancient, most holy effusion; who engendered the engendered things through the precedent, holy effusion; and who made eternity manifest through temporality, and temporality through eternity" (text in S. H. Askari, *Reflection of the Awakened*, p. 3). Despite the fact that Ibn al-ʿArabī does not explicitly formulate this pair of terms, his commentators and followers frequently discuss it, typically ascribe it to him, and draw the explication of what the terminology means from his writings. For example, he makes the same distinction in the second chapter of the *Fuṣūṣ* in terms of "essential gifts" and "name-derived gifts" and in the twelfth chapter in terms that are also being discussed here, that is, the two self-disclosures that are the "absent" and the "witnessed."

57. The common expression "May dirt fill your mouth!" can have an imprecatory sense and can also mean, "Keep your mouth shut!" or "Be ashamed of what you have said." Richard offers a mystical interpretation that is farfetched.

7. Displaying the Concealment of the Real Realm

1. Compare this verse from the Zen *Platform Scripture*: "The heart is the tree of perfect wisdom. /The body is the stand of a bright mirror./ The bright mirror is originally clear and pure./ Where has it been defiled by any dust?" (Chan, *Source Book*, p. 432).

2. There is a reference here to a Neo-Confucian discussion based on a passage from the ancient *Book of Documents* (2.2.15): "The human heart is in danger, the Tao heart is concealed; be refined, be one! Hold fast to the center!" For Chu Hsi's explanation of the two hearts from his introduction to the *Doctrine of the Mean*, see Kalton, *To Become a Sage*, p. 167.

3. This refers back to the sentence, "In talk of endeavor, righteousness is there, and in talk of righteousness, endeavor is lodged within." The second half will be explained shortly.

4. The allusion here is to a passage in Mencius (2A.2): "Let the heart not forget, but let there be no helping by force." Mencius illustrates what he means about "not helping" with a story:

> There was a man from Sung who pulled at his rice plants because he was worried about their failure to grow. . . . 'I am worn out today,' he said to his family, 'I have been assisting the rice plants to grow.' His son rushed out to take a look and there the plants were, all shrivelled up. There are few in the world who can resist the urge to help their rice plants grow. (Translated by Lau, *Mencius*, p. 78)

5. Ching-ch'u, also known as Yüan Kuo-tsu, was editor and publisher of several of Liu Chih's works. See Leslie, *Islamic Literature in Chinese*, p. 107, number 179.

6. The term is *chung-yung*, which is the title of the Neo-Confucian classic that is commonly translated as *The Doctrine of the Mean*. In his *Source Book*, Wing-tsit Chan tells us that *chung-yung* means literally "centrality and universality," though he translates it there sometimes as "equilibrium and harmony" and sometimes as "Mean." In the relevant chapter in *Neo-Confucian Terms Explained*, he translates it as "central and ordinary." Tu Weiming calls his study of the text *Centrality and Commonality*. Ch'en writes,

> Chu Hsi interpreted *chung-yung* as being ordinary. It is not that outside *chung*, there is another *yung*. It simply means that when what is central is manifested externally . . . that is the ordinary daily principle. The ordinary and the strange are opposed to each other. . . . All that are practiced by people daily and cannot be abolished are ordinary principles. . . . Those practices are unchangeable throughout the generations. . . . *Chung-yung* refers to moral activity, combining both action and affairs. (*Neo-Confucian Terms Explained*, pp. 125–26)

7. These are the philosophers Yang Chu and Mo Ti, whom Mencius and others hold up as exemplifying erroneous doctrines, as in *Mencius* 3B.9.

8. The reference is to the last four steps of the Confucian *Great Learning* (see p. 69).

9. On Liu Chih's use of the terms *penetration* and *obstruction* here, see the note on the original Persian passage.

10. It was noted earlier that Neo-Confucians strive to achieve "one body with heaven, earth, and the ten thousand things."

11. Jāmī means that the secret relation, which is inner concentration on the Real through remembrance (*dhikr*), needs to be intensified by ridding oneself of all attention to the things of the manifest world. One needs to empty oneself of concern for the forms and thoughts that normally fill the heart and replace them with recollection of God. Liu Chih seems to have missed the point. Or, if he has understood the point, he has preferred to interpret this self-emptying in terms of the "investigation of things," the first of the eight steps of the Confucian *Great Learning*.

12. As noted in chapter two, this expression derives from the *Analects*.

13. There is an allusion here to Mencius (7A.4): "The ten thousand things are all provided in myself."

14. "Non-awareness" (*pu-chio*) seems to be the same as the awareness and consciousness attained at the level of the "no-heart," which, as Wang explains in book one, chapter nineteen of the *Real Commentary*, is the highest stage of realization, beyond even the "true heart."

15. "Colors and guises" (*se-hsiang*) is a common Buddhist expression. *Se* was used to translate the Sanskrit *rupa* and means "appearance, matter, color, form, thing" (Chan, *Source Book*, p. 339). Chan thinks that in technical Buddhist language, *hsiang* can best be translated as "characteristic." It is whatever can be

described, as opposed to the hidden suchness. In ordinary usage, it means "sign, feature, appearance, form, etc." (*Source Book*, p. 786).

16. Compare the *Doctrine of the Mean* (1:3): "Nothing is more seen than what is hidden, nothing is more manifest than what is concealed."

17. "Ruling" translates *fa*, which has a variety of meanings, including "law, punishment, custom, duty, discipline, method, technique, and model" (Chan, *Source Book*, p. 786). In the philosophical context, it is used to render the Buddhist term *dharma* in the sense of the things that are considered to be existent, whether with or without form. Liu Chih uses the term several times in the text, in each case to refer to the specific attributes and properties of things, or their ruling characteristics.

18. On Liu Chih's avoidance of the proper names here, see p. 126.

19. The Chinese for "humanity" is of course *jen*, which, as we know, has a pre-eminent status among the virtues and manifests directly the goodness of heaven. That Liu Chih should employ it to refer to the category of the gentle and beautiful names of God should not be surprising, especially when we remember that *jen* has also been translated by terms such as love, benevolence, and perfect virtue.

20. Compare Chu Hsi: "Fundamentally there is only one Great Ultimate, yet each of the ten thousand things has been endowed with it and each in itself possesses the Great Ultimate in its entirety" (Chan, *Source Book*, p. 638).

21. Liu Chih seems to have missed the point of Ibn al-ʿArabī's text here, though his reading is plausible. In his commentary on the *Fuṣūṣ*, Jāmī glosses this passage as follows: "*The* possible *entity has no act. Rather, the act belongs to its Lord within it*, so it is the locus of manifestation for the act, not the agent. *So the entity is at peace*, or silent, *from the attribution of any act* in the mode of agency *to it*."

22. There is an allusion here to the first sentence of the Confucian *Great Learning*: "The Tao of the great learning exists through clarifying the clear virtue, loving the people, and abiding in the utmost good."

23. Liu Chih's expanded translation of this passage may be for the sake of bringing in the Neo-Confucian concept of "completeness." Compare this passage from Chu Hsi:

> Considering the fact that all things come from one source, we see that their principle is the same but their vital-energy is different. Looking at their various substances, we see that their vital-energy is similar but their principle utterly different. The difference in vital-energy is due to the inequality of its purity or impurity, whereas the difference in principle is due to its completeness or partiality. (Chan, *Source Book*, p. 637)

Glossary of Chinese Words

a-heng / aheng 阿衡
A-tan / Adan 阿丹
ai / ai (love) 愛
ai / ai (obstruction) 碍
an-la / anla 諳喇

Ch'a-mi / Chami 查密
ch'a-shih / chashi 察時
Ch'ang Chih-mei / Chang Zhimei 常志美
Ch'ang Tsai / Zhang Zai 張載
Chao-yüan Pi-chüeh / Zhaoyuan Mijue 昭元秘訣
chen / zhen (real) 眞
chen / zhen (upright) 貞
chen-chu / zhenzhu 眞主
Ch'en Ch'un / Chen Chun 陳淳
Ch'en Ts'ang-ch'i / Chen Cangqi 陳藏器
chen-chung / zhenzhong 眞忠
chen-hsin / zhenxin 眞心
chen-hui lao-jen / zhenhui laoren 眞回老人
chen-i / zhenyi 眞一
chen-sheng / zhensheng 眞聖
chen-tsai / zhenzai 眞宰
chen-tz'u / zhenci 眞賜
chen-yu / zhenyou 眞有
cheng / zheng (witnessing) 証
ch'eng / cheng (sincerity) 誠
cheng-chiao / zhengjiao 正教
Ch'eng Hao / Cheng Hao 程顥
cheng-hsüeh / zhenxue 正學
Ch'eng I / Cheng Yi 程頤
ch'eng-i / chengyi 成一
cheng-ming / zhengming 正命
chi / ji 極
ch'i / qi (unity) 契
ch'i / qi (vital-energy) 氣
Chi-tsang / Jicang 吉藏
chi-lo / jile 極樂
Ch'i-meng yao-lüeh / Qimeng yaolüe 啓蒙要略
chieh / jie 界
chiao-liang / jiaoliang 較量
ch'ien / qian 乾
chien-i / jianyi 見一
chien-jen / jianren 見認
ch'ien-ting / qianding 前定
chih / zhi (disposition) 質
chih / zhi (knowledge) 知
chih / zhi (utmost) 至
chih / zhi (will) 志
chih / zhi (wisdom) 智
ch'ih / zhi 治
chih-hsiao / zhixiao 至孝
chih-i / zhiyi (knowing one) 知一
chih-i / zhiyi (only one) 止一
chih-jen / zhiren 知認
chih-sheng / zhisheng 至聖
ch'in-ch'a / qinchai 欽差
chin-shih / jinshi 今世
Chin Shih-ho / Jin Shihe 金世和
ching / jing 經
ch'ing-chen chiao / qingzhen jiao 清眞教
ch'ing-chen pi-jen / qinzhen biren 清眞鄙人
ch'ing-chen shu-pao-she / Qinzhen shubaoshe 清眞書報社
ch'ing-chen-ssu / qingzhensi 清眞寺
Ching-chio / Jingjue 淨覺
Ching-ch'u / Jingchu 景初 (袁國祚)
chio / jue 覺
ch'iu / qiu 求
chiung-i / jiongyi 迥異

cho / zhuo 濁
Chou Tun-i / Zhou Dunyi 周敦頤
chü / ju 聚
Chu Hsi / Zhu Zhi 朱子
ch'ü-she / qushe 取舍
chung / zhong (loyalty) 忠
chung / zhong (central) 中
Chung-hua / Zhonghua 中華(書局)
chung-yung / zhongyong 中庸

en / en 恩

fa / fa (ruling) 法
fa / fa (issuance) 發
feng-shui / fengshui 風水
fu-fu / fufu 夫婦
fu-lu / fulu 附錄

Hao-wa / Haowa 好媧
ho / he 合
Ho Han-ching / He Hanjing 何漢敬
hou-shih / houshi 後世
hou-t'ien / houtian 後天
hsi / xi 習
hsi-i / xiyi 習一
hsiang / xiang (guise) 相
hsiang / xiang (image) 象
hsiao / xiao 孝
Hsieh Sheng-wu / Xie Shengwu 薛省吾
hsien / xian (appearance) 現
hsien / xian (worthies) 賢
hsien / xian (manifestation) 顯
hsien-shen / xianshen 仙神
hsien-t'ien / xiantian 先天
hsin / xin (faithfulness) 信
hsin /xin (heart) 心
hsing / xing (form) 形
hsing / xing (nature) 性
hsing-li hsüeh / xingli xue 性理學
Hsing-li ta-ch'üan / Xingli daquan 性理大全
hsing-ming / xingming 性命
hsiu / xiu 修
hsü / xu 虛
hsü-jen / xuren 續認
Hu Kuang / Hu Guang 胡廣
hua / hua 化
huan-yu / huanyou 幻有
hui-hui / hui-hui 回回
hun / hun 渾
hun-su / hunsu 葷素
huo / huo 活

i / yi (change) 易
i / yi (righteousness) 義
i-chen / yizhen 易眞
i-kuan / yiguan 一貫
i-ma-na / yi-ma-na 以媽納
i-t'i-ha-te / yi-ti-ha-de 一體哈德

jen / ren (human) 人
jen / ren (humanity) 仁
jen-chi / renji 人極
Jen-ching ching / Renjing jing 人鏡經
jen-i / renyi 認一
jen-p'in / renpin 人品
jen-tsu / renzu 人祖
jen-tz'u / renci 仁慈
ju / ru 儒

Ko-chih ch'üan-ching / Gezhi quan-jing 格致全經
ko-wu / gewu 格物
kuang / guang 光
Kuei-chen pi-yao / Guizhen biyao 歸眞必要
kuei / gui 鬼
kuei-i / guiyi 歸一
k'un / kun 坤
k'ung / kong 空
kung / gong 功

li / li (principle) 理
li / li (propriety) 禮
li / li (strength) 力
li-ku / ligu 利穀
li-ming / liming 利名
li-pai / libai 禮拜
li-pai ssu / libaisi 禮拜寺
Liang I-chün / Liang Yijun 梁以濬
ling / ling 靈
Liu I-ts'an / Liu Yican 劉一參
Lu Hsiang-shan / Lu Xiangshan 陸象山

Ma An-li / Ma Anli 馬安禮
Ma Chung-hsin / Ma Zhongxin 馬忠信 (君實)
Ma Kai-k'o / Ma Kaike 馬開科
Ma Ssu-yüan / Ma Siyuan 馬思遠
mei-chen / meizhen 昧眞
miao / miao 妙
ming / ming (clarity) 明
ming / ming (mandate) 命
ming / ming (name) 名
ming-te chih yüan / mingde zhi yuan 明德之源
mo / mo 魔
Mu-han-me-te / Mu-han-mo-de 穆罕默德

neng / neng 能
ni / ni 擬

pen / ben 本
pen-ching / benjing 本經
pen-fen / benfen 本分
pen-jan / benran 本然
pen-wei / benwei 本爲
P'eng Hui-o / Peng Huie 彭輝萼
pien / bian 辨
p'in / pin 品
P'o Na-ch'ih / Po Nachi 破納痴
po-yin / boyin 博飲
pu-chio / bujue 不覺
p'u-tz'u / puci 普慈

san-chi / sanji 三極
san-kang / sangang 三綱
se / se 色
se-hsiang /sexiang 色相
Sha Chen-ch'ung / Sha Zhenchong 沙振崇
shan-o / shane 善惡
Shao Yung / Shao Yong 邵雍
She Yün-shan / She Yunshan 舍蘊善
shen / shen (body) 身
shen / shen (spirit) 神
shen-kuei / shengui 神鬼
sheng / sheng (production) 生
sheng / sheng (sage) 聖
sheng-hsien / shengxian 聖賢
sheng-ssu / shengsi 生死
sheng-yü / shengyu 剩語
shih / shi (discernment) 識
shih / shi (freedom) 釋
shih / shi (reality) 實
shih-ming chen-ching / shiming zhenjing 實命眞經
shou-ling / shouling 首領
shou-mo / shoumo 首魔
shou-p'u / shoupu 首僕
shou-shen / shoushen 首神
shu-i / shuyi 數一
shun-i / chunyi (unmixed one) 純一
shun-i / shunyi (following one) 順一
ssu / si 私
ssu-chen / sizhen 似眞

t'ai-chi / taiji 太極
tai-li / daili 代理
tai-shu / daishu 代書
tao / dao 道
t'ao-hei-te / tao-hei-de 討黑德
t'ao-po / tao-bai 討白
te / de 德
t'i / ti 体
ti-chin / dijin 地禁
ti-i / diyi 第一
t'i-i / tiyi 体一
ti-yü / diyu 地獄
t'ien-ching / tianjing 天經
t'ien-chu / tianzhu 天主
t'ien-fang / tianfang 天方
t'ien-hsien / tianxian 天仙
t'ien-kuo / tianguo 天國
t'ing-ming / tingming 聽命
tsai-sheng / zaisheng 宰性
ts'an-wu / canwu 參悟
tsao / zao 造
tso-cheng / zuozheng 作証
tu / du 獨
tun-ya / dun-ya 吨丫
tung / dong 動
t'ung / tong (penetration) 通
t'ung / tong (totality) 統
tung-ching / dong jing 動靜
tzu / zi 子
tz'u / ci 慈

tzu-i / ziyi 自一
Tzu-ssu / Zisi 子思

wa-ha-te-te / wa-ha-de-te 空哈德特
wan / wan 万
Wang Chan-ch'ao / Wang Zhanchao 王占超
Wang Shou-ch'ien / Wang Shouqian 王守謙
Wang Yang-ming / Wang Yangming 王陽明
Wei Kang Ch'ui-ch'ih / Wei Gang Chuichi 危𡽪吹篪
wu / wu (nonbeing) 無
wu / wu (thing) 物
wu-ch'ang / wuchang 五常
wu-chi / wuji (non-ultimate) 無極
wu-chi / wuji (no-self) 無己
wu-hsin / wuxin 無心
Wu Lien-ch'eng / Wu Liancheng 伍連城
wu-se-chieh / wusejie 無色界

Yang Tsan-hsün / Yang Zanxun 楊贊勳
yeh / ye 業
yen / yan 言
Yen-chen ching / Yanzhen jing 研眞經
yin-yang / yinyang 陰陽
yin-yüan / yinyuan 因緣
yu / you 有
yü-pei / yubei 預備
yu-se-chieh / yousejie 有色界
yu-tao / youdao 友道
yüan / yuan 緣
yüan-hsün / yuanxun 元勳
yüan-shih / yuanshi 元始
yung / yong 用

Bibliography

Islamic Texts in Chinese

I list below all the Chinese Islamic texts that I have used in my research. For a more complete bibliography, see Leslie, *Islamic Literature in Chinese*. Asterisks designate the fifteen books that were reproduced by photo-offset in the fifty-five volume set *Hui-tsu ho chung-kuo i-szu-lan chiao ku-chi tzu-liao hui-pien* 回族和中國伊斯蘭教古籍資料匯編 ("A collection of materials in Chinese classical Islam"). Ningxia, 1987.

Chang Shih-chung 張時中. *Kuei-chen tsung-i* 歸眞總義. Beijing, 1923.

* ———. *Ssu-p'ien yao-tao* 四篇要道. Beijing, 1923.

Chin T'ien-chu 金天柱 (北高). *Ch'ing-chen shih-i* 清眞釋義. 1876.

Hei Ming-feng 黑鳴鳳. *(T'ien-fang) Hsing-li pen-ching chu-shih* (天方) 性理本經註釋. Canton, 1875.

* *Hui-hui yüan-lai* 回回原來. Beijing, 1894.

Lan Hsü Tzu-hsi 藍煦子羲. *T'ien-fang cheng-hsüeh* 天方正學. Beijing, 1923.

Liu Chih 劉智 (介廉、一齋). *Chen-ching chao-wei* 眞境昭微. Beijing, 1925

* ———. *Tarjama-yi Mustafa: T'ien-fang chih-sheng shih-lu* 天方至聖實錄. 1872. Japanese translation by Ippei Tanaka. *Tempo shisei jitsuroku*. Tokyo: Dainihon Kaikyo Kyokai, 1941.

* ———. *T'ien-fang hsing-li* 天方性理. Shanghai, 1863, 1928.

———. *T'ien-fang san-tzu-ching yu-i* 天方三字經幼義. 1858. English translation by F. J. M. Cotter and L. Reichelt. "The Three Character Classic for Moslems." *The Chinese Recorder* 48 (1917): 645–52; also in *Moslem World* 8 (1918).

* ———. *T'ien-fang tien-li [tse yao-chieh]* 天方典禮 (擇要解). Shanghai, 1740, 1923, 1924.

———. *Wu-kung shih-i* 五功釋義. Beijing, 1924.

Ma Ch'i-Yung 馬啓榮. *Hsi'-lai tsung-p'u* 西來宗譜. Zhenjiang, 1918.

* Ma Chu 馬注. *Ch'ing-chen chih-nan* 清眞指南. 1869, 1988.

Ma Fu-chu 馬復初 (德新). *Han-i tao-hsing chiu-ching* 漢譯道行究竟. 1870.

———. *Ssu-tien yao-hui* 四典要會. Beijing, 1922.

———. *Ta-hua tsung-kuei* 大化總歸. Beijing, 1922.

———. "The Three-Character Rhymed Classic on the Kaʿbah." Translated by J. Peter Hobson. *Studies in Comparative Religion* 14 (1980): 181–94.

Ma Fu-chu 馬復初 and Ma An-li 馬安禮. *Chen-ch'üan yao-lu* 眞詮要錄. Yunnan, 1864.

Ma Lian-yüan 馬聯元 (Muḥammad Nūr al-Ḥaqq ibn al-Sayyid Luqmān). *Hsing-li wei-yen* 性理微言 (*Laṭā'if*). Yunnan, 1898.

———. *Sharḥ-i laṭā'if*. Cawnpore, 1320/1902–3.

Ma Ming-lung 馬明龍. *Jen-chi hsing-yü* 認己醒語. 1919.

Ma Po-liang 馬伯良. *Chiao-k'uan chieh-yao* 教款捷要. 1874.

P'o Na-chih 破衲痴. *E-shen-erh-ting* 額慎㖠哼. 1930.

* Sun K'o-an 孫可庵. *Ch'ing-chen chiao-k'ao* 清眞教考. Beijing, 1921.

* T'ang Chuan-yu 唐傳猷. *Ch'ing-chen shih-i pu-chi* 清眞釋義補輯. 1881.

* Wang Ching-chai 王靜齋. *Ku-lan ching i-chiai* 古蘭經譯解. Shanghai, 1946.

Wang Tai-yü 王岱輿. *Cheng-chiao chen-ch'üan* 正教眞詮, *Ch'ing-chen ta-hsüeh* 清眞大學, *Hsi-chen cheng-ta* 希眞正答. Edited by Yu Zhengui. Ningxia, 1987.

* ———. *Cheng-chiao chen-ch'üan* 正教眞詮. 1642, 1657, 1873; Beijing, 1921.

* ———. *Ch'ing-chen ta-hsüeh* 清眞大學. Beijing, 1921 (under the title *Ch'i-meng yao-lüe* 啓蒙要略), undated (see part 3, note 17). Japanese translation by Kadono Tatsudo. *Kaikyo-ken* 1941 (5/4): 31–43; (5/5): 12–24.

* ———. *Hsi-chen cheng-ta* 希眞正答, together with *Fu-lu* 附錄 and *Sheng-yü* 剩語. Editions of 1827, 1925, 1987.

* Wu Tzu-hsien 伍子先. *Hsiu-chen meng-yin* 修眞蒙引. Beijing, 1921.

* ———. *Kuei-chen yao-tao* 歸眞要道. Editions of 1911 and undated.

* Yü Hao-chou 余浩洲 (attributed to Liu Chih 劉智). *Chen-kung fa-wei* 眞功發微. Sichuan, 1884.

Other Sources

Abarqūhī, ʿAbd al-Salām ibn ʿAlī ibn Ḥusayn. *Nihāyat al-masʾūl fī riwāyat al-rasūl*. Edited by Muḥammad Jaʿfar Yāḥaqqī. Tehran: Shirkat-i Intishārāt-i ʿIlmī wa Farhangī, 1366/1987.

Algar, H. *The Path of God's Bondsmen from Origin to Return*. Delmar, NY: Caravan Books, 1982.

Askari, S. H. *Reflection of the Awakened*. London: Zahra Trust, 1983.

ʿAṭṭār, Farīd al-Dīn. *The Conference of the Birds*. Translated by A. Darbandi and D. Davis. New York: Penguin, 1984.

———. *Muslim Saints and Mystics*. Translated by A. J. Arberry. Chicago: University of Chicago Press, 1966.

———. *Tadhkirat al-awliyāʾ*. Edited by M. Istiʿlāmī. Tehran: Zuwwār, 1346/1967.

Aubin, Françoise. "En Islam chinois: Quels Naqshbandis?" In *Naqshbandis: Cheminements et situation actuelle d'un order mystique musulman*, edited by M. Gaborieau, A. Popovic, and Th. Zarcone. Istanbul: Éditions Isis, 1990, pp. 491–572.

———. "La Chine." In *Les Voies d'Allah*, edited by A. Popovic and G. Veinstein. Paris: Fayard, 1996, pp. 261–67.

———. "Taṣawwuf 8. In Chinese Islam." *The Encyclopaedia of Islam*. Vol. 10, pp. 337–39.

———. "Les traductions du Coran en chinois." *Etudes orientales* 1994 (no. 13/14): 81–87.

Bay Shouyi 白壽彝. *Chung-kuo i-ssu-lan shih ts'an-k'ao* 中國伊斯蘭史存稿. Ningxia, 1983.

———. *Hui-tsu jen-wu chih* 回族人物志. Ningxia,1992.

Birdwhistell, Anne D. *Transition to Neo-Confucianism: Shao Yung on Knowledge and Symbols of Reality*. Stanford: Stanford University Press, 1989.

Chan, Wing-tsit. *A Source Book in Chinese Philosophy*. Princeton: Princeton University Press, 1963.

Ch'en Ch'un 陳淳. *Neo-Confucian Terms Explained*. Translated by Wing-tsit Chan. New York: Columbia University Press, 1986.

Chin Chi-t'ang 金吉堂. *Chung-kuo hui-chiao shih yen-chiu* 中國回教史研究. 1935.

Chittick, William C. "The Five Divine Presences: From al-Qūnawī to al-Qayṣarī." *The Muslim World* 72 (1982): 107–28.

———. "Ibn ʿArabi's own Summary of the *Fuṣūṣ*: 'The Imprint of the Bezels of Wisdom.'" *Journal of the Muhyiddin Ibn ʿArabi Society* 1 (1982): 30–93.

———. "Notes on Ibn al-ʿArabī's Influence in India." *Muslim World* 82 (1992): 218–41.

———. "Rūmī and *Waḥdat al-wujūd*." In *Poetry and Mysticism in Islam: The Heritage of Rūmī*, edited by A. Banani, R. Hovannisian, and G. Sabagh. Cambridge: Cambridge University Press, 1994, pp. 70–111.

———. "The School of Ibn ʿArabī." In *History of Islamic Philosophy*, edited by O. Leaman and S.H. Nasr. London and New York: Routledge, 1996, pp. 510–23.

———. *The Self-Disclosure of God: Principles of Ibn al-ʿArabī's Cosmology*. Albany: SUNY Press, 1998.

———. *A Shiʿite Anthology*. Albany: SUNY Press, 1981.

———. *The Sufi Path of Knowledge: Ibn al-ʿArabī's Metaphysics of Imagination*. Albany: SUNY Press, 1989.

———. *The Sufi Path of Love: The Spiritual Teachings of Rumi*. Albany: SUNY Press, 1983.

———. "*Waḥdat al-shuhūd* and *waḥdat al-wudjūd*." *The Encyclopaedia of Islam*, forthcoming.

Chittick, William C., and Peter Lamborn Wilson. *Fakhruddin ʿIraqi: Divine Flashes*. New York: Paulist Press, 1982.

Chō Shōsi (Zhang Chengzhia 張承志). *Kaikyō kara mita chūgoku*. Tokyo: Chuokoronsha, 1992.

Chō Shōsi (Zhang Chengzhi) and Umemura Hiroshi. *Junkyō no chūgoku isulamu*. Tokyo: Akishobō, 1993.

Chodkiewicz, Michel. "Quelques aspects des techniques spirituelles dans la *ṭarīqa* naqshbandiyya." In *Naqshbandis: Cheminements et situation actuelle d'un order mystique musulmane*, edited by M. Gaborieau, A. Popovic, and Th. Zarcone. Istanbul-Paris: Éditions Isis, 1990, pp. 69–82.

Chodkiewicz et al., *Les Illuminations de La Mecque/The Meccan Revelations*. Paris: Sindbad, 1988.

Cleary, Thomas. *Shōbōgenzō: Zen Essays by Dōgen*. Honolulu: University of Hawaii Press, 1986.

Farghānī, Saʿīd al-Dīn. *Mashāriq al-darārī*. Edited by S. J. Āshtiyānī. Tehran: Anjuman-i Islāmī-i Ḥikmat wa Falsafa, 1358/1979.

———. *Muntaha'l-madārik*. Cairo: Maktab al-Ṣanāʾiʿ, 1293/1876.

Fletcher, Joseph F. *Studies on Chinese and Islamic Inner Asia*. Aldershot: Valiorum, 1995.

Forbes, A. D. W. "Liu Chih." *Encyclopaedia of Islam*. Vol. 5, pp. 770–71.

Ford, J. F. "Some Chinese Muslims of the Seventeenth and Eighteenth Centuries." *Asian Affairs* 61 (1974): 144–56.

Fu T'ung-hsien 傳統先. *Chung-kuo hui-chiao shih* 中國回教史. Japanese translation by Ito Ken as *Chūgoku kaikyōshi*. Tokyo: Okakura Shoten, 1942.

Ghazālī, Muḥammad. *Iḥyāʾ ʿulūm al-dīn*. Cairo: Maṭbaʿat al-ʿĀmirat al-Sharafiyya, 1326–27/1908–9.

———. *Kīmiyā-yi saʿādat*. Edited by H. Khadīw-jam. Tehran: Jībī, 1354/1975.

Gladney, Dru C. *Muslim Chinese: Ethnic Nationalism in the People's Republic*. Cambridge: Harvard University Press, 1991.

Ḥakīm, Suʿād al-. *al-Muʿjam al-ṣūfī*. Beirut: Dandara, 1981.

Ibn al-ʿArabī. *Fuṣūṣ al-ḥikam*. Edited by A. ʿAfīfī. Beirut: Dār al-Kutub al-ʿArabī, 1946.

———. *al-Futūḥāt al-makkiyya*. Cairo, 1911. Reprinted Beirut: Dār Ṣādir, n.d.

Ibn Qaḍīb al-Bān. *al-Mawāqif al-ilāhiyya*. In *al-Insān al-kāmil fi'l-islām*, edited by ʿAbd al-Raḥmān Badawī. Kuwayt, Wikālat al-Maṭbūʿāt, 1976, pp. 148–219.

Ibn Sīnā. *al-Najāt*. Edited by M. Ṣabrī al-Kurdī. Cairo: Maṭbaʿat al-Saʿāda, 1938.

———. *al-Shifāʾ: al-Ilāhiyyāt*. Edited by G. C. Anawati and Saʿid Zayed. Reprinted Tehran: Intishārāt-i Nāṣir Khusraw, 1363/1984.

Izutsu, Toshihiko. *Sufism and Taoism*. Tokyo: Iwanami Shoten, 1983.

Jāmī, ʿAbd al-Raḥmān. *ʿAbdorrahmān b. Ahmad Jāmi: Les Jaillissements de Lumière; Lavāyeh. Texte persan édité et traduit avec introduction et notes* par Yann Richard. Paris: Les Deux Océans, 1982.

———. *Lawāʾiḥ*. Edited by M. Ḥ. Tasbīḥī. Tehran: Kitābfurūshī-yi Furūghī, 1342/1963.

———. *Lawāʾiḥ: A Treatise on Sūfism*. Translated by E. H. Whinfield and M. M. Ḳazvīnī. London: Oriental Translation Fund, 1906.

———. *Nafaḥāt al-uns*. Edited by M. ʿĀbidī. Tehran: Iṭṭilāʿāt, 1370/1991.

———. *Naqd al-nuṣūṣ fī sharḥ naqsh al-fuṣūṣ*. Edited by W. C. Chittick. Tehran: Imperial Iranian Academy of Philosophy, 1977.

———. *The Precious Pearl*. Translated by Nicholas Heer. Albany: SUNY Press, 1979.

———. *Sharḥ Fuṣūṣ al-ḥikam*. On the margin of al-Nābulsī. *Sharḥ Fuṣūṣ al-ḥikam*. Cairo, 1304–23/1887–1905.

———. *Sharḥ-i rubāʿiyyāt*. In Jāmī. *Lawāmiʿ wa Lawāʾiḥ*. Edited by Īraj Afshār. Tehran: Kitābkhāna-yi Manūchihrī, 1360/1981.

———. *Sharḥ-i rubāʿiyyāt*. Edited by M. Harawī. Kābul: Anjuman-i Jāmī, 1343/1964.

Jandī, Muʾayyid al-Dīn. *Sharḥ Fuṣūṣ al-ḥikam*. Edited by S. J. Āshtiyānī. Mashhad: Dānishgāh-i Mashhad, 1361/1982.

Jin Yijiu. "Notes of the Quarter." *Muslim World* 82 (1992): 332.

Kalton, Michael. *To Become a Sage*. New York: Columbia University Press, 1988.

Knysh, Alexander D. *Ibn ʿArabi in the Later Islamic Tradition: The Making of a Polemical Image in Medieval Islam*. Albany: SUNY Press, 1999.

Kuwabara Jitsuzō, *Chūgoku no kōdō*. Tokyo: Kodansha, 1977.

Lāhījī, Muḥammad. *Mafātīḥ al-iʿjāz fī sharḥ gulshan-i rāz*. Edited by M. Barzigar Khāliqī and E. Karbāsī. Tehran: Intishārāt-i Zuwwār, 1371/1992.

Lau, D. C. *Mencius*. London: Penguin Books, 1970.

Legge, James. *Confucius: Confucian Analects, The Great Learning, & The Doctrine of the Mean*. Oxford: Clarendon Press, 1893.

Leslie, Donald. *Islam in Traditional China*. Canberra: Canberra College of Advanced Education, 1986.

———. *Islamic Literature in Chinese*. Canberra: Canberra College of Advanced Education, 1981.

Leslie, Donald, and M. Wassel. "Arabic and Persian Sources Used by Liu Chih." *Central Asiatic Journal* 26 (1982): 78–104.

Lin, Chang-Kuan. "Three Eminent Chinese ʿUlamaʾ of Yunnan." *Journal of the Institute of Muslim Minority Affairs* 11:1 (1990): 100–17.

Lynn, R. J. *The Classic of Changes*. New York: Columbia University Press, 1994.

Mason, Isaac. *The Arabian Prophet*. Shanghai, 1921.

———. "Notes on Chinese Mohammedan Literature." *Journal of the North China Branch of the Royal Asiatic Society* 56 (1925): 172–215.

Matsumoto, Akiro. "Ma Rengen cho 'Tenpō seili abun chūkai' no kenkyu." *Toyōshi Kenkyu* 58/1 (1999): 1–36.

Murata, Sachiko. *The Tao of Islam: A Sourcebook on Gender Relationships in Islamic Thought*. Albany: SUNY Press, 1992.

Murata, Sachiko, and William C. Chittick. *The Vision of Islam*. New York: Paragon, 1994.

Naqshband, Bahāʾ al-Dīn. *Qudsiyya*. Edited by A. Ṭ. ʿIrāqī. Tehran: Ṭahūrī, 1354/1975.

Nasā'ī. *al-Sunan*. Beirut: Dār Iḥyā' al-Turāth al-ʿArabī, 1348/1929–30.

Nohara Shiro. "Tempō tenrei taku yōkai no hōyaku ni saishite." *Kaiyyōken* 4/2 (1940): 81–100.

Nurbakhsh, Javad. *Spiritual Poverty in Sufism*. London: Khaniqahi-Nimatullahi Publications, 1984.

———. *Sufism: Fear and Hope, . . . Gathering and Dispersion. . .* New York: Khaniqahi-i Nimatullahi Publications, 1982.

Palmer, E. H. *Oriental Mysticism: A Treatise on the Sufistic and Unitarian Theosophy of the Persians*. London, 1867.

Qūnawī, Ṣadr al-Dīn. *Nuṣūṣ*. Edited by S. J. Āshtiyānī. Tehran: Markaz-i Nashr-i Dānishgāhī, 1362/1983.

Rāzī, Najm al-Dīn. *Mirṣād al-ʿibād*. Edited by M. A. Riyāḥī. Tehran: Bungāh-i Tarjama wa Nashr-i Kitāb, 1352/1973.

Richard. See under Jāmī.

Rossabi, Morris. "Islam in China." *The Encyclopedia of Religion*. Vol. 7, New York: Macmillan, 1987, pp. 377–90.

Rūmī. *The Mathnawī*. Edited by R. A. Nicholson. London: Luzac, 1926–34.

Saguchi Toru. "Chugoku isuramu no kyōten," *Toyōgakukō* 32 (1950): 480–508.

———. *Shinkyo musulim kenkyu*. Tokyo: Yoshikawa Kōbunkan, 1995.

Suyūṭī, Jalāl al-Dīn al-. *al-Jāmiʿ al-ṣaghīr*. In al-Munawi. *Fayḍ al-qadīr fī sharḥ al-jāmiʿ al-ṣaghīr*. Beirut: Dār al-Maʿrifa, 1972.

Tazaka Kōdō. *Chugoku ni okeru kaikyō no denrai to sono gutsū*. Tokyo: Tōyō Bunko, 1961.

Tu Weiming. *Centrality and Commonality*. Albany: SUNY Press, 1989.

———. *Confucian Thought: Selfhood as Creative Transformation*. Albany: SUNY Press, 1985.

———. "Embodying the Universe: A Note on Confucian Self-Realization." In *Self as Person in Asian Theory and Practice*, by Roger T. Ames et al. Albany: SUNY Press, 1994, pp. 177–86.

Waḥīdī, Suʿād al-. "Al-Falsafat al-islamiyya fi'l-ṣīn: Waḥdat al-wujūd wa naẓariyyat al-insān al-kāmil ʿind Liyū Tishī." *Etudes orientales* 1994 (no. 13/14): 72–111 (Arabic section).

Whinfield. See under Jāmī.

Wilhelm, Richard. *I Ching*. London: Routledge & Kegan Paul, 1968.

Yang Huaizhong 楊懷中 and Yu Zhengui 余振貴. *I-ssu-lan yü chung-kuo wen-hua*. 伊斯蘭與中國文化 Ningxia, 1995.

Yu Zhengui 余振貴 and Yang Huaizhong 楊懷中. *Chung-kuo i-ssu-lan wen-hsien chu-i t'i-yao* 中國伊斯蘭文獻著譯提要. Ningxia, 1993.

Zürcher, Erik. "Jesuit Accommodation and the Chinese Cultural Imperative." In *The Chinese Rites Controversy: Its History and Meaning*, edited by D. E. Mungello. Nettetal: Steyler Verlag, 1994, pp. 31–64.

Index of Chinese Names and Terms

(Contemporary names are found in the General Index.)

Index of Persian and Arabic Names and Terms

taqyīd, 226
ṭarīqa, 227
Tarjama-yi mawlūd-i Muṣṭafā, 34, 215
Tarjama-yi Muṣṭafā, 34, 215
tashbīh, 8, 71, 124

General Index

(Includes anglicized Arabic and Chinese words as well as modern proper names.)

Relationships, 81, 107, 108, 109; Five, 23, 95
remembrance (*dhikr*), 116, 138, 150, 152, 226–28, 234
representative (*tai-li*), 18, 75–76, 84, 91, 93, 95
respects (*iʿtibār*), 154, 156, 160, 162, 176, 178, 184, 196, 200
return (to God), 16, 51, 54, 57, 98, 102, 108, 131, 151; and origin, 23, 53, 163 → beginning
reward, 65, 98; and punishment, 103, 111
Ricci, Matteo, ix, x, 24
Richard, Yann, 120, 126–27
right, and wrong, 66, 82, 110
righteousness (*i*), 39, 49, 81, 88, 98, 108, 110, 122–23, 129, 131, 135, 153
Rites, Book of, 69
root (Ch. *pen*, Ar. *aṣl*) → nature
ruler, 88, 98, 110; and minister, 45, 46, 53, 84, 108, 109
Rules and Proprieties → Liu Chih
ruling (*fa*), 161, 163, 183, 235; images, 163, 177, 185, 187
Rustic of the Pure and Real, 79, 81, 219

sage (*sheng*), 9, 18, 41, 44, 50, 59, 73, 76–77, 100, 103; ten thousand, 48; utmost, 18, 49, 50, 75, 83, 84, 86, 93, 96, 99, 100, 104, 106; and worthies, 18, 27, 97, 101, 103, 104, 161, 220
Saguchi Toru, 214
saints (*awliyāʾ*), 18 → friends
Sanskrit, 234
Satan, 18, 62–63
self (*tzu*), -awareness, 147; -being, 98, 99; -nature, 51, 59, 60, 82, 107; -one, 76, 98; -satisfaction, 103, 105; no-self (*wu-chi*), 54, 57, 77, 98, 99
selfish, selfishness, 40, 42, 56, 64, 99, 137, 147, 151
selflessness (*bī-khwudī*), 77, 132, 146
sensation (*ḥiss*), 150, 162
servant, chief, 18, 84, 86, 93, 95, 101
severity, 157, 189 → mercy
Shahadah, 8, 18, 55, 65, 70, 71, 73, 117
Shariah, 4, 14, 16, 22, 33, 65, 70
signs of God, 71–72, 221
similarity (*tashbīh*) → incomparability
similitive (*ni*), 159, 177, 181; marks, 157, 159, 161, 163, 171, 179, 184
sincerity (*ch'eng*), 53, 68, 82, 97, 129 → intention
social, society, 10, 23, 40, 70
solicitude (*tz'u*), 50, 58, 62, 65–68, 108
Sophists, 126, 186, 188
soul (*nafs*), 52, 144, 164, 198, 226; rational, 142; universal, 29, 30
species (*nawʿ*), 125, 164
specificity (*khāṣṣiyya*), 160, 164, 166, 202, 229
spirit (Ch. *shen*), 18, 45, 53, 63, 76, 92, 94, 110, 165; (Ar. *rūḥ*), 30, 52, 162, 227; spiritual (Ch. *ling*), 93; ten thousand spirituals, 88, 91, 93, 96, 103, 109; (Ar. *rūḥānī*)→ corporeal
station (*maqām*), 130; of no station, 77, 119
strength (*li*), 85, 147
subjugation (*qahr*), 188, 232
subsistence (*baqāʾ*), 56, 77, 140, 146, 190
substance (Ch. *t'i*), 145, 147, 185, 193, 197; (Ar. *jawhar*), 125; Root, 155, 159, 171, 197; and function, 19, 37–38, 42, 49, 50, 88, 91, 102, 104, 125, 129, 157, 161, 165, 169, 171, 175, 177, 205, 207, 209, 222; universal, 29; and accident, 164, 172, 184, 186, 190, 192
subtle (Ch. *miao*), 27, 48, 57, 62, 75, 81, 83, 85, 88, 91, 92, 93, 96, 97, 98, 99, 102, 104, 112, 131, 145, 151, 153, 161, 163, 165, 169, 177, 181, 220; (Ar. *laṭīfa*), 52, 142, 196
Sufism, 8, 15, 16–17, 23, 25–26, 29, 31–33, 35, 52, 113–14, 125, 214
Summary of the Important Points, 78, 83
Sunnah, 14, 15

Tao, 56, 58, 66, 82, 89, 93, 102, 104, 107, 109, 139, 145, 147, 151, 153, 220; of the True Teaching, 46, 53, 60

Printed in the United States
98273LV00003B/137/A